Hotspur

Hotspur

Sir Henry Percy and the Myth of Chivalry

L'audace, l'audace, toujors l'audace (Danton)

John Sadler

Foreword by Ralph Percy,
12th Duke of Northumberland

Pen & Sword
MILITARY

AN IMPRINT OF PEN & SWORD BOOKS LTD.
YORKSHIRE – PHILADELPHIA

First published in Great Britain in 2022 by
PEN & SWORD MILITARY
An imprint of
Pen & Sword Books Ltd
Yorkshire – Philadelphia

ISBN 9781399003889

A CIP catalogue record for this book is available from the British Library

Typeset in 10.5/13 Ehrhardt by Vman Infotech Pvt. Ltd.
Printed and bound by CPI Group (UK) Ltd, Croydon CR0 4YY

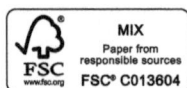

FSC
MIX
Paper from
responsible sources
FSC® C013604
www.fsc.org

Pen & Sword Books Ltd incorporates the imprints of Pen & Sword
Archaeology, Atlas, Aviation, Battleground, Discovery, Family History, History,
Maritime, Military, Naval, Politics, Social History, Transport, True Crime,
Claymore Press,
Frontline Books, Praetorian Press, Seaforth Publishing and White Owl
For a complete list of Pen & Sword titles please contact

PEN & SWORD BOOKS LTD
47 Church Street, Barnsley, South Yorkshire, S70 2AS, England
E-mail: enquiries@pen-and-sword.co.uk
Website: www.pen-and-sword.co.uk

Or

PEN AND SWORD BOOKS
1950 Lawrence Rd, Havertown, PA 19083, USA
E-mail: Uspen-and-sword@casematepublishers.com
Website: www.penandswordbooks.com

Contents

Dedicated to Jasper Sidney Meadows

Foreword

by Ralph Percy, 12th Duke of Northumberland

I was brought up on tales of Hotspur's bravery, heroism, and chivalry without questioning his heady reputation, gained on fields of battle and in corridors of power. Historians, poets, and playwrights have been generous to Harry Percy, imbuing him with legendary charisma and popularity, and Shakespeare has perpetuated this shining reputation for nobility despite Hotspur's many flaws. John Sadler takes a deeper and more critical look at Hotspur's character, and the flow of events that created his legend and ultimately led to disaster. It shows other, less attractive characteristics; petulance, arrogance, bullying, cruelty, and overwhelming ambition, a trait shared with his father, the 1st Earl of Northumberland, that raised the Percies to dizzying heights and precipitated a disastrous fall. This book also seeks to make sense of historical events, questioning previous assertions that were often based on scant knowledge and repeated as gospel over generations. It takes a fresh, forensic look at one of the most fascinating and bloody periods in our history, a history that could have been very different but for the flight of a single, deadly arrow.

Ralph Northumberland
January 2022

Introduction and Acknowledgements

Tragedy: branch of drama that treats in a serious and dignified style the sorrowful or terrible events encountered or caused by a heroic individual.[1]

If the Border Marches were the furnace in which the identities of England and of Scotland were forged, Henry Percy, 'Hotspur' (1364–1403), was the red-hot steel. His life and achievement would be the mirror in which every Christian knight wished to see himself reflected.

In his hometown of Alnwick, not far from the castle, there's a great bronze statue of him. He's depicted, slightly larger than life size, in full late fourteenth-century armour, sword at the ready, just as you'd imagine. If you miss that one, don't worry – there's another inside. He looks a bit of an automaton, a fighting machine, rather impersonal, like it's all about the armour, nothing special inside. Shakespeare loved Hotspur, the epitome of chivalry, noble, brave, and not very bright. A more revisionist approach is just to see him as a glaring example of magnatial thug, a gentleman bruiser, arrogant, essentially vicious, and self-obsessed. He was a bit of both.

Homeric heroes are currently out of fashion, yet Hotspur would have fitted admirably onto the pages of the *Iliad*. Had anyone compared him to Achilles, he probably would have been cheered. But my purpose is to try and get inside the visor and see a real man. He did live in a nasty age. He, with his family, contributed substantially to that nastiness and profited handsomely from it. He was a fighter, but pacifists didn't exist then and if they had, wouldn't have lasted awfully long. Being 'judgemental', as our Transatlantic friends might say, is very much in vogue but exporting the moral attitudes of Islington drawing rooms back into a fourteenth-century frontier *Threap* (waste-land) is pure self-indulgence. We must judge the man by the standards of his time not ours.

There's a problem with history. Napoleon observed it was 'but a fable agreed upon', and many of us who call ourselves historians might, in an unguarded moment, or in drink, be inclined to agree. Wellington somewhat agreed with his enemy, he viewed describing the course of a battle as pointless as describing the sequence of a ball. The Iron Duke, having vanquished Bonaparte, was sniffy about people trying to write the story of his great victory. He urged historians to be wary of eyewitness testimony, which we normally prize so highly, too much vanity, hogwash, and false recollection at play. Wellington would know a thing or two about that as his own dispatches were intended if not to disparage his allies (without whom there'd have been no great triumph), then certainly to minimise their role and boost his own.

Hotspur doesn't leave us any dispatches or instructions to future biographers. We have some pieces of official correspondence, and that's it. We have what others said about him, and most had their own agendas but he leaves no single clue as to what was going on in his head at any given time. The bard, brilliant as he is, doesn't help. His portrayal in the history plays is pure Hollywood, he creates a cinematic, two-dimensional figure, put there as a literary device and takes vast liberties with history. Why not, he's a storyteller after all?

But the longer time goes by, the more the stereotype sticks and the further we get from any true glimpse. We see flashes of character in the letters and moments such as the immediate aftermath of Homildon where our hero takes time to wreak personal vengeance on two luckless knights who've offended him and it's plain that is what matters, the perceived personal slight and betrayal. This is arbitrary, clearly unlawful, even by the elastic standards of the time and nastily vindictive. It shows hubris with more than a dash of cruelty.

Having said that, times were very cruel and the 'feid' (feud) or vendetta, the mandatory seeking for vengeance, a hallowed border tradition. If we come to judge Hotspur, we must judge him primarily as a borderer, a marcher, raised in a school of endemic violence. He did not create this environment, it was his cultural inheritance, and it was harsh, unforgiving, and relentlessly savage. Yes, he seems to fit the mould perfectly but if he hadn't, he'd never have made it out of his teens.

Meanwhile, Alnwick Castle has more recently made much of its fictional hero Harry Potter, having featured in most of the movies as Hogwarts and done very well indeed out of the connection, broomstick training is still immensely popular. When that attraction fades as surely it must and there are no more broomsticks to fly, Hotspur is the evergreen replacement. Tricky, and while Shakespeare has kept him in the literary superhero league, he's never exerted quite the pull of Harry Potter, very few have. I'm none too sure what he'd have thought of broomstick training as grounding for knighthood either. He probably believed in witches, though.

*   *   *

Thanks are due to the following: Geoffrey Carter, David Austen, Phil Philo, Tony Fox, and other colleagues at the UK Battlefields Trust, the late Beryl Charlton, Jo Scott and Elaine Ryder at Elsdon church, George Common and the Friends of Harbottle Castle, Chris Jones, Ruth Dickinson, Rachel Baron and Karen Collins of Northumberland National Park Authority, Mark Hornsby, Katie Bridger and

Karen Collins from Revitalising Redesdale, The National Archive, Kew, staff at the Literary & Philosophical Society Newcastle upon Tyne, colleagues at the Society of Antiquaries of Newcastle upon Tyne, staff at the Wallace Collection, London, to Dr Tobias Capwell, Dr David Caldwell, Douglas Archives at Drumlanrig, Tower Hawick, James Boyd, Lisa Little, Chris Hunwick and colleagues at Alnwick Castle, to Bob Brooks and Hotspur School of HEMA, the Revd Ken Steventon, Rob Dingle, Ulfric Douglas, Derek Stewart, Arran Johnson, Paul Macdonald from Macdonald Armouries, Andy Scott, Phil Abramson of the MoD, the late Alec Bankier, the late Professor George Jobey, the late Wilf Dodds, the late Jock Tate, Anne Telfer, Dave Grey of Kimmerston Design, Margaret Eliott from Clan Eliott, Fiona Armstrong of the Clan Armstrong Trust, Sir Humphry Wakefield of Chillingham Castle, Anne-Marie Trevelyan MP, Karen Larkin from Bamburgh Castle, Graham Hepburn and colleagues at Historic Scotland, English Heritage, colleagues at the Explore Programme, Newcastle upon Tyne, staff at Newcastle Central Library, Gateshead Library and Northumberland Libraries, Mark Jackson and colleagues at Royal Armouries, Leeds, Pearl Saddington, Ann McAlpine, Doug Chapman, Graham Trueman, Charles Wesencraft, Dr Ian Roberts, Emma-Kate Lanyon, Giles Carey and colleagues at Shropshire Museums.

Especial thanks are due to Gerry Tomlinson, Trevor Sheehan, Anthony Edward Fairey, Jo Scott, Beverley Palin (also for indexing), Alan Grint and Adam Barr for photographs; as ever to Chloe Rodham for the maps, Julia Grint and Chris Hunwick for editing.

As ever, the author remains responsible for any errors or omissions and if any reader should notice any of these please contact me via the publisher and I will undertake to make the necessary corrections.

John Sadler
March 2022

Timeline

1066	Battle of Hastings
?–1067	William de Percy I (d.1096) comes to England
c. **1072–***c*. **1135**	Alan de Percy
?–*c*. **1174/5**	William de Percy II
?–1202	Maud de Percy
?–1203/4	Agnes de Percy
?–1198	Henry de Percy I
1196	Birth of William de Percy III
1215	Signing of Magna Carta; outbreak of First Barons' War
1216	First siege of Dover, sieges of Windsor and Rochester
1216, October	Death of King John
1217	Second siege of Dover; Battles of Lincoln, Dover and Sandwich
1217, September	Treaty of Lambeth
1244	Death of Richard de Percy
1235	Birth of Henry de Percy II
1245	Death of William de Percy III
1258	Provisions of Oxford
1261	Henry III obtains a papal bull releasing him from the Provisions of Oxford
1263	Simon de Montfort identified as leader of baronial faction
1264, May	Battle of Lewes, King Henry and Prince Edward captive; de Montfort in control
1264, May	The Mise of Lewes concluded
1264, June	Constitution established by de Montfort in place, the council of nine

1265, January	First meeting of the English Parliament in the Palace of Westminster
1265, August	The Battle of Evesham
1266, October	Terms agreed with the surviving rebels; the dictum of Kenilworth
1267	End of the war, terms of the dictum of Kenilworth ratified
1272	Death of Henry III; accession of Edward I
1272	Death of Henry de Percy II
1273	Birth of Lord Henry de Percy I
1296	Start of the Three-Hundred Years War
1297	Battle of Stirling Bridge
1298	Battle of Falkirk
1301	Birth of Lord Henry Percy II
1309	Percies acquire Barony of Alnwick
1314	Battle of Bannockburn
1314	Death of Lord Henry Percy I
1320	Birth of Lord Henry Percy III
1333	Battle of Halidon Hill
1341	Birth of Henry Percy, 1st Earl of Northumberland
1346	Battle of Neville's Cross
1352	Death of Lord Henry Percy II
1359	Henry Percy accompanies the Duke of Lancaster on his French expedition
1360	Treaty of Brétigny
1364	Birth of Henry Percy ('Hotspur')
1368	Death of Lord Henry Percy III
1369	Resumption of French and Scottish Wars
1372	English defeat off La Rochelle
1375	Percy gains control of part of the Umfraville lands in Northumberland
1377	Henry becomes Marshal of England
1377	Death of Edward III; accession of Richard II

1377	Percy elevated to his earldom
1381	Peasants' Revolt in England; Gaunt seeks sanctuary in Scotland
1383	Hotspur (nearly) joins the Baltic Crusades
1384	Raid against Scotland by John of Gaunt
1384	Earl Percy marries his second wife, Maud, heiress of Gilbert de Umfraville
1385	Richard II leads a major raid into Scotland
1386/7	Hotspur does tour of duty in the Calais Pale
1388, 5 August	Battle of Otterburn, Hotspur defeated and captured
1393/4	Hotspur undertakes tour of duty in Aquitaine
1395	Earl of Northumberland acquires the extensive Hylton holdings
1399	Usurpation of Henry IV
1400	Henry IV expedition against the Scots
1402	Scots defeated at Nesbit Muir
1402, 14 September	Battle of Homildon
1403, 21 July	Battle of Shrewsbury and death of Hotspur
1408, 19 February	Fight at Bramham Moor; death of 1st Earl of Northumberland

Dramatis Personae

James Douglas, 2nd Earl Douglas (*c.* 1358–88)

James Douglas was the son of William Douglas, 1st Earl Douglas and in 1371 (or 1373) married Isabel, a daughter of King Robert II of Scotland. With George Dunbar, Earl of Dunbar and March (see below), he led a strong diversionary force down into Northumberland and Durham in the high summer of 1388 and commanded the Scottish flank attack during the subsequent Battle at Otterburn. This manoeuvre was successful, Henry Percy ('Hotspur') and his brother Ralph were defeated, and both captured, though Douglas himself died in the fighting.

Archibald Douglas, 4th Earl Douglas (*c.* 1369–1424)

Known by the unfortunate nickname of 'Tineman' or loser, he was the son of Archibald the Grim, 3rd Earl Douglas and married Margaret, a daughter of the future King Robert III of Scotland. In 1400 he won a skirmish against his Scottish rival George Dunbar who'd defected to the English. Thereafter, militarily, it was all downhill. He was suspected, in cahoots with the regent, King Robert's brother Robert, Duke of Albany, of being guilty of, or certainly heavily implicated, in the murder of Robert III's oldest son, the Duke of Rothesay, though he escaped censure. His luck ran out at Homildon in 1402 where he was defeated and captured. He fought with Percy in another losing fight at Shrewsbury. He wasn't freed from English captivity till 1413 and finally fought his last losing battle at Verneuil in 1424 when the English were commanded by John, Duke of Bedford.

George Dunbar, 10th Earl of Dunbar and March (1338–1422)

A key player in the Hotspur saga, George Dunbar was also 12th Lord of Annandale and Lord of the Isle of Man and prime architect of the Scots' military revival after 1370. In 1395 he negotiated the betrothal of his daughter Elizabeth to the Duke of Rothesay. So far so good but Archibald the Grim intervened, jealous of the influence this would bring to March and was instrumental in getting the marriage contract annulled, then scooping the pot by marrying his own daughter Marjory to the duke, trumping Dunbar. This was a double blow as Elizabeth had effectively lived as the duke's wife for two years (while papal dispensation was sought); not only had he now lost the alliance, but his daughter would be deemed second-hand goods (in fact she never married). This skulduggery prompted his defection to England.

Owen Glyndwr (Glendower) (*c.* 1354–*c.* 1416)

The star of Welsh national resurgence, he was a complex character and self-styled Prince of Wales. Though his rebellion ultimately foundered, he was a significant thorn in the flesh of both Richard II and Henry IV and was, for a long period, extraordinarily successful. He's still very much an icon of Welsh nationalism. Hotspur's role in the fight would exacerbate tension between him and the throne and lead to the final rift.

Henry IV, King of England (1366–1413)

Henry of Derby, Duke of Hereford, Henry Bolingbroke and, on the death of his father John of Gaunt (see below), Duke of Lancaster, finally rebelled against the perceived tyranny of Richard II. He then usurped the throne, being almost certainly responsible for Richard's death in captivity, almost equally certainly by murder. He thus became the first of the three Lancastrian kings (Henry V and Henry VI being the other two) and this act of usurpation was long perceived as the ultimate catalyst for the Wars of the Roses. Though the Percies facilitated his takeover, they became disenchanted, then hostile and finally rebellious.

Henry, Prince of Wales (Henry V of England) (1386–1422)

Shakespeare's Prince Hal, whose apparently libertine youth forms the dramatic contrast with Hotspur's chivalric zeal (in fact there was a substantial age difference), and Prince Henry would not only lead the decisive counterattack at Shrewsbury but would complete his military apprenticeship in the war against Glyndwr. He would then go on to win undying renown and a reputation for utter ruthlessness in France with Agincourt (October 1415), as perhaps his finest hour.

John of Gaunt, Duke of Lancaster (1340–99)

Gaunt (a corruption of the name of his birthplace Ghent) was also Earl of Richmond and from 1390, Duke of Aquitaine, fourth son of Edward III and third surviving. He acquired the vast Lancastrian inheritance in right of his first wife and served consistently if unsuccessfully as a senior commander in the war with France. With his youthful nephew's accession, he became senior statesman and *éminence grise*, though he had few friends among his fellow magnates. Latterly and in right of his second wife he inherited a claim to rule Castile which he attempted, again unsuccessfully, to promote via military intervention, though he did manage to marry his daughter to the future Henry III of Castile.

Ralph Neville, 1st Earl of Westmorland (1364–1425)

Like the Percies, the Nevilles were important northern magnates, centred on Raby (where they remain to this day). Ralph was the son of John Neville, 3rd Baron Neville and his mother Maud was a Percy. Hotspur and he were first cousins and he campaigned in France under Thomas of Woodstock, another of Edward III's sons. He also served on the border being responsible for the collection of amounts outstanding from David II's ransom and acted as Governor of Carlisle and West March Warden. He fulfilled a slew of important roles and Richard II created him Earl for his support against the Lords Appellant (though he was also Gaunt's son-in-law). Like Percy, he supported Henry Bolingbroke and received a lifetime's grant of the office of Earl Marshal. His rivalry with the Percies intensified and he did well out of his continued and significant support for Henry IV. The ongoing sparring with his Percy relatives would swell to a major feud during the middle decades of the fifteenth century.

Henry Percy, 1st Earl of Northumberland (1341–1408)

Hotspur's father and the Percy who took the family's fortunes to their very zenith, completed their careful transition from gentry and lords to great magnates. A stellar player in his time who held many important offices on the border including March wardenships and who, with his sons Henry and Ralph, was the great bulwark against re-ignited Scottish aggression after 1370. He held the line and, at the same time, judiciously and steadily increased his vast estates. Initially an ally of but latterly at odds with Gaunt, he became a kingmaker, promoting the cause of Henry Bolingbroke and active in the unseating and death of Richard II. Craftily, he tried latterly to portray himself as a wise senior statesman, above the rash importunities of his eldest son, disavowing his final doomed revolt only to die an ignominious traitor's death himself five years later.

Henry Percy ('Hotspur') (1364–1403)

The very doyen of chivalry, stuff of heroic if flawed legend; immortalised, inaccurately, by Shakespeare, who by his portrayal guaranteed Hotspur's fame. Harry Percy was born into an era of increased violence along an already fractious border, born to shoulder the family responsibility for fighting the Scots, taking the fight to them, perfecting a role in the dangerous art of hobiler warfare. He served on numerous significant missions abroad and against the Welsh rebels. His name was a byword for courage and decisiveness if occasionally flawed by rashness and a taste for cruelty. His finest hour was Homildon in 1402 which also partly lit the fuse which detonated his doomed insurrection against Henry IV, his own defeat and death at Shrewsbury a year later and the eclipse of his family's hitherto luminous fortunes.

Thomas Percy, Earl of Worcester (*c.* 1344–1403)

Brother to the 1st Earl and Hotspur's uncle/mentor, he campaigned with considerable distinction in France during Edward III's reign, held offices in the north and served as Admiral of the Fleet under Richard II. He joined his brother in forsaking Richard in favour of Bolingbroke in 1399 but became a major mover in the Percy rebellion four years later. He fought at Shrewsbury, was captured, and paid the price. The earldom became extinct on his execution.

Richard II, King of England (1367–1400)

Richard was born at Bordeaux and inherited the grand tradition of his father and grandfather, though this proved to be something of a poisoned chalice. The war with France when it resumed went badly, Bertrand du Guesclin adopting more Fabian tactics as did Dunbar on the Anglo–Scottish borders. The king was perpetually hard up and frequently at odds with his nobles, his cause spluttered on all fronts, but it was his attempt to seize the vast Lancastrian estate from his cousin Bolingbroke that did for him though the crown never sat easy on that usurper's head.

List of Maps

List of Plates

The bronze statue of Hotspur in Alnwick

'Arms of Sir Henry Percy'

Alnwick Castle

Warkworth Castle

Bamburgh Castle

The walls of Berwick-upon-Tweed

The remains of the castle at Berwick

Dunstanburgh Castle

Facsimile armour of the fourteenth century

Newcastle Keep

The Otterburn battlefield memorial

A general view of Otterburn battlefield

Looking east at Otterburn

The Silloans Sword

The replica Silloans Sword

Elsdon church

The Neville effigies, Staindrop church

A medieval spur, recovered from the vicinity of Albright Hussey

Otterburn battlefield walk participants

An aerial view of Battlefield church and its environs in Shrewsbury

Battlefield church

The effigy of Simon Mewburn, Church of St John of Beverley, St John's Lee

List of Abbreviations

CDS	J. Bain (ed.), *Calendar of Documents relating to Scotland*, Vol. IV, 1357–1509, Edinburgh, 1881–8
De Fonblanque	E.B. De Fonblanque, *Annals of the House of Percy: From the Conquest to the opening of the nineteenth century*, London, R. Clay & Sons, 1887, Vol. 1
Froissart	Jean Froissart, *Chronicles of England, France etc.*, trans. Lord Berners, ed. G.C. Macaulay, London, Macmillan & Co., 1924
Hardyng	J. Hardyng, *The Chronicle of John Hardyng*, ed. F.C. and J. Rivington, England, 1812
Ridpath	G. Ridpath, *The Border History of England and Scotland*, Edinburgh, Mercat Press, 1979
Scotichronicon	Walter Bower, *Scotichronicon*, ed. D.E.R. Watt, Edinburgh, John Donald, 2012, Vol. 7
Usk	*Chronicles of Adam of Usk 1377–1421*, trans. C. Given-Wilson, Oxford, Oxford Medieval Texts, 1997
Walsingham	Thomas Walsingham, *Historia Anglicana*, ed. H.T. Riley, Rolls Series, Cambridge Library, 2015

Prologue

A Storm of Arrows

The Army Warrior Ethos states, 'I will always place the mission first, I will never accept defeat, I will never quit, and I will never leave a fallen comrade.' The Warrior Ethos is a set of principles by which every soldier lives. In a broader sense, the Warrior Ethos is a way of life that applies to our personal and professional lives as well. It defines who we are and who we aspire to become.[1]

Over two-and-a-half thousand years before Harry Percy, Homer recounts how Sarpedon and Glaucos, cousins and officers in the Trojan army, prepare to take on the Greek besiegers' leaguer and, hopefully, burn their ships – death to the invader! Glaucos complains or queries why it is they who always get the dangerous jobs. Sarpedon reminds him that this is their assigned role, why they are favoured above others and why those others labour in peacetime to provide luxuries and why they are raised above other men and revered – this is payback time, and their warrior code demands they lead the show from the front. We don't know if Hotspur read the *Iliad*, but he may well have done and that's one passage that would have resonated. Being in the front line defines privilege and obligation, for the warrior there's never any real option. Whatever is said about Hotspur, that's one ideal he never defaulted from.

* * *

Along the valley floor, the River Glen twists and bends away eastwards, slow still at this time of year, a warm high summer with no whisper of incipient autumn. A lone kite wheels lazily in a blue sky, wheatears and swallows dart over lazy water, perhaps the most beautiful time of year in north Northumberland. Henry Percy, who his enemies have nicknamed Hotspur, catchy and it's stuck, sits upon his destrier. Just south-west of where his cavalry stand, a large Scottish army is deploying clumsily, crowding the lower slopes of steep-sided Homildon Hill, the conical massif covers their rear.

These English knights opposite are ranged over the flat alluvial plain with another hill, Harehope, looming above them. Topography has fashioned the arena and the main English force, primarily dismounted archers, are between the Scots and the river. They're also between them and Scotland. The Earl of Douglas, latterly to have his own sobriquet the 'Tineman' (or 'loser'), is in charge and seemingly he has no idea what to do. Gilded, late summer light glances mockingly perhaps from his burnished plate and Scottish banners. Officers await his orders, but he doesn't seem to have any to give.

Douglas' men, all or the vast majority now on foot, are drawn up in dense, bristling brigades of packed spears, the famous Scottish *schlitron* – their traditional formation for both attack and defence. Douglas understands that when spears meet arrows the results tend to be one-sided. At Falkirk (1298), Dupplin Moor (1332), Halidon Hill (1333), and Neville's Cross (1346) English war-bows have shot Scottish spearmen to pieces. True, he outnumbers the English, perhaps by as many as two to one but he knows what an arrow storm can do, the hurricane fury and terror of the tempest that has shattered Scottish and French armies time and again for over a century.

It is warm, muggy; men sweat inside their harness. Most Scots lack armour, maybe a steel helmet and padded jack, twin layers of canvas stuffed with rags or tallow, enough if you're lucky to turn a blade. Yet none of these young men have had to face the coming storm, the last great battle at Durham was in their grandfathers' day. Theirs will be a very cruel initiation. It's not as though Douglas hasn't had warning. His grand chevauchée, however impressive in numbers, wasn't likely to go unchallenged. Two months earlier, Sir Patrick Hepburn of Hailes, leading a softening up raid, was intercepted at Nesbit Muir (Moor) in the Merse (Scottish East March) before he could get clear, and his force badly cut up. Hepburn was among the many dead and more knights were captured. This day has the potential to be a great deal worse.

Does Hotspur chafe to be at them, to launch his lightning cavalry in a great mounted charge? Maybe, but he doesn't. He's under the guidance of wily George Dunbar, Scottish Earl of March, his earlier nemesis at Otterburn, fourteen years before and now a turncoat ally of convenience. The Percies and Douglases are natural rivals. March is at odds with Douglas, the prime reason for his defection. Both Hotspur and his father Northumberland respect their new partner, the prime architect of a Scottish military revival that began over thirty years before. Harry Percy isn't a boy; that rash, impetuous youth of Shakespeare's myth is almost 40. In this battle he'll show neither rashness nor impetuosity. His cavalry is there as a blocking force, to seal off any attempt by the Scots to squeeze past and head for home. If March is indeed the master tactician guiding his former enemies against current rivals, he's planning a battle of annihilation. Douglas obliges.

March and Hotspur have the perfect tool, the English yeoman with his great war-bow, one of the most efficient weapons of mass destruction ever devised. These phenomenal men of the grey goose feather can shoot up to a dozen arrows a minute, from bows with draw-weights of anything from 120 to 200lb, staves as thick as tree trunks needing vast strength and mastery to draw. With say 5,000 bowmen, that's 60,000 shafts a minute. They'll be using needle-tipped, armour piercing bodkins against armoured knights and barbed broad heads for the rank and file. Their killing power is tremendous and dense-packed bodies of infantry, relying on contact to use their spears, are a dream target. Arrows will blot out the sun, a hailstorm of untidy death, striking as hard as a .303, punching men off their feet, studding their shrieking, writhing bodies. It's not a quick death, no numbing shock like a bullet but terrific force and resulting terrible agonies.

These mainly young Scotsmen have experienced nothing like it, it is a horror almost beyond our imagining, compounded by utter helplessness. Perhaps the nearest modern parallel would be the first day of the Somme when many thousands of young men, some possibly the descendants of those who'd fought on both sides here, advanced in solemn doomed dignity into the teeth of sustained and accurate fire from German Maxims. Any attempt to advance is stillborn, great shuddering gaps are torn in the ranks, the mini forest of standing shafts, a minefield in themselves; even those that miss create a major obstacle.

You can see them coming; you've little protection and no cover. You see the man next to you, perhaps on both sides, plucked down, shot through the face or body or both, his feet perhaps nailed to the dry earth below. You probably grew up with him and now you watch his inhuman suffering, his raw, primeval terror, smell his stink. Sergeants bellow to close, dead or dying men strewn everywhere. There is no hope of maintaining any cohesion. Your leaders seem impotent. They are impotent. Death is coming out of that darkening sky. The reek of blood, of piss and shit and fear fills your nostrils.

When the dam bursts and the lines disintegrate, men stampede like rabbits, the same fellows who have stoically withstood the terrible and sustained barrages, they down their spears, so the ground looks like a chaotic, abandoned lumberyard and it's every man for himself. Douglas, severely injured, is taken prisoner; he's fast earning his nickname. He's suffered numerous wounds.

Hotspur's role isn't glorious in the chivalric sense but it's tactically effective. His lances bear down on the herd of frantic fugitives killing some, herding others into the water's embrace and keeping them under as they drown or watch them be pulled down by the weight of their kit, building a sagging pontoon of waterlogged corpses. Others are just ridden over, swiped backhanded with sword or axe, lopping skulls like eggs. The alluvial ground is a carpet of corpses, blood leaks in steady rivulets, even mini torrents, into the river staining the water, a late summer flood of blood and spilt entrails. The smell will be biblical, one that haunts restless dreams ever after.

Now, Harry Percy did not necessarily devise this strategy and enjoyed a subsidiary role in its execution. Possibly he was never in overall command – that was either his father or March – but he gets a lot of the credit for this, his most famous victory even if it isn't his. It is in fact the most perfect longbow victory and, most telling of all, not even Agincourt can boast such a clean-cut triumph, the kill-ratio fantastically slewed. At least a thousand Scots are dead, and hundreds more are prisoners. Whatever is left of their army is in pieces, the pride of their chivalry dead, wounded or taken, never having struck a blow. No English casualties are recorded. It is indeed a conquest for a prince to boast of. And Hotspur intends to boast.

Shakespeare leads us to think of this Harry Percy as being a victim partly of events and partly of his own hot-tempered nature. In fairness, the Percies weren't famed for reticence or self-denial. It's not who they were, these mightiest of over mighty subjects. Nobody had heard of 'celebrities' in the fourteenth century, but Hotspur would have understood, and we think he was in fact a master of the art, that his life wasn't some doom-laden adrenalin rush but a carefully planned exercise in self-aggrandisement. If he'd just stopped at Homildon, history might have offered a different verdict and Shakespeare would have had to re-invent him completely. By and large, he was rather good at flagrant self-promotion and yet less than a year after Homildon he himself would be struck down by an arrow on the field of Shrewsbury, not as a chivalric hero meeting a noble end but a miserable and despised traitor who led his family into the dust.

But who is he, this Harry Hotspur, an English Achilles whose quest for glory, like the Greek hero, led to a shorter but renowned life: 'don't try to console me for my death, for I would rather toil as the slave of a penniless, landless labourer, than reign here as lord of all the dead'? Was he a hot-tempered aristocratic thug or has he been a victim of historical bias? Shakespeare has a lot to answer for. Or, just possibly, was he an astute player, one who could be rash and certainly made mistakes yet played a clever double act with his senior statesman father, saying the things the old man couldn't but one who finally overreached himself and made one mistake too many?

And indeed, was he ever a 'hero'? That's a much-abused term, everyone who ever served in a war is now heroic, if you rescue next door's cat stuck up a tree then you're lauded in the press. Our society craves heroes but then we tend to whitewash them, see them as icons not as real people. A recent UK Channel 5 TV biography of Lord Louis Mountbatten, very much a totem of the mid-twentieth century, attempted to show him as a deeply flawed human being with feet of clay, as so many people are.

Kalos thanatos – the glorious death, ideally and perhaps uniquely available to a Greek hero on the field of battle. Hotspur perfectly fulfils this idealised stereotype, and we like that. In the spectacularly bastardised view of the 'Three-Hundred Spartans', brilliantly realised in the film *300*, Michael Fassbender's gung-ho Spartan hoplite describes this ideal of a noble end which Xerxes' 'army of slaves' is about to bestow; this how a Spartan, dedicated to war, and like Horatius at the bridge, should die.

Spanish author Javier Cercas, in his *Lord of All the Dead* (2017), tracks a great uncle who fought for the Falange during the bloody Spanish Civil War of 1936–9; venerated in his one-horse village and by his family as a true hero, one who fulfils all the criteria for the beautiful death. The truth Cercas meticulously and painfully uncovers presents a different or certainly contradictory reality where death in battle is in fact agonising, slow, and terrible, no beauty whatsoever in sight. His great uncle emerges as an ordinary young man called upon to do extraordinary things in extraordinary times, any glory deflected because, in Cercas' estimation, he was fighting for the 'wrong' side and that neither was truly worthy of the sacrifice.

This is the reality of Henry Percy I hope to uncover.

Act 1

Worm-eaten Hold of Ragged Stone –
The House of Percy

> Yea, there thou makest me sad and makest me sin
> In envy that my Lord Northumberland
> Should be the father to so blest a son
> A son who is the theme of honour's tongue
> Amongst a grove, the very straightest plant
> Who is sweet Fortune's minion and her pride . . .
> William Shakespeare,
> *The First Part of King Henry IV*, Act I, sc. i

So, a beleaguered Henry IV bewails, groaning under the weight of his stolen crown and lumbered with a good-for-nothing a son. He envies Northumberland whose own eldest boy is Chivalry's idol, Chaucer's perfect knight. This is Shakespeare of course and he's building up his Prince Hal towards his achievement as king to be. His fictional Hotspur is just a foil, a literary device, to be discarded when necessary. Harry Percy's heroic death in single combat against the prince is crafted for Hal's advancement not his. Besides which, it never happened.

Not much remains of the pretty and commodious manor William de Percy built at Spofforth in North Yorkshire in the epicentre of his burgeoning acres. It was said that the draft of Magna Carta was hammered out there by the northern barons. Though licence to crenellate was later granted in 1308, the place was more country house than fortress, though it does enjoy a dominant position, overlooking the village below from its rocky eminence as a castle should.[1]

Hotspur's biographer, Andrew Boardman, asserts he was born there on 13 June 1364, the date confirmed by the *Chronicles of Alnwick Abbey*: 'Henry was born of the said Lady Margaret the 13th of the Kalends of June, in the year of our Lord 1364'.[2] There is some confusion here as Harry himself (presumably) while giving evidence at a trial in 1386 (see Act 6) and as shown in the court papers offers a later date of 20 May 1366. There may be politics in this, and I agree with Andrew Boardman that this earlier date is more compelling. Boardman also concludes he was born at Spofforth, a more comfortable house for his mother's confinement. But this may not be convincing. Alnwick was the heart of his father's northern empire, and it would seem probable if not certain his heir would be born there and the birth is recorded in the *Alnwick Abbey Chronicle*.

The Threap

Henry Percy, to be called Hotspur and whose name, fame, and achievement were to be forever linked to the Anglo-Scottish borderland, was a Northumbrian icon even to the extent he's been anecdotally linked to the distinctive dialect, although in fact it predates him by centuries.[3] Any understanding we may have of the man depends on grasping the wider context of his background, both personal and geographical. This Anglo-Scottish border was an incredibly wild frontier, no young Lochinvars of Scott's romantic tradition but a bitter, vindictive, and unrelenting struggle at state and sub-state levels; magnates, gentry, and commoners were all involved. Edward I of England ('Longshanks') had begun the Three-Hundred Years War in 1296 so it had simmered for three score and more years before Hotspur was born. It was nasty from the start. Edward had ravaged Berwick-upon-Tweed, then a major Scottish port, with frenetic violence, murdering, it was said 7,000 of its citizens, men, women, and children. That pretty much set the tone. It wasn't, as Alastair Macdonald points out, a sustained continuum; the wars burnt, flickered, and flamed with varying intensity. It went from bad to unbelievably bad, awful, and catastrophic.[4]

In 1369 it flared up again after a period of, by local standards, relative calm since the defeat and capture of David II at Neville's Cross in October 1346. This local *Ragnarök* was linked to Edward III and his son the Black Prince's wars in France; the Three-Hundred Years War as a facet of the Hundred Years War. The prince's stunning triumph against the odds at Poitiers, adding the King of France to his father's cache of high-value prisoners, set the seal on a successful epoch. After 1369, as the French wars kicked off again, there was resurgence in Scots military activity. Like Bertrand du Guesclin, the King of France's 'hog in armour', George Dunbar, the Scottish Earl of March led the charge from north of the border but with much more caution than elan. He'd seen where that led. He knew just what he was doing and did it very well.

So Hotspur was born into this era of heightened tensions and increasing marcher violence. He didn't create a broken frontier but he helped keep it that way. He also arrived in a new era of localized tactical innovation, the day of the 'hobiler', border light cavalry. Edward III's abortive Weardale campaign of 1327 had clearly shown that a traditional deployment of barded knights, heavily armoured, superbly mounted but dependent on an extensive logistical 'tail', didn't work well on the borders.[5] Local marchers mounted on sturdy garrons, self-reliant, hard riding and hard hitting, were now the real arbiters of this harsh and unforgiving school, young Percy's boot camp. It didn't offer second chances.

Name was all important; those later to be dubbed the riding names, the infamous reivers, lived by a ruthless and expedient code which relied wholly on blood and affinity. There were no other loyalties; nationhood was an academic concept, reality adjusted at will. In time the riding names from these hard uplands would coalesce into cross-border criminal gangs chaired by local leaders or 'heid-men', certainly hard men. To get them to follow you, you'd have to earn their respect and it took a very particular type of man (or woman) to achieve that. Naturally, if you offered loot it helped. Hotspur proved to be such a man. If he was rough, callous, vain, and swaggering then he was just fitting in with what the role required.

There was his *own* name as well. A century before and the Percies would barely be known in Northumberland, by young Harry's time they were pre-eminent; a meteoric rise which would burn most brightly during his lifetime before crashing. The Percies went from being local players to regional and then national. At each bound their wealth and prestige soared by another prodigious leap so their fall, when it came, was also prodigious. It was the Border Wars, the ruin of so many, that gave them their chance to excel as knights, to swell and prosper as landowners. By the time Harry Percy came into the world, his father pretty much had control of the border, aside from the Nevilles of course.

Now, by the term 'Borders' I'm referring to the northern English counties of Northumberland in the east and Cumbria in the west – this latter is an amalgamation (much resented by locals) of the ancient shires of Cumberland and Westmorland. North of the border it's even worse; the Scottish counties of Berwickshire, Roxburghshire, Selkirkshire, Peeblesshire, and Dumfriesshire have been re-packaged simply as Scottish Borders in the east with Dumfries & Galloway in the west. Long ago distant, seismic upheavals formed a distinctive landscape or set of landscapes with bony ridges of high ground, Cheviots humped in the centre of the English side, Southern Uplands over on the Scottish. Old high hills, endlessly rolling and rounded, usually still with only the wind that scours across from chilled lands north and east and that lamenting lilt of curlews haunting the emptiness.

For a robust man of action with a constant eye to the main chance, the second half of the fourteenth century would provide opportunities as well as threats, both in equal abundance. Sixty odd years of near constant international warfare and endemic local violence, the seeding of a makeshift warrior caste in the Northumbrian dales, was now exacerbated by deteriorating climatic conditions and the horrors of the Black Death.[6] The landscape of conflict, this blood divide, was already formed and the Scots, from an initially inferior position, were bouncing back. Not just to reclaim those areas of the Scottish Marches, the English Pale, which Edward III had created to form a forward defensive line but once again to

THE BORDER MARCHES

--- THE BORDERS OF THE MARCHES

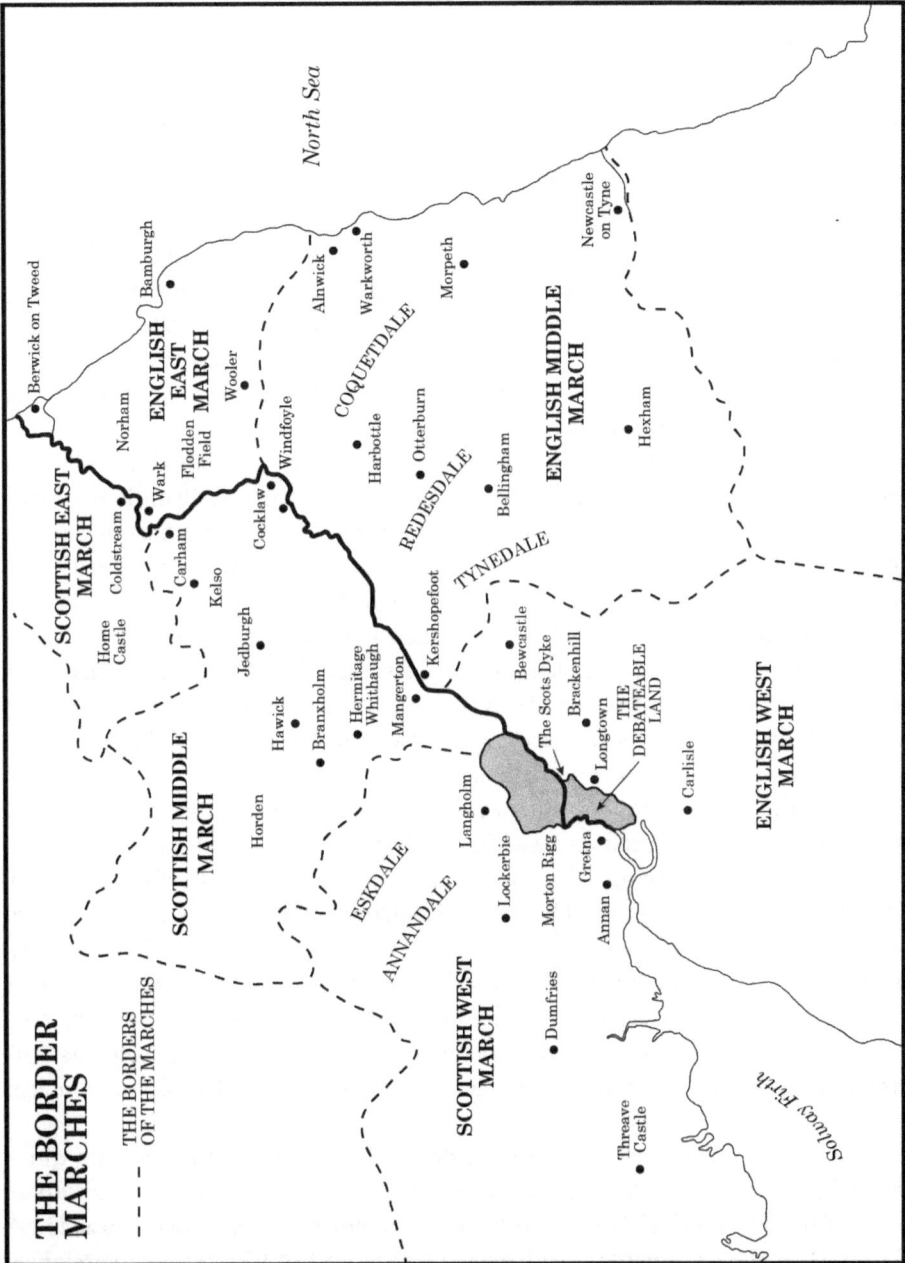

North Sea

Solway Firth

Berwick on Tweed

Bamburgh

Newcastle on Tyne

Alnwick

Warkworth

Morpeth

ENGLISH EAST MARCH

SCOTTISH EAST MARCH

Norham

Wooler

Coldstream

Wark

Flodden Field

Carham

Kelso

Windfoyle

Cocklaw

Harbottle

Otterburn

COQUETDALE

REDESDALE

Bellingham

Hexham

ENGLISH MIDDLE MARCH

Home Castle

Jedburgh

Hermitage

Whithaugh

Branxholm

Mangerton

Kershopefoot

TYNEDALE

Bewcastle

Brackenhill

The Scots Dyke

THE DEBATABLE LAND

Hawick

SCOTTISH MIDDLE MARCH

Horden

Langholm

ESKDALE

Lockerbie

Morton Rigg

Gretna

Longtown

Carlisle

ENGLISH WEST MARCH

ANNANDALE

Amman

SCOTTISH WEST MARCH

Dumfries

Threave Castle

threaten Northumberland, Durham, Cumberland, and Westmorland as they'd done so devastatingly in the wake of Bannockburn, a proper Scottish hegemony. But this time they'd have to get past the House of Percy, charged with holding the line and for all their slippery avarice they did a rather good job.

House of Percy

'The ancient Percies were from the necessities of their position as well as the character of the age more distinguished for moral and physical vigour and energy than for political genius'.[7] This is unfair and inaccurate. Up to the 1st Earl and his son Hotspur, they rarely put a foot wrong while steadily and impressively accumulating vast holdings. Henry Percy, 1st Earl had a glittering career up to the moment of that fatal rift with Henry IV. Then he lost it and the family spent a generation in the wilderness clawing their way back, sparking their deadly and damaging feud with the Nevilles.

No Percy fought at Hastings, the real bonanza for opportunist knights (see Note – Percy and Hastings at the end of this chapter). It's probable William Percy I (not many magnatial families are numbered like royalty) crossed the Channel in the following December, certainly in time to become enmeshed in the situation in the north in 1069. It's also likely the family hailed from Percy-en-Auge, located in the Calvados Department, 15½ miles (25km) south-east of Caen in the valley of the River Dives.[8] De Fonblanque suggests that the Percies may have been descended from a Manfred de Percy, a Dane who followed Viking Rollo into Normandy and that he was baptised by the Bishop of Rheims in 912.[9] A handy tale and one which might contain more than a germ of history.

William (born sometime in the decade between 1030 and 1040) swiftly made his mark, being appointed as castellan at York – a tough assignment by any standard while also serving as deputy-sheriff for the county. It's also suggested, intriguingly, that he was established in England before the Conquest, one of Edward the Confessor's Norman imports and was hustled out again by Harold II. His apparent nickname was 'als Gernons', implying he had facial hair – contrary to prevailing Norman fashion but in line with English (the name Algernon, popular with Percies, is a subsequent derivation). It's been suggested his wife Emma, despite her Norman name, was a daughter of Earl Cospatric, which is thought-provoking but unlikely.[10]

William clearly did well and was rewarded with substantial grants of land which he held as tenant-in-chief, i.e., directly from the Crown, steadily building up an estate of 60,000 acres (25,000 hectares). His immediate feudal superior was Hugh d'Avranches, the Conqueror's nephew and future Earl of Chester, and Percy held a further 10,000 acres (4,170 hectares) from him.[11] In Lincolnshire he netted as many again.[12]

To cap it all, he married well. His wife Emma was in fact almost certainly the daughter of a Norman neighbour, Hugh de Port, Lord of Basing who held wide lands in fertile Hampshire. William's arrival, or return, had neatly coincided with a second burst of Norman expansion. Plum fiefs in the south had gone to those who sweated and bled on Senlac Hill, so this second wave had to be content to carve out holdings in the cold and hostile northlands. But King William rewards carried obligations. As a feudal lord you were obliged to provide your quota of knights and men-at-arms to swell the royal muster. Percy certainly understood the message and parcelled out his newly acquired manors judiciously and by the time of Domesday Book (1086) he had seventeen knights on his rent-roll.[13]

The hub of his burgeoning local empire was his pleasing manor of Topcliffe, north of York, which sits aside a strategic crossroads (today A1/A19). The name means literally 'Top-of-the-Cliff'. It's a commanding elevation with long views all round and overlooking the River Swale where Percy threw up a motte and bailey castle; its clear footprint survives.[14] He built another wooden fort at Tadcaster and a third at Spofforth – where his descendant Henry Percy might have been born in 1364. A neat triangulation, and he kept a decent sized town house in York as well. In 1087, King William died to be succeeded in England by his son William Rufus who had to fight to secure his inheritance. Percy judiciously backed the right horse and remained loyal; his star continued its steady ascent.

Like many of his baronial contemporaries, William Percy appears as a pious man – relentless self-promotion wasn't at odds with a deep and genuine spirituality, moreover this was an era which witnessed a significant boost in monasticism. Monasteries had flourished during the earlier Saxon period, though Viking raids and rule had prompted a steep decline. These new Norman lords cannily helped set their seal on the landscape by sponsoring a major and sustained revival. William became a generous patron of a refreshed house at Whitby (though this doesn't appear to have been an entirely stress-free programme).[15] His piety extended to joining the ranks of Pope Urban's great crusade, despite the fact he would be at least in his fifties, fairly old for his times. Nonetheless, he made it to the Holy Land but never got back, dying in 1096 in sight, it was said, of Jerusalem. All in all, he'd done well going from hopeful immigrant to major regional landowner in a generation. The Percies had arrived.

Alan de Percy who succeeded his father was born in 1072 so took as an adult, avoiding the evils of wardship. He came into his inheritance at the same time as King Henry I who was immediately embroiled in bother with his older brother Robert, getting the upper hand and a decisive result on the field of Tinchebrai in 1106. Alan, like his father, chose his side wisely; those who didn't lost their lands. Alan fought so well some of his contemporaries tagged him as 'the Great'.[16] By dint of 'tenurial engineering' the king redistributed attainted land among those who'd stayed staunch. New figures arrived in Yorkshire (including one Robert de Brus) and Alan netted a further 23,000 acres (9,580 hectares).[17]

David I of Scotland spent many years as a pensioner of the English court; his chances of reigning seemed distant but matured unexpectedly when both his older brothers died childless. He was the last of Malcolm III (Canmore's) sons, a man of great ability and something of an Anglophile. Having spent so long at the English court it was thought 'he had rubbed off all the tarnish of Scottish barbarity'.[18] It was he who introduced Norman feudalism into Scotland more by infiltration than invasion; the de Brus were significant beneficiaries as, more tangentially, were the Percies. One of Alan Percy's bastards was granted lands in the Scottish borderland but unlike so many others, there was no Scottish line of Percies, the minefield of cross-border estate and divided loyalties would not entangle them as it did so many others.

Alan Percy died in the same year as King Henry, 1135, leaving his heir William de Percy II as an adult successor (we're not sure of the year of this William's birth but he was clearly mature). Alan might not have had the stellar career his father had enjoyed but he'd continued the family's seemingly inexorable rise, leaving his son a very solid foundation. Just as well, Yorkshire was about to become the new front line. King David had first pounced in 1136 but Stephen had obliged him to back down. Two years later and Matilda was in a superior position – time for a second try. This was a well-planned and executed two-pronged invasion, a thrust (extraordinarily successful) into Cumbria and a major blow in the east aimed at asserting his rights in Northumberland. The new marcher lords said no.

On 22 August 1138 English knights and men-at-arms deployed a couple of miles (3.2km) north of Northallerton in North Yorkshire, looking uphill at a dazzling array of Scottish lords, banners blazing and backed by a tough-looking crew of Gallowegians from the south-west. A wild downhill charge from the Scots was met with an archery barrage which decimated King David's unarmoured Gallowegians, their bodies so studded with arrows they seemed 'like hedgehogs with quills'.[19]

Though William de Percy II served with the northern saints his illegitimate relation fought for King David – perhaps not so much a case of divided loyalties as hedging your bets. While the wily King of Scots might have lost the war, he did win the peace. Stephen was too weak to open a second front on his northern border, so granted Northumbria's earldom to David who installed his son Henry as proxy, thus achieving his goal of a border hegemony, his writ running down to the Tees. William de Percy who held lands in Craven meanwhile had to adjust to Scots' supremacy in the west where David's deputy and winner of another, if smaller, fight at Clitheroe, William Fitz Duncan, enjoyed quasi vice-regal status. In fact, and this is a tribute to William's charm and acumen, the two men rubbed along very well and established a lasting amity.

King Stephen, hopeless and worn out, was probably happy to hand over the reins to Matilda's son by Geoffrey of Anjou, charismatic and able Henry II. By now King David of Scotland was dead too, as was his son Henry, leaving a boy, Malcolm IV, on the throne. Henry II intended to fully reclaim the north and browbeat young Malcolm into agreeing a deal whereby he was bought off with the Earldom of Huntingdon and Regality of Tynedale. William de Percy was no longer a borderer, the line was restored; peace prevailed, at least for the moment. A great patron of monastic revivals, William who died in 1174/5 was buried in Fountains Abbey.[20]

Despite leaving the Percies in a healthy position, William departed childless, in spite his two marriages. His first was to Alice de Tunbridge, a daughter of Richard, 3rd Earl of Clare – an excellent match and though he had no surviving male heirs, there's a hint he had at least one son, Ralph (who may perhaps have been illegitimate). Nonetheless, Ralph, at least according to legend, exhibited all the Percy inclination toward hot-tempered and violent solutions. One day he along with two chums was hunting in Whitby Forest, chasing a boar they'd wounded. The pig fled into St Hilda's Chapel, where the priest was minded to offer sanctuary. Percy was so enraged by this that he killed the clergyman, incurring a hefty penance.[21]

Whatever the truth, William did leave two surviving daughters by Alice: these were Matilda and Agnes, both eligible heiresses. Matilda married William, Earl of Warwick and when her husband pre-deceased her, she elected to stay a widow and bought out the Crown's reversionary interest in her portion of the family lands. She survived till 1202, just outlasted by her sister Agnes who'd married very well indeed. Her husband was Jocelin, Count of Louvain, who could trace his line clear back to Charlemagne. His half-sister Adeliza had been first King Henry's second wife and her large estate centred on Arundel came, in due course, into Jocelin's grasp. These holdings, making up the Barony of Petworth, roughly 25 per cent of the vast Arundel lands, were real plums and this acquisition began the process of transforming the Percies from regional into national players.[22] When Jocelin died Agnes, like her sister, stayed in widow's weeds retaining her portion of her patrimony, though Petworth reverted to the Crown.

Agnes left two male heirs, Henry (probably the elder) and Richard. Henry bought Petworth back having wed the daughter of another Yorkshire landowner before dying in 1198. His heir, another William III, took as a minor and ward of King John. Greedy and needy, the king sold William's wardship on to one of his affinity, William Brewer, who next got his hands on Matilda's portion when she died. When Will Percy came of age, he married his ward's daughter and laid claim to Agnes' portion which her surviving son and William's uncle Richard had been enjoying. Their dispute endured a generation and made many lawyers happy. Uncle and nephew remained in de facto possession and enjoyment of their respective portions until Richard died childless in 1244 (ironically perhaps his first wife of two was a Neville). William who only survived him by a year took as his second spouse a Baliol and produced an heir, Henry II in Percy chronology. He got everything.

King John's has not enjoyed a positive reputation. Richard Percy was one of those who came to oppose him, abandoning the family's steadfast loyalty. Aside from his slide into tyranny, John, who was far from incapable, seems to have tried to exert greater influence in the north than his predecessors. Northerners had got rather used to a fair degree of home rule and didn't care too much for royal interference. Richard was heavily implicated in the swelling tide of baronial opposition, even going so far as to join a plot to have the king murdered while engaged on his Welsh chevauchée. In the aftermath of Runnymede, Richard was appointed as one of a committee or cabal of twenty-five barons set up to keep a watchful eye on the king. Nobody trusted John to keep his word and they certainly weren't mistaken.

King John died, embittered and broken, at Newark on 18 or 19 October 1216. The accession of the 9-year-old Henry changed the complexion of the civil war with the barometer of baronial support swinging away from French Prince Louis in favour of the boy king. Richard de Percy was one of the last rebel lords to lay down his arms but once reconciled remained loyal to young Henry III. On his death Richard too was buried at Fountains. William de Percy, his nephew, had stuck by King John throughout the First Barons' War. This division of loyalties might have mirrored the bad blood between the two knights, but it might also have represented a further hedging of bets; during civil war it paid to have a foot in both camps. Henry Percy II also succeeded as a minor but bought out the royal wardship in his mid-teens.[23]

On a warm summer's day in 1265, during a fierce electrical storm, Henry III of England found himself a helpless spectator to the furious battle being fought for control of his kingdom just outside the town of Evesham. A puppet of the baronial faction, he had been led onto the field in full harness and now wandered, impotent and largely irrelevant, as the violent denouement of the Second Barons' War flared around him. Wounded in the shoulder and in peril of being cut down in the frenzy, he was finally rescued by his eldest son, as a contribution to the restoration of his authority.

Now, Henry Percy stayed firmly wedded to the Crown as part of John de Warenne, the Earl of Surrey's affinity (Petworth being the connection). His service on the field of Lewes was far from glorious and he was captured thus missing the subsequent bloodbath at Evesham – still nobody could question his level of support. At the relatively advanced age of 33, he married de Warenne's daughter, being far more adroit in the wedding stakes than on the field. Though he only lived for three years after his marriage, Henry produced two sons, the elder, John, little is known about and he was certainly dead by 1293. The younger, destined to be Henry Percy III, was born on 25 March 1273.[24]

War on the Marches

For others, particularly the House of Percy, opportunity, in the shape of the Scottish Wars, was about to come knocking. Now they were grand; soon they'd be great. The north of England might be rough, wild, and dangerous but it offered unlimited potential. Much of this focused upon the office of warden which allowed the magnate to build up a private army, often courtesy of the public purse and to aggrandise himself while acting on behalf of the state. The Percies were exceptionally good at this but no different or less rapacious than the other great northern names: Neville, Umfraville.[25] Or, on the Scottish side, Douglas, or Dunbar. From 1345 the English Marches became designated simply as East and West. Forty odd years afterwards the eastern half was further divided into a coastal and 'middle' section, though these were habitually administered by one warden.[26]

Henry Percy was born in 1273 and inherited on the death of his older brother (date uncertain).[27] Young Henry was active in the lists and served during Edward's earlier Welsh campaigns. In 1295, just before things blew up in Scotland, he accompanied de Warenne on a diplomatic mission (the earl was his grandfather). Hostilities began on 26 March the following year, a providential birthday gift to young Percy who'd now reached the age of 29. He bloodied his sword at both Berwick and Dunbar.

Later, during Longshanks' 1298 campaign against Wallace, a roll of arms or muster list, the Falkirk Roll, was created by Percy's herald, Walter le Rey Marchis – heralds were, at this formative point, something of a novelty. Percy was one of 110 bannerets who'd serve.[28] Edwards' army was formidable: 2,500 cavalry, as many as 12,000 foot soldiers, a heterogeneous force with archers from Wales and crossbowmen from Gascony. By July, this leviathan was plodding northward advancing up the east coast, an English fleet in close support. In the battle that ensued Edward proceeded to win an impressive all-arms victory using heavy cavalry, infantry, and bowmen, utterly defeating Wallace whose army was destroyed. Percy was with de Warenne's brigade and clearly fought with distinction, earning his title of Lord Percy the next year. From now on the fortunes of his name would be inextricably linked to the border wars and this bitter fury Longshanks had unleashed would rage for three centuries.

Lord Percy, on the other hand, was doing very well. He served at the siege of three-sided Caerlaverock in 1300 and that of Stirling four years later. Two years after that he was district commander for the West March, with civic responsibilities for Cumberland and occupied zones of Dumfriesshire. He had ample incentives. In 1299 he'd been handed the confiscated estates of Ingram de

Baliol, all in the south-west of Scotland. Baliol had fallen foul of Longshanks, but Percy and he were related as both were grandsons (by different wives) of William de Percy III (d.1245).[29]

Ageing Edward was shrewdly binding his English subjects into the realities of the Scottish conquest by granting cross-border estates, from which, overall, much grief would flow. Percy also gained the earldom of Buchan, stripped from the de Comyns but held it only briefly till they reverted after Red Comyn's taking off and Percy had to hand back their estates. But the very savagery of repression just fed the patriot cause and in the following year, the old warrior king died almost literally in the saddle at Burgh by Sands as he prepared for yet another campaign. Though dead, his spirit seemed destined to live on – he left instructions for his son, now crowned Edward II, to continue the offensive and that the king's coffin, like some malevolent talisman, be carried before the army.[30]

Lord Henry Percy would now be one of those who could feel the earth move and realise there wasn't a lot he could do about it. To succeed the English drive had to be relentless, no room for a dilettante approach. This new Edward's sybaritic indifference must have been galling, not to mention costly. As David Lomas observes, it's hardly surprising that Percy's resentment, like that of others, boiled over and he joined those disaffected magnates, the 'Ordainers', who in 1311 sought to curb the king's prerogative. He participated in hated Gaveston's seizure at Scarborough but seems to have stood aloof from his subsequent judicial murder.

Bannockburn changed everything. Battle was joined south of Stirling Castle on 23 June 1314 and continued the next day. Edward's lumbering army was broken and scattered, Stirling fell, and Scotland was free. It was a pivotal moment. Henry Percy was summoned to serve during the ill-starred English campaign but, despite being only 41, died almost certainly before the battle. He certainly wasn't killed or captured there; he might possibly have died of wounds but probably succumbed to unknown natural causes. He was also interred in Fountains Abbey. After all, the Percies were still very much a Yorkshire family.

Lords of Alnwick

What Henry had done which would influence the family fortunes forever was to acquire the Barony of Alnwick from Anthony Bek, the colourful Bishop of Durham. This estate, already the grandest in Northumberland, had been created by Henry I in around or before 1130 and had, for a considerable time, been owned by the de Vesci family. It is not known how much Percy paid but it was likely a great deal, and there is evidence that he had to borrow from Italian bankers to complete the purchase.[31] A taint of corruption clung to the sale; testamentary provisions within the de Vesci family were complex and Bek's capacity has been questioned.

Certainly, Henry's heir, yet another Henry, 2nd Lord Percy, paid a hefty premium to the surviving de Vesci heir for affirming that his father's acquisition had all been above board, which clearly suggests it may not have been. From the 1st Lord Percy's point of view Alnwick was a desirable and significant addition, linking his traditional Yorkshire holdings to his hoped-for satrapy in southern Scotland, a handy base for future campaigning. At the same time, he'd kept one eye on the south where he was careful to strengthen links with the powerful Fitz Alans, latterly Earls of Arundel. Affinity, after all, was everything.[32]

This new Lord Percy was a child of the East Riding. As he took as a minor, he'd not come into his own till December 1321 when Edward II knighted him at York. The king was not popular. Frustrations with Edward's seeming mix of indifference and incompetence drove Sir Andrew de Harcla from the English West March (who'd save the king's honour by defeating the Earl of Lancaster's rebels at Boroughbridge in 1322) to mediate a separate peace with Bruce. Lancaster had, as early as 1313, been in treasonous communication with the Scottish king and Harcla's efforts, undoubtedly genuine, still cost him his head. Nonetheless, the Treaty of Northampton was the crowning moment of Bruce's highly eventful career; he was recognised by his inveterate enemies as a free prince and, as his health failed, he bequeathed an orderly realm to his successor.

Despite having given his name to the treaty, Edward III was determined to avenge the humiliation of Bannockburn and to recover Berwick, upon which so much English treasure had been lavished and which remained, as always, the key to the East March. Bower warned the Scots: 'An Englishman is an angel who no one can believe; when he greets you, beware of him as an enemy'.[33] He may, of course, have been prone to bias. This class of redundant Scottish nobles led by Edward Baliol, son of the unlamented King John, provided a ready-made insurgency and the English king was happy to provide a fleet of eighty-odd ships, in which the adventurers set sail from the Humber in the summer of 1332. The 'Disinherited' made an unopposed landing at Kinghorn and boldly marched inland to Dunfermline, aiming for Perth where on Dupplin Moor they won a major battle.

Meanwhile, Edward III had other priorities, particularly the pursuit of his claim to the throne of France. This was the spark which ignited the Hundred Years War which effectively expanded the Anglo-Scottish Wars into a European conflict. Edward wasn't bothered about conquering Scotland; he just wanted to keep the back door nailed shut. That meant creating a pale, or occupied zone, in southern Scotland and backing this with northern English ready, willing, and able to take on the Scots without the support of southern armies. Those wasted upland dales were re-settled by freelances who held their land with the sword not by the plough. They would need leaders and fortunately the Percies were here, as were the Nevilles and Umfravilles. Poor knights from the shires couldn't maintain their much-wasted manors but a powerful magnate with extensive holdings could buy out these lesser fry and build up a vast hegemony. The new Lord Percy owned Alnwick and he still held extensive and profitable lands in Yorkshire.

Lord Henry Percy was a constant and zealous servant of his king. He held office as keeper of royal fortresses at Scarborough, Skipton, and Bamburgh, a wide-ranging portfolio and served as March Warden. He frequently raised local forces for various campaigns against the Scots, favouring the contract system refined by King Edward. Such paid, professional forces were infinitely more effective than the old feudal levy and English marchers were fast becoming experts. Percy himself was rarely out of the saddle. He wasn't at Dupplin Moor as he wasn't really one of the 'Disinherited' but got stuck in with gusto once hostilities proper got going, fighting at Halidon Hill and helping to recover Berwick.

During subsequent brawling on the Marches, Percy was obliged to work alongside Ralph Neville, Lord of Raby, a fellow northern magnate. Between them they saw off a major Scots raid against Redesdale. That leading lords would be acting in concert was necessary, but Nevilles and Percies would be competing as rivals and finally enemies; their relationship would, in the fifteenth century, turn toxic. Percy fought during three years of rigorous campaigning, 1336–8, and something is known of his actions during the muster of May 1337 when 25 leading knights agreed to raise a total of just over 500 men-at-arms. As befitted a most powerful lord, the Earl of Warwick as commander brought 120 soldiers, but it was Percy who supplied the second largest contingent.[34] He was back over the border still in harness in 1342 and again two years later.

It wasn't all armour-bashing. In 1328 he'd been one of a quartet sent to negotiate terms with Bruce. This was timely as the Scottish king had confiscated the lands he'd amassed in the south-west of his country. Percy persuaded him to return these so avoided ever becoming one of the Disinherited (astutely, and just to be sure, he bought off Baliol as these had been part of his family's patrimony). Next, he'd done his bit in arranging the marriage alliance between David II and Edward III's sister Joan. A few years later he was senior ambassador at Edward Baliol's one and only threadbare Scottish parliament.

In October 1346, David II, trying to ease the pressure on his French allies, humiliated at Crécy, invaded northern England. The marcher lords prepared to resist, and battle was joined at Neville's Cross just outside Durham. Drawn up in their customary three battles with a body of archers in front, Henry Percy took the right; Neville the centre; and Rokeby, bolstered by spiritual guidance from the Archbishop of York, commanded the left. What followed, after a hard-fought engagement, was another famous English victory with the Scots vanquished and worse, King David captured. This loss was a disaster for his country, and he remained a prisoner in the Tower for those eleven years while both sides haggled over his ransom.

All in all, Henry, 2nd Lord Percy did very well out of both war and peace. In 1332 King Edward rewarded his services with the grant of Sir John Clavering's estate which had reverted to the Crown upon his death, a great acquisition and Percy traded in his annuity, bestowed for good service.[35] A bare two years later and he acquired the manor of Thirston, followed by the significant plum of the Earl of Dunbar's English holdings. Obliged to choose between the northern or southern kingdoms, the earl had opted for his Scottish estates and those extensive lands he held in Northumberland dropped into Percy's lap. In a generation the family had gone from newcomers to the county's biggest landowner.

Earlier, after Baliol had won so unexpectedly at Dupplin Moor, Lord Percy cheerfully offered him his sword and netted Annandale and Moffatdale as part of the contract. But King Edward wanted those lands transferred to the de Bohuns on the basis his grandfather had made an original grant back in 1306. Percy wasn't left empty handed; the king rewarded his ever-loyal subject with Jedburgh and Jedforest (a cue for conflict with the Douglases), the keepership of Berwick and a revived cash annuity payable from the town's customs revenue. Despite the prohibition on cross-border estates, Percy was a de facto leading landowner in Scotland. Four years after Neville's Cross he was sent to broker a lasting truce. Nonetheless, his had been an outstandingly successful career, a steady but inexorable rise. He died, in his bed, at Warkworth in February 1352 in his 51st year.

Percy was buried at Alnwick, surely evidence of the family's northern migration, and survived by his widow Idonea, herself a daughter of Lord Clifford, the leading family of Westmorland, Henry's old comrade-in-arms who'd been killed at Bannockburn. They produced a healthy brood, Henry their eldest boy succeeded as Henry Percy III (the only non-royal name to be so numbered). A second son became Bishop of Norwich while one daughter married into the Umfravilles and another the Nevilles: such marriage alliances were a central tactic in affinity building.

This new third Lord Percy had been born perhaps in 1320 so was already in his early thirties when he succeeded and an experienced knight. He'd served under the Earl of Arundel (he may well have been apprenticed in his illustrious kinsman's household) and most of his early exploits occurred in the French war, winning his spurs in such famous English victories as Sluys (1340), Morlaix (1342), and Crécy (1346). He took part in the epoch-shifting capture of Calais and served in Gascony under the brilliant Earl of Lancaster. His father's death meant his personal emphasis shifted back to England and the northern frontier. This was fast becoming a Percy monopoly.

Henry soon took on the governorship of Berwick, was appointed Warden of the Marches, Keeper of Roxburgh (a vital bastion in Edward's forward defence strategy) and acted as Sheriff of Roxburghshire; a useful appointment for keeping an eye on family estates round Jedburgh. Neville's Cross had been such a resounding victory and with King David imprisoned the Marches were, by local standards, quite quiet. Local standards were pretty flexible, in 1355–6, the winter of 'Burnt Candlemas', there was more bother and the Scots, albeit briefly, recovered Berwick. Percy may, in this instance, have been absent, returning with the king to France as effectively chief of staff, a very prestigious assignment. He may have been involved in the campaign of Poitiers but missed the battle itself. Percy was still in France three years later preparing to take part in Edward's major expedition to capture Rheims which if he succeeded would have ended the French war. It didn't and the king had to be satisfied with the terms of the Treaty of Brétigny.

Once this deal was done, Percy returned to Northumberland. His first wife Mary was Henry of Lancaster's sister, but she predeceased him, and his second spouse was Joan, heiress of John, Lord Orreby. This was in 1365 and three year later, aged only 48, Henry Percy himself died. Both he and his first wife were interred at Alnwick, most likely in the Premonstratensian canonry.[36] His too had been an illustrious and phenomenally successful career, the Percies could be said to be flying but they were in fact about to soar.

Note – Percy and Hastings

I am indebted to Chris Hunwick for the following discussion. Traditionally, it has been asserted that William de Percy was not present at the Battle of Hastings but came over the following year in 1067. The source for this statement is an entry in a Whitby Abbey cartulary: 'Memorandum quod A.D. millesimo sexagesimo septimo, Hugo, Comes Cestrensis, et Willelmus Percy, venerunt in Angliam cum Domino Willelmo, Duce Normannorum, Conquestore.' 'In the year 1066, Hugh, the Marshal of the Camp and William Percy came to England with William Duke of Normandy, the Conqueror.'

This is given as entry number 376 in the Surtees Society edition of cartularies of Whitby Abbey. It is footnoted in that edition as follows:

> This is rather an extraordinary document, inasmuch as the statements it makes are in some instances entirely incompatible with known facts, and even, as will be noticed below, with the direct and most distinct statements conveyed or involved in not a few of the Charters contained in the preceding parts of the book itself. This is unfortunate, as having a direct tendency and force towards rendering its statements, when more in consistency with truth and evidence, of less authority. Were it otherwise, the statements involved in the sentences to which this note is appended would be of great value as well as importance.

Interestingly, the edition also notes that the chartulary breaks off abruptly in the middle of the previous entry, followed by a blank verso, a leaf cut out, and then two blank folios. The authenticity of number 376, therefore, is called into doubt by its late position in the volume and its separation from the earlier text by a missing leaf and blank folios, not to mention its inaccuracies.

Even if the 1067 date is accurate, this does not preclude William Percy from having been at Hastings. After all, William the Conqueror himself is also noted in this same source as returning to England in 1067, as he is known to have returned to France to celebrate after the Battle of Hastings. The same might equally be true of William de Percy. One might question why William de Percy would have been 'so beloved' by William the Conqueror and rewarded with the grant of a significant proportion of Yorkshire had he not been at the Battle of Hastings.

Battle Abbey, founded by William the Conqueror on the spot where Harold was slain, is said once to have contained a commemorative list of the Companions of the Conqueror. The original has been lost since at least the sixteenth century and its contents are only known from sixteenth-century published copies by Leland, Holinshed, and Duchesne, whose versions contradict each other, leading to estimates of the numbers of Companions varying between 149 and 629.

The more recent discovery of the Auchinleck Manuscript in the National Library of Scotland provides a perhaps more accurate mid-fourteenth-century copy of the Battle Abbey Roll. Folio 106r of the Auchinleck MS clearly lists 'Percy' as one of the 551 surnames. It is, however, only a surname and does not prove William's presence, as it is known, for instance, that Reinfred de Percy, William's cousin, was part of William the Conqueror's war band. Bishop Thomas Percy, the eighteenth-century chaplain to the 1st Duke and Duchess, discovered a list of those of repute who came over with William the Conqueror in Harleian MS 293. The original source of the list is given as a copy of Matthew Paris' *Flores Historiarum* belonging to All Souls College, Oxford. The first leaf of this MS is missing (since the nineteenth century) and there is now no trace of the 'list'. Bishop Percy's notes give the following opening of the list: 'Dominus Percye magnus constabellarius, dominus Mowbraye mariscallus . . .'. The evidence is inconclusive either way, but the burden of proof would seem to lie with those seeking to deny William de Percy a place in the battle line.

Act 2

Sensible of Courtesy –
A Knightly Apprenticeship

What is it good for
Absolutely nothing
Uh-huh
War, huh, yeah
What is it good for
Absolutely nothing
Say it again, y'all
War, huh, good God
        'War' by Edwin Starr

How that red rain hath made the harvest grow
And is this all the world hath gained by thee
Thou first and last of fields! King making victory?
      Byron, *Childe Harold's Pilgrimage*, canto III

In a side chapel in the Church of St John of Beverley, St John's Lee in Northumberland, is a beautifully carved marble effigy of a 'knight', in fact a young man called Simon Mewburn who died in Palestine during the First World War but who lies in his home parish inside this splendid tomb.[1] His effigy, slightly larger than life size, is superbly detailed down to the nails of his boots and he's laid out as one of his fourteenth-century ancestors might have been.

This memorial is a fine and very conscious tribute to the cult of chivalry, still alive six centuries after Hotspur. Here lies a true knight, one who served God and England and fell in the good fight, a proper *Kalos thanatos*. A century on and knightly ideals, smacking of elitism and imperialism, are a good deal less exalted, yet the sad and moving vigils of the citizens of Wootton Basset as each flag-draped casualty of the war in Afghanistan came through the town shows the notion is not completely dead, and probably never will be. Hotspur might have wondered at Simon Mewburn's kit, but he'd surely have recognised what he represented.

Age of Chivalry

Chivalry – the knightly class of feudal times: the primary sense of the term in Europe in the Middle Ages is 'knights,' or 'fully armed and mounted fighting men.' Thence the term came to mean the gallantry and honour expected of knights. Later the word came to be used in its general sense of 'courtesy.' In English law 'chivalry' meant the tenure of land by knights' service. The court of chivalry instituted by Edward III, with the Lord High Constable and Earl Marshal of England as joint judges, had summary jurisdiction in all cases of offences of knights and generally as to military matters.

This concept of chivalry in the sense of 'honourable and courteous conduct expected of a knight' was perhaps at its height in the 12th and 13th centuries and was strengthened by the Crusades, which led to the founding of the earliest orders of chivalry, the Order of the Hospital of St. John of Jerusalem (Hospitallers) and the Order of the Poor Knights of Christ and of the Temple of Solomon (Templars), both originally devoted to the service of pilgrims to the Holy Land: in the 14th and 15th centuries the ideals of chivalry came to be associated increasingly with aristocratic display and public ceremony rather than service in the field.[2]

Hotspur is portrayed as a fanatical devotee of chivalry or rather the cult of chivalry and had he not been, this would have been surprising. This was something young men of his caste were likely to be obsessed with. Ideas of chivalry had been maturing for a long time and changed over the centuries, and Harry's era was perhaps its greatest or certainly most flamboyant phase. Its roots were ancient, and its tenure kept rippling long after, the Eglinton Tournament of 1839 was a nineteenth-century romantic revival while jousting is still alive and well as part of today's living history movement. Chivalric ideals were the essence of feudal superiority, a code owned by the warrior elite, the lifeblood of pan-European aristocracy. Kings such as Edward I and especially his grandson were obsessed by and promoted the cult of King Arthur. This part mythical hero and his Knights of the Round Table were England's *Iliad*, our homegrown legend and timeless barometer of noble conduct.

Knighthood in a basic form had also been in existence for a long time – the idea of a privileged warrior elite, whose status lifted them clear of more workaday mortals, 'rude mechanicals', but also imposed a set of binding obligations. In Homer's *Iliad*, as discussed, the Lycian hero and Trojan ally Sarpedon spells it out for his comrade Glaucos.[3] The archaeological evidence for Northern Europe's own version, the so-called Battle of Tollense (*c.* 1300–1200 BC), echoes this theme. Interpretation of human and equine remains suggests that possibly both sides in this unsung fight, which claimed as many as a thousand victims and probably involved five times that number of combatants, were led by mounted warrior elites. Unfortunately, no literary or historical records of this battle remain.

At the outset, before the Church imposed a civilising and controlling hand, it was indeed all about the warrior; the strong man whose function was to bear arms and face danger without flinching. And if there isn't any danger lurking, he needs to go out and find some. Edward III, who'd also created the Order of the Garter, promoted a near fanatical obsession with Arthur and his knights. Much of this may be myth but glimmers of a Dark-Age past do keep surfacing before the Church laid on a restraining hand.

Sir Tristan, serving his uncle Mark of Cornwall whose kingdom is in thrall to Irish warlords, challenges the oppressors' champion, Marhaus. The two meet on a small island which they reach by coracles. If one succumbs to fear and runs for his boat, he's lost. When the big Irishman taunts Tristan, sneering he needs to tie the boat up properly so it's there when he needs to flee, the hero simply pushes it away into the stream, the message being that only one of them is going back alive (it's not the Irishman). Hotspur would have been raised on such fine tales and Northumberland abounds with Arthurian resonances, Bamburgh was said to have been Lancelot's Joyous Garde, where he shelters Guinevere. Why would such tales not thrill lads bred to be covetous of honour?

Saxon kings and thegns built up retinues of professional fighting men, trained warriors for every working day and rewarded their feats with silver arm rings and, above all, land. The association with status and landholding is already established; ultimately that is what the fighter craves. His career span is relatively short before age and/or wounds take him out from the game. Without land he's just a beggar. But the more successful the king, the greater his war-band and then the resultant pressure to acquire more land increases. Once the early Church is added to the mix and proves even more acquisitive, satisfying the warrior elite becomes a real problem.

Knighthood as an estate properly arrives with William the Conqueror and slides neatly into those upper tiers of his feudal pyramid, below the magnates and senior clergy with their raft of rights and obligations neatly defined. This is the medieval solar system, but the problem is knights become a curse. There are too many landless warriors and unemployed younger sons, whose only trade is war; having no war at all isn't that much of an option. Then, in 1095 Pope Urban II had a brilliant idea, how to match his twin objectives of freeing up the Holy Places and curbing this boisterous and dangerous excess of testosterone. At Clermont, he unveils his strategy and lectures Europe's fractious chevaliers:

> This land which you knight inhabit . . . is too narrow for your large
> population, nor does it abound in wealth . . . hence it is that you murder

and devour one another, that you wage war and that so frequently you perish by mutual wounds. Let, therefore, hatred depart from among you, let your quarrels end . . . take the road to the Holy Sepulchre and wrest that land from the wicked one.[4]

This is a perfect example of creative genius. Urban sets out to recover these Holy Places and teach the Infidel a lesson, gets rid of his knightly overpopulation *and* takes control of knighthood as an institution. From now on Church and sword are carefully fused and, in name at least, the Church now fully controls its quarrelsome subjects. What they do in the Holy Land is up to them. Some, like the gloriously reprehensible Bohemund, will go with the express desire of carving out kingdoms for themselves but even as they stumble incompetently across Europe and the Levant, these first crusaders become the sword of the lord. Their suffering only sharpens their edge and, in 1099, they achieve God's holy purpose, taking Jerusalem, admittedly in a deluge of blood but they win. It's steadily downhill after that but Urban's twin objectives have been met.

Knighthood is transformed, sanctified by the good fight to see off the heathen and a slew of knightly orders, austere, monastic, and seriously avaricious, come into being. Some, like the Templars, become so powerful they threaten the French state or are perceived to, besides King Philip needs their treasure. Crusading remains the ideal even if relatively few ever trouble to experience its reality. Yet Hotspur, like his uncle Thomas, wants to serve in the Baltic Crusades in 1383.[5] His younger sibling Ralph takes part in the disastrous campaign and Battle of Nicopolis thirteen years later (this time God isn't on their side and the crusading army is shattered by Sultan Bayezid). Percy's long-term rivals, the Nevilles, also took part in the northern crusades as did Henry Bolingbroke, the future Henry IV.[6]

Crusader poet Aymer de Pegulhan sums it up: 'Behold, without renouncing our rich garments, our station in life, all that pleases and charms, we can obtain honours down here and joy in paradise'.[7] It is a highly beneficial situation. In his will, Henry, 2nd Lord Percy makes a bequest of 1,000 marks (£666.67p) – at least £100,000 today – to endow a pilgrimage to the Holy Land.[8] King Henry IV always wanted to go on a real crusade, though dying in his Jerusalem Chamber was the closest he got. Even as late as the sixteenth century with Machiavelli's stark realpolitik starting to become prominent, King James IV of Scotland often expressed his desire to crusade – in his case Flodden Edge was the nearest he achieved, and he didn't come back.

None of this happy idealism impacts too much on the earthly business of winning lands and settling private scores. An anecdote is told of Sir John Hawkwood, a notorious mercenary *condottiere* whose White Company formed a perfect example of all that was bad. Sir John, who'd amassed a vast fortune from Italy's endless civil wars, riding through Florence, tossed a coin to a mendicant friar, whereupon the grateful priest wished him eternal peace. Angrily, the knight snatched the silver back, retorting that he'd no use for peace, war was what he needed.

In practical terms, chivalry allowed the knight to participate fully in national and sub-state violence where he was fighting the Crown's Christian enemies or indeed rebels and defining who was a rebel largely depended on the outcome. This describes the cockpit Harry Hotspur lived and fought in. As a true knight he would fight the king's enemies in Scotland, France, or even Wales. He wasn't branded a rebel for his part in Bolingbroke's usurpation, just when his own subsequent attempt at king un-making foundered.

From the romantic troubadour culture of Languedoc, chivalry gained the further ideal of courtly love. This was Lancelot and Guinevere again, where the knight loved chastely but passionately, setting up the object of his desire as a temple to ideal womanhood, writing her poems and letters without necessarily indulging in carnal activities. As Andreas the Chaplain expressed in his *De Arte Honeste Amandi*: 'Love is a certain suffering denied from the sight of and excessive meditation upon the beauty of the opposite sex'.[9] Was Hotspur a devotee, probably yes but did the reality of his life measure up?

Probably not, such ascetic infatuations only extended to women of the same social class; Longshanks had gibbeted Bruce's women, hung them in cages from his battlements. Hotspur took part in endless border raids where he'd have seen women casually abused, raped, and murdered:

> They spared neither man nor wife
> Young or old of mankind that bore life
> Like wild wolves in fury
> Both burnt and slew with great cruelty.[10]

Hotspur may even have ordered such atrocities or at least condoned them. Courtly love was an ideal, at best an aspiration; realities of medieval warfare shaped up very differently.

That other great ideal was comradeship; knighthood fostering true brotherhood. This wasn't new; Achilles and Patroclus, Roland and Oliver, tinged perhaps in some instances with homo-eroticism, but such bonds were clearly forged:

> We have been brothers-in-arms from the very beginning and we have been and still are bound to one another in such a way, that each will stand by the other to the death if need be, saving his honour, and thus true affection has brought me to his assistance, to aid him by my body and with all my goods, as he would do the same for me if I had need of him.[11]

Shakespeare gives us his version when Prince Hal laments Hotspur's death at Shrewsbury:

> If thou wert sensible of courtesy
> I should not make so dear a show of zeal
> But let my favours hide thy mangled face
> And, even in thy behalf I'll thank myself
> For doing these fair rites of tenderness
> Adieu, and take thy praise with thee to heaven
> Thy ignominy sleep with thee in the grave
> But not remember'd in thy epitaph.[12]

Obviously, this never happened, there was no climatic duel and Hotspur, shot down by an anonymous archer, died in the muck alongside so many of his affinity. We can doubt that Prince Hal, diverted by the painful business of having a bodkin point extracted from his face, felt anything other than relief that his enemy was dead.

One thing is certain, becoming a knight was not a vocation for dilettantes; it was a very tough process, part boot camp, part finishing school, part martial arts and all hard work. At the age of about 7 the boy began his long apprenticeship as a page where he'd begin with the rudiments of combat and equitation. He'd serve at table, learn the arts of courtesy and gentlemanly behaviour; a knight must know how to behave as well as fight. Only those from the correct social strata were able to undertake this. It wasn't or would ever be a comprehensive system; it was designed to promote elitism, to foster a breed apart. After about seven years of this preparation, by now in his mid-teens, his real training would begin and this would likely be in the household of some great lord, part of his wider family affinity, that vital web of alliances and allegiances that defined a man's place, power, and position.

He'd now be a squire apprenticed to an experienced knight who was mentor, disciplinarian, and role model. He'd clean weapons, burnish mail with sand till it shone, assist his master in arming either for the fight or the joust, and socialise with other boys undergoing this very same induction. He'd be encouraged to be harshly competitive, to excel and to understand that personal honour was all. Spartan the training may have been, but this was about the individual rather than his being part of a wider corporate identity, yet his class conferred membership of a European-wide fraternity. You were your name and name mattered more than anything else but at the same time you were a paid-up member of a wider international oligarchy of the highest status.

A select 'band of brothers' indeed, who lived and trained for war together and if there weren't any wars, they'd fight in the lists. Before he qualified, the initiate spent a whole night in silent vigil, his sword upon the altar, so the Church could remind him of where his spiritual allegiance lay. In the morning or perhaps before battle he'd be dubbed by his feudal superior. Then he'd be a knight, be he a magnate's son or a poorer knight from the shires, he'd achieved the exalted status. Yet in its own way knighthood was a great leveller within its own exalted caste; status had to be won by hard work, dedication, and achievement, it wasn't strictly a birth right.

Wargames

An unknown fifteenth-century artist has left us an image of the celebrated tournament at St Inglevert, 10 miles (16km) south-west of Calais. The spectacle portrayed is just what you'd expect a proper high-medieval joust to look like. Amid glittering pavilions knights in full plate harness, destriers gorgeously caparisoned in glowing fabrics, charge boldly at full tilt, lances levelled over the barrier. Lords and ladies, decked out in their finest silks, watch from the stands. Naturally, the sun is shining, no mud and no horse dung anywhere. Successful jousters became superstars.

By Hotspur's day jousting was far more than a sport; it was training for war and could easily get close. Yet it was also this exclusive fraternity where members could meet and socialise, perhaps even going as far as to plot sedition, a perfect cover to mask more clandestine intentions. It hadn't always been this formal; the beginnings of what was primarily an Anglo–French experience went as far back as King Stephen's day, boosted by the Arthurian revival of Longshanks and his grandson Edward III. It was the first Edward who by his *Statuta Armorum* in 1292 laid down regulatory provisions for the management of jousts. This was timely as many early tournaments were mass brawls, fought in open fields and often spilling into adjacent countryside, with wounds, more severe injuries, and even deaths commonplace.

It was later in the thirteenth and fourteenth centuries that single combats, on foot or mounted between individual knights, morphed into the main attraction. Jousting became for some a trade; that grand and formidable thug William the Marshal, latterly Earl of Pembroke, became a living legend. Lords, their household knights, and squires competed as teams, which was helpful in developing *esprit de corps* as well as an ideal proving ground, assuming one survived. This could refine itself into private wars. The notorious Piers Gaveston, Edward II's alleged catamite, and his crowd, not quite 'our' sort of people as far as his magnatial critics were concerned, competed avidly and worse, successfully, in the lists. Significant events such as St Inglevert were also political; knights from England, Scotland, and France competed effectively as state-sponsored gladiators.

In the same year Sir David Lindsay and John, 5th Baron Welles banged it out over London Bridge on horseback, but this French do was an altogether bigger match. John II le Maingre (known as 'Boucicaut' for 'Brave'), latterly Marshal of France and destined to die at Agincourt, together with Reginald de Roye and Lord Sempy, King Charles' chamberlains:

> . . . manfully performed a deed worthy of recitation. For performed this deed against all foreigners, from England, Denmark, Germany, Bohemia, Poland and all regions and countries of Christendom who gathered at the end of February at St. Inglevert, a religious house located between Boulogne on the sea and Calais: These people came from everywhere having news of the upcoming deed through herald of the Duke of Lancaster, who was called in French 'Lincastre', namely that the three were prepared to meet every one of whatever condition, as long as they were nobles, who would come to them over a thirty-day period, beginning on the first of March, and excepting Sundays and holy days, and who wished to perform courses with sharp lances or others with blunt ones.

And the following conditions were set forth: that if any of the three of them for whatever cause should be rendered unable to joust during the thirty days of the festival, the other two would be obligated to fulfil the courses of the rest of the comers, however many there were; and that if two of them were incapable the third nevertheless would have all those courses of the lances aforesaid for withstanding the comers and fulfilling their courses. And it was added that he who ran out of bounds, either within or without, should lose his horse; and if anyone killed the horse of his opponent, he should give full compensation, either out of his own funds or from that of the comers as a group.[13]

Hotspur certainly wasn't one to miss out on such an opportunity and accompanied Bolingbroke as part of his retinue. Jean Froissart (1337–1405), a Hainulter who came to England in the service of Queen Philippa, Edward III's consort, writes enthusiastically about this; the very gist of chivalric spin and he goes into great detail about how the various combatants fared. The English generally do well all told and though he doesn't specifically mention Harry Percy, we can certainly see him getting stuck in.

Percy was related to Sir John Arundel whose prowess Froissart glowingly describes:

> The next that presented himself was a young gay knight from England, who shone in tournaments, in dancing, and in singing, called Sir John Arundel. He sent his squire to touch the war-shield of Sir Reginald de Roye. The knight replied that he wished for nothing more agreeable than to tilt with him. Having received their spears, they galloped off at the same moment, and gave and received hard blows on their shields; but they kept their seats handsomely and continued their career.

Their lances having fallen from their hands, were restored to them by those appointed for that purpose; and they began their second course with blows on the helmets that made the fire spark, but they passed on without further hurt. At the third onset, the horses swerved; and the knights, in their attempt to strike, lost their lances, and with difficulty recovered themselves. At the fourth they struck the helmets, but without harm or un-helming. At the fifth course, they hit each other on the targets, and broke their lances, without any other damage. Sir John Arundel completed his career and returned to his friends.[14]

All told, this gentlemanly scrapping continued for a full thirty days and broken bones aside, it was all very sporting. While this was the highest level of fixture, many others were fought out in the same era. Late fourteenth-century Scottish rolls contain numerous references to the issue of licences and safe conducts for Scottish knights to brawl for their country and win honours in both France and on the Anglo-Scottish borders. Percy was a product and a leading one of this sharp-edged competitive culture. It was what he was born for and, and this theme will be revisited, the era into which he was born and lived fits neatly into the time frame for an upsurge in cross-border violence. It wasn't that this ever went away but some periods were even more violent than others.

After 1370, the Scots in tandem with France experienced a military revival in sharp contrast to their earlier reverses and the resulting, comparative, calm of mid-century. For a while, carefully guided, they maintained the initiative and kept an upper hand until they crashed disastrously at Homildon in 1402. Harry Percy would be a prime player in this extended broil and his knightly training the perfect preparation, even if the war itself would be the very antithesis of chivalric *courtesie*.

And What About Harry?

How does Harry Percy measure up, does he match the chivalric ideal and did he aspire to? Clearly the answer to the first question is no. He died a traitor's death and so failed to live up to the fine ideals of the cult. He betrayed one king and rebelled against another. His conduct in singling out prisoners for personal vengeance after Homildon demonstrates a bloody minded and vindictive streak extremely far from any notion of courtesy. None of this means he didn't try, he was, above all and like all of us, a man of his times, bred to and conditioned by the sentiments of the age. He wasn't an innovator or a game changer but then those times were hard, and his temperament was forged in a brutal and bloody school of border war flaming up in one of its worst interludes. In Coppola's *Apocalypse Now* the protagonist exclaims cynically that talking about war crimes in Vietnam was like 'handing out speeding tickets at the Indy 500'.[15] The same cynicism certainly goes for the Anglo–Scottish border.

What we're called upon to do, and it isn't easy, is to put ourselves, insofar as we're able, into the fourteenth-century gentleman's mindset, not just any knight or lord but one raised in the ravenous cockpit of those Anglo–Scottish–French wars that had begun in Hotspur's great-grandfather's day and would last for another two centuries after Homildon. To play a leading role and to be leading from the front was his inheritance. He wasn't offered a choice; indeed, he wouldn't have wanted one, but we must fuse nasty reality with an ideal of chivalry underscored by deep piety. Percy could kill, maim, condone, or order, rape, mutilation, arson, and theft while never missing Mass and believing he did God's work. He would constantly seek to aggrandise himself and his name, acquiring titles and honours like a covetous miser while aspiring to the perfect courtesy of a chivalric hero. Tricky to get our modern heads around but this is who Henry Percy was and none of his contemporaries would have expected him to be any different.

Chivalry was also about the cult of celebrity, not narcissistic posturing reported in today's tabloids but about real fame and renown in the heroic sense. Achilles was still the model and if you didn't play the game there was no point in ever becoming a knight. War and its facsimile, the tourney, were the only career paths open and the only ones that mattered. You could live a noble, priestly life of contemplation, be a wise and learned judge but you might as well be a farm labourer for all the reputation you'd earn. People liked their heroes, and this has always been the case, and medieval sportsmen starred only on the field of Mars. In this he did well, the most famous knight of his day, one who others measured up to, who they wanted to be.

Hotspur's track record on the battlefield as commander was poor. He fought in three major battles, two of which he lost, last time cost him his life. The one he's credited with winning may really have belonged to someone else, *but* he never ran away, nobody ever called Hotspur a coward, he fought to the last every time. Though he was defeated at Otterburn, his vast ransom of 7,000 marks (£4,620), over £½ million today, was quickly raised and his credibility didn't suffer. In these terms he was a success, the contemporary embodiment of Chaucer's ideal:

> A Knyght ther was, and that a worthy man
> That fro the tyme that he first bigan
> To riden out, he loved chivalrie
> Trouthe and honóur, fredom and curteisie
> Ful worthy was he in his lordes were
> And thereto hadde he riden, no man ferre
> As wel in cristendom as in hethenesse
> And evere honóured for his worthynesse.[16]
> Hotspur would have been happy with that.

Act 3

Storm Clouds Brewing – A Scottish Resurgence

> For deer to hunt and slay
> and see them bleed
> any hardship adds to his courage and
> In his mind he takes heed
> imagining taking them by surprise
> aged sixteen years to wage war
> to joust and ride with castles to assail
> to skirmish and to scourge
> and setting watches for nightly perils
> > *The Chronicle of John Hardyng*

> That some night-tripping fairy had exchanged
> In cradle clothes our children where they lay
> And called mine 'Percy' and his 'Plantagenet'
> Then would I have this Harry, and he mine.
> > William Shakespeare,
> > *The First Part of King Henry IV*, Act I, sc. i

Young Harry Percy's education in arms and the role of a gentleman was not just blind adherence to convention, it was a necessary preparation. He would be catapulted from the training ground to the battlefield at a frighteningly early age, as severe a testing as can be imagined and whatever is said of Hotspur, he passed the test and kept on passing. To achieve this, he had to be bred to it, the sum of all his ancestors' parts.

What we cannot know, and it is almost pointless to speculate, was the cumulative emotional cost of going to war at 9 years of age. Was there any? It would be possible to attribute some of Hotspur's more bellicose even cruel aspects to post-traumatic stress disorder (PTSD). Identification of this is a modern recognition, no such idea existed in the fourteenth century. Harry Percy lived in an age harsher than our worst imagining, for gentleman and commoner alike. Death was a constant companion, an everyday occurrence, even without endemic warfare. Faith too, a far more concrete reassurance. People like Hotspur believed in God and in his divine wrath but also in the notion of salvation. It would be fascinating to explore the psychological impacts of war and killing on the mental health of medieval knights, but we simply don't know.

The Old Fox

Hotspur's father and a pivotal influence, Henry, 4th Lord Percy was born 10 November 1342, so aged 26 when his own father died. He most probably spent his formative years in the household of an uncle, Henry of Grosmont, latterly Duke of Lancaster, a great and enormously wealthy magnate. He was first blooded when accompanying his mentor during a French campaign in 1359 when he was 17, easily old enough. De Fonblanque places Percy on the field of Poitiers on 19 September 1356 where he 'fleshed his maiden sword', which while tempting to believe is far from certain.[1] We can be sure he'd like to have been, and gentlemen still-a-bed should think themselves accursed they were not here, as Shakespeare expressed it. In fact, Henry Percy wasn't knighted until 1361, five years after the Black Prince's great victory, and he'd become one of only twenty-six Knights of the Garter, a highly prestigious honour.[2]

Following family tradition, Hotspur's parent gained experience of border affairs with his father, and this was fast evolving into the family business. De Fonblanque, as biographer, does veer towards hagiography: '. . . He was possessed of that "noble port" and commanding presence then considered a natural attribute of rank and power. More than one writer refers to his courteous and winning manners, and if we may trust to the authenticity of his portraits, he must have been a strikingly handsome man.'[3] Judging from his subsequent career his courteous manners tended to slip when, as frequently, driven by a furious temper, twinned with an irritating and overbearing hauteur.

Henry Percy spent a decade enmeshed in France. For England and the English polity, this was always the principal theatre of war, Northumberland and the border were just the margins, a back door that had to be kept closed. The Treaty of Brétigny was little more than a truce, never a ceasefire. Hostilities broke out again in 1369 and this time the English would not have it all their own way. John of Gaunt was now the leading captain, third surviving son of Edward III, who'd married Blanche, Grosmont's daughter and heiress. On her father's death in 1362 he was elevated Duke of Lancaster.[4] Rich he might be, but Gaunt lacked any of that military genius so often displayed by his father and older brother, and as English fortunes began to unravel, he lacked any talent to stem the rot.

Gaunt's strategic incompetence, compounded by repeated tactical failures, was exacerbated by steely French resilience under Bertrand du Guesclin, the King of France's 'hog in armour', who adopted Fabian tactics to fight what might now be called more of an asymmetric war and achieved commendable success.

Gaunt's main tactical gambit was the extended raid or chevauchée, flashy even sensational but largely futile and very costly. Just as bad, war at sea also did not go well. Nonetheless, at least at the outset, Lancaster's relationship with Henry Percy, two years his junior, appears to have been extremely cordial, even friendly. That wasn't to endure. Two such towering egos were bound to collide.

Henry's younger brother Thomas (1343–1403), destined to be a strong influence in his nephew's career, accompanied his elder sibling on numerous campaigns and earned equal plaudits. The Percy biographer writes well of him: 'he seems to have possessed all his elder brother's warlike spirit and military accomplishments with a more politic temper and greater intellectual culture'.[5] Thomas was a comrade-in-arms to the redoubtable Sir John Chandos and took part, even if in a rather passive way, in the final skirmish where the old warrior's luck finally ran out.

Walsingham tells us a stirring tale of high adventure in the Channel when Thomas with Sir Hugh Calveley and Sir William Elmham, storm tossed for days and weakened by lack of provisions, 'more in need of a hammock', were set upon by a large Spanish vessel.[6] In fine seadog tradition, despite the unfortunate odds and their own lamentable state, Thomas and his comrades dragged on harness and fought it out. For three hours the battle raged till the Spaniards finally struck their colours. Shakespeare subsequently paints him as a more duplicitous character, slyly manipulative. Perhaps he was and used those greater intellectual gifts De Fonblanque boasts of to exert control. In the biographer's description of Henry, 1st Earl, we can see much of Hotspur as well. He was not stupid but probably wouldn't be offered any form of academic distinction like his uncle.

Nonetheless, Thomas' career in arms suffered a severe downturn when he was captured by the French, back fighting on land. Just before and serving with the other great English or nearly English legend the Gascon Jean III de Grailly, Captal de Buch, he'd taken part in the victory at Soubise.[7] He became a prisoner soon after but was swiftly ransomed by 1373, the ageing Edward III trading ground to retrieve his valiant knight. A year after that, his star undimmed, he was created a Knight of the Garter with the gift of a handsome annuity.

England in general and taxpayers in particular were losing their enthusiasm for the war, hitherto sustained by so many stellar victories. Gaunt's task was an unenviable one, but he did at the outset receive great support from Henry Percy who by 1376 had been appointed Marshal of England, a prestigious post but no plum, as he'd have to fight extremely hard for it. If France was tough, the border was about to get tougher still. In 1369 a fourteen-year truce between England and Scotland was negotiated. This should have endured till 1383 but the death of Edward III and accession of his grandson Richard II as a minor provided the springboard for a Scottish resurgence.

A Distant Roar

Richard of Bordeaux appeared to inherit a measure of stability, though this soon proved a chimera. Edward III had consolidated his northern border with a string of brilliant successes, topped by the resounding triumph of the northern English at Neville's Cross in October 1346 which netted King David II of Scotland among the spoils. The subsequent establishment of a buffer zone throughout southern Scotland, the 'Pale', shielded the north from raids and indeed the years immediately after Neville's Cross marked an era of relative prosperity. Border violence never went away. It simply oscillated, from all-out relentless interstate war to magnatial quarrels and low-level endemic thievery from the riding names. In many cases lords behaved no better than common reivers but aristocratic thuggery was wont to be enacted on a larger scale and had a consequentially more de-stabilising effect. The later Percy/Neville feud of the mid-fifteenth century is a good example; this not only affected the region but had national implications. Hotspur's father married a Neville, but the rivalry remained, though not yet marked by violence.

Hostilities along the line were intricately linked to events in France, English performance across the Channel forming a barometer for events in the north. France's recovery was Scotland's opportunity. A lull or truce in France implied a backing off along the border. Subtle strategists like George Dunbar (see below) saw the value in stealth while maximising the shield offered by England's difficulties abroad.

By 1369, this English grip, the 'Pale', was largely confined to three bulging salients. In the west, like a fat finger pointing north from the Solway and taking in Annandale, the Pale here had Lochmaben very nearly at its apex. Teviotdale, in the centre, was mainly under English influence with important centres and castles such as Hawick, Kelso, Roxburgh, and Jedforest holding garrisons. Same with most of the Merse, up from Berwick to the rise of the Lammermoors, gaunt and lonely Fast Castle in the north-east with prosperous Coldingham below.[8]

These tracts weren't delineated on any map, they were zones of influence rather than hard occupation. Castles were manned and held but control was limited by who was in the ascendancy at any one time. Locals were compliant only if they were intimidated or bribed, and Scottish lords who'd been alienated (such as the Douglases) hovered on the edges awaiting their chance. Weakness was corrosive. As the old king of England slid into the abyss of senility, his strong hand and that of his equally enfeebled eldest son, the Black Prince, slackened their collective grip. The Pale began to contract, shrinking by bite-sized chunks. A handy reference is the Berwick Chamberlain's accounts which detail rents received from lands under control. The entry for 1369–70 refers to nine manors no longer held, and the next year's returns speak of another two which have just been lost.[9]

Despite his humiliation on the battlefield and years of incarceration, David II remained something of an Anglophile. He shared Edward III's obsession with chivalry and bore no grudge against his captors, remaining on cordial terms with England until his death, at a relatively early age, in 1371.[10] This doesn't imply he was blind to opportunities and if he did not overtly support the hawks, neither did he hinder them from flying. His successor Robert II, not a direct heir as David died childless, has often had a poor press, seen as rather weak and ineffective, royal power undermined by aggressive magnates. He had plenty of these, but a revisionist view suggests the king was adept in channelling their ardour while appearing to keep a safe distance. Allowing Dunbar to maintain an active front against the Pale worked well for both and avoided provoking large-scale English retaliation.

It just got worse. In 1372, the unthinkable occurred, England was defeated at sea. A Castilian squadron beat the Earl of Pembroke's ships at La Rochelle, and he was captured. King Robert then moved to renew the old Franco-Scottish alliance and his policy began to harden, there were reservations over payment of the outstanding balance of King David's ransom. By now Scots were aware that their powerful friend used them as allies of convenience, a handy distraction against England, one that had led them to disaster at Neville's Cross. Though they might want to damage England, Scots were increasingly aware that French aid could carry a hefty price tag. This would rather come to a head during the invasion of 1385 when the two found out not only that they had quite different tactical objectives, but a vastly different cultural outlook (see below).

One of the prime players who'd have a major role in Hotspur's saga was, as mentioned above, the presiding genius of this resurgence, George Dunbar, 10th Earl of Dunbar and March, 12th Lord of Annandale, titular Lord of the Isle of Man. Machiavelli would have loved George Dunbar, a brilliant general of marvellous fluidity. He understood that meeting the English head-on was a path to catastrophe, his predecessors' failures at Dupplin Moor, Halidon Hill, and Neville's Cross, not to mention the many reverses of their French allies, had shown that all too clearly, all too many times. He too would adopt a subtle, Fabian strategy, clawing back, piece by piece, the whole of the English Pale, mirroring Robert Bruce's successful campaigns in the lead up to Bannockburn. Attrition, something the French when in Scotland during the 1385 campaign signally failed to appreciate, was a far surer policy than confrontation. Staying below the radar conferred pain-free dividends.

Dunbar would be partnered with James Douglas, 2nd Earl Douglas, the son of William, 1st Earl Douglas who in 1371 (or 1373) married Isabel, daughter of King Robert. There is a mirror reflecting on Douglas and Percy:

> Two households, both alike in dignity
> From ancient grudge break to new mutiny . . .[11]

On the Scottish side the rise of the House of Douglas seemed equally inexorable. Jamie 'Black' Douglas had been the Achilles of Bruce's wars, formidable, clever, bold, and ruthless; a dark hero for a dark time. Still, his family's rivalry with Percy wasn't any chivalric contest but a more mundane matter of real property, dear to any magnate's heart.

This concerned title to Jedburgh and Jedforest, a grand swathe of territory stretching from Teviot Water to Carter Bar. King Robert had granted this to Jamie Douglas, but a year after his major win at Halidon Hill in 1333, Edward III handed the whole lot to Henry, 2nd Lord Percy and the family had enjoyed possession since Neville's Cross. Continuing English hegemony had ensured Percies remained in occupation, but Douglas didn't have to like it. Honour and flying pennons may be the stuff of romantic legend, but control of profitable acres was what counted. It is certainly possible there was some periodic sparring on the ground between Douglas and Percy retainers.

On 16 February 1373, an English commission was appointed to investigate; the Scots were requested to do the same and this commission renewed its brief the following year.[12] As ever on the Marches, national policy was inextricably linked to local interest to the extent the tail frequently appears to have been wagging the dog. Edward III, even if he was past his prime, saw this and appointed non-marchers to his commission.[13] For the Douglases, clawing back Jedforest was both a personal and national cause. They wanted to recover what they believed to be theirs which had, as a bonus, the effect of further shaking the English grip. Meanwhile, Henry Percy had no intention of letting go.

Just to set the tone of relations, Percy had had a bruising encounter with Dunbar in the summer of 1370. He'd been appointed Governor of both Berwick and Roxburgh on attaining his majority, so was in charge when a fracas erupted at the annual fair. Drink was usually a factor and both sides indulged liberally. In the ensuing scrap, the Scots were bested and several of Dunbar's retainers lay among the dead when the smoke cleared. The Scottish earl appealed to Percy as castellan for redress but got none. A bad man to disappoint, he led a big raid against the English West March, dragging back livestock and hostages. Percy retaliated and took a large force over the border to even the score. He got as far as Duns. Hector Boece says he commanded 7,000 mainly mounted fighters. Dunbar, canny as ever, appears to have resorted to what would now be classed as psychological warfare by creating such a nocturnal racket that the English horses broke free and bolted in fear, shortly followed by their owners.[14]

Marchers, on both sides of the fence, had finely attuned antennae, essential for continued survival. While there had been some element of stability during the couple of decades before 1369, a sense that the mood was shifting and that the bad old days were firmly on their way back quickly surfaced. If this English Pale was finally and fully eliminated, then the northern frontier was once again a front line. Those terrible years after Bannockburn would not have been forgotten. This new paradigm ushered in a spate of frantic building and re-building. John of Gaunt undertook a phase of further construction at his great northern fortress of Dunstanburgh, a key coastal redoubt. Lochmaben, Berwick, and Bamburgh received extensive makeovers, as did a slew of manorial castles and towers.

For a short time, mid-decade, hostilities cooled as a putative ceasefire between England and France appeared possible. The Scots took heed, all too aware that France wouldn't hesitate to sacrifice their interest if expediency dictated. In fact, there was no rapprochement likely, the French were just buying time to restock their arsenals and allow their able and energetic admiral John de Vienne to construct a fleet of galleys copying the specifications that had worked so well for Castile. It was still very much game on and this game, from the borderers' perspective, would continue for thirty years. It would be Hotspur's inheritance, his proving ground, and it would be he who, in 1402, brought this Scottish renaissance crashing down.

That was a long way off in 1377 and the future paladin only 13, though he'd soon be playing his part. But that year saw a significant shift in the scale of activity along the border and it was the Scots, orchestrated by Dunbar, who were making the running.[15] Historians debate whether this upsurge reflected Crown policy or just George Dunbar forcing the pace, perhaps a shaded combination of both, with the Scottish earl in the driving seat.

It's surely no coincidence that this offensive was timed to capitalise on a further deterioration in Anglo-French relations. Sir John Gordon, Scotland's new Achilles, got the better of an English contingent at Carham and captured its captain, Sir John Lilburn. Gaunt came north again with a significant array and again achieved remarkably little. As Froissart perhaps flippantly but correctly comments, 'Scotland was the place in the world whereby England might be most annoyed'.[16] To add further injury Thomas Musgrave, keeper of Berwick, along with his grandson was captured by the hyper-active Gordon that same summer.[17] As Alistair Macdonald points out, this was a palpable shift away from a previously almost unbroken line of English successes.[18] Lands were wasted and renders declined, a revival of that dark spectre of Bruce's hegemony loomed. This time it would be different. Edward III's forward policy and his astute re-stocking of Northumberland's upland dales with good fighting stock had forged a new race, those hobilers. There'd be no easy pickings this time around.

Baptisms of Fire

Just as his father had been mentored by Henry of Grosmont, the 9-year-old Hotspur followed his parent to France. Part of a knight's education was to witness war at first hand. He would have been learning all about theory but there's no school like harsh reality. Imbued as he clearly was by notions of chivalry, what he saw in France would have been hugely different. This brand of campaigning was proceeded by frightfulness, terrorism as we'd call it today, pillage, and mass destruction in a bid to impress or at least cow the French. This was, on a grander scale, like his future apprenticeship in border warfare, where brutal reality was the name of the game.

Knighthood wasn't just about skill at arms and derring-do, it was a practical military induction. On campaign in France, the boy would learn to comprehend the necessities of war rather than the frills; logistics and concentration, the real sinews of conflict, mastery of which mattered as much as tactical skill or strategic purpose. Command of subordinates, liaison with allies, control of supply, the politics of leadership, who to trust, who to advance, who to be wary of, who to listen to and ponder, who to hear out but ignore. It was unfortunate that the commander in chief – John of Gaunt – came into the latter category.

Young Henry's mother was a Neville, a marriage alliance about as close as you can keep your enemies, and while there was no sign of any real feud between these two magnatial families emerging, they both wanted to be cocks of their own midden. As a taste of things to come, the future Hotspur's introduction to continental warfare was none too inspiring. He arrived at the tail end of English hegemony, which was crumbling at an alarming rate, exposing fully Gaunt's weaknesses as generalissimo. There'd be no return to the glory days, with all those ransoms and fiefdoms, England was now in full retreat.

De Fonblanque tells us that Percy crossed over to France early in the new year after the debacle at Duns. That was 1370 and taking Hotspur's date of birth as 1364, he'd only have been 7 not 9. Andrew Boardman dates Lord Percy's arrival at Calais as late July 1373 and this makes more sense. We're told Henry Percy led a sizeable following comprising 12 knights, 47 squires, and160 mounted bowmen.[19] Hotspur was in time to witness England's defeat on land by du Guesclin in his native Brittany and the Spanish defeating Pembroke (with whom Uncle Thomas was serving) at sea. Autumn rains just underlined the futility. Gaunt's expedition had achieved nothing, and a grim retreat showed young Harry the folly of bad management.

Henry Percy senior was soon back on the Anglo-Scottish border and just as quickly back in the saddle. In his absence the Scots had taken another crack at Roxburgh and smashed the town up. Percy retaliated against the lands of firebrand Sir John Gordon which prompted yet more tit for tat.[20] Younger Henry was getting a balanced and fruitful introduction to the realities of cross-border violence twinned with the liberal application of 'frightfulness' by both sides. This would be his arena, and on this terrain his legend would take root. All the chroniclers agree that this was war without pity or, for that matter, much in the way of honour. For those in the south this was just an uncouth, largely forgotten frontier.

This present bout wasn't just low-level cross-border raiding, but activity openly encouraged and led by the leading magnates, unrestrained by royal authority on either side. This was war *with* hate, short-term gain, and revenge being the principal motivations, though, from the Scottish side, Dunbar was steadily nibbling away at the Pale and whittling down those vestiges of English hegemony.

Meanwhile, the inexorable waning of Gaunt's star rebounded on Percy. Military failure abroad, coupled with high taxation to fund it, fuelled a swelling public discontent which focused on Lancaster. Some suspected that as the old king weakened and as his son was visibly dying, Gaunt might hope to supplant his nephew Richard of Bordeaux. When, in April 1376, the 'Good Parliament' met, more than a whiff of reform was in the air. Despite his closeness to the now generally despised John of Gaunt, Henry Percy was appointed as a commissioner to promote and facilitate this reforming process which naturally now stood him in the opposite corner to his former comrade-in-arms.

The ailing Black Prince did his younger sibling an inestimable service by dying, creating a void that Gaunt alone could fill. By this timely demise, the Duke of Lancaster regained his seat at the head of the constitutional table and Parliament, which assembled in January 1377, proved far more pliant. Percy, by this point, had earned his marshal's baton and succeeded in hanging on to it. By now, he was firmly back in Gaunt's camp and looking forward to becoming an earl, the next step up the baronial ladder, far higher than any of his ancestors, however diligent and illustrious, had attained.

Then Percy blundered. He espoused the cause of the heretic John Wyclif.[21] This was strong stuff, but he was just echoing Gaunt's own stance and it can safely be assumed that clerical reform wasn't necessarily a cause dear to his heart. The duke himself was no theologian, but he had fallen out with the clerical faction when the Bishop of Winchester insinuated he was illegitimate. This was a serious slur and reflected sharp battle lines drawn between barons and bishops, feudal and ecclesiastical parties. Wyclif, as a handy reformer and agitator, provided an ideal stooge. The prelates, duly alarmed, weren't slow to pick up the gauntlet and, in February 1377, this rebel priest was summoned before convocation to answer for his temerity and alleged heresy. Lancaster saw this as a weapon being deployed against him personally and Henry Percy weighed in on his friend's side. This wasn't due to theological conviction but personal interest, the Earldom of Northumberland rather than Kingdom of Heaven was his objective. Just in case the situation wasn't clear, he strutted around, fully harnessed, as Wyclif's minder.

Such bluster might work on the streets but less so inside the sanctified precincts of St Paul's Lady Chapel. Percy's brand of thuggery didn't suit theological debate, however heated, and he snarled at the bishops in full street-fighting mode. Walsingham, no friend of Gaunt's and therefore by association not one of Northumberland's partisans, was outraged. Both Henry Percy and John of Gaunt had misread the general mood which their high-handedness had merely stoked. Percy's town house on Aldersgate was sacked, an unlucky priest, mistaken for him in disguise, was murdered.[22] This was followed by more larceny at Gaunt's sumptuous Savoy Palace. The time for braggadocio had passed and both had to run for their lives. Happily, the Princess of Wales with whom they'd sought refuge, interceded on her uncle's behalf and the danger subsided. Still, Percy had seriously damaged his standing.

If his father's star had slipped from its stellar orbit, that of his son, young Harry Percy, was about to rise. At age 13 he was knighted by the ageing king at Windsor that April. Kneeling with him were Richard of Bordeaux, soon to be King Richard II, and Gaunt's own son, Henry Bolingbroke. The lives of these three youths were to be inextricably entwined thereafter. Two would be kings, one a kingmaker and one the death of both the others. Harry's younger siblings, Thomas and Ralph, were also dubbed yet within two months Edward III would be dead and Richard of Bordeaux the new sovereign.

John of Gaunt now came into his own, neatly sweeping his past failures under the carpet and ensuring his loyal pal Henry Percy profited from steadfast loyalty. On 15 July 1377, Lord Percy was elevated to his long-coveted earldom. He had finally arrived. This time round he bathed himself in humility, no more swaggering, at least not too much. The new earl continued to fill the office of Marshal of England, though not strictly his to take on much to the vociferous annoyance of the Earl of Norfolk's eldest daughter, Margaret. This was embarrassing, it ill-behoved Percy to assume offices that weren't his and he was glad to depart rapidly for less troubled waters on the borders. Less troubled politically, but George Dunbar had drunk the young king's health in the flames of Roxburgh.

Blooding at Berwick

Inadvertently, the wily Scot had helped dig his adversary out of the hole and Percy returned the compliment with interest, spurring over the line for a three-day spree of arson. Ridpath tells us he 'entered Scotland at the head of 10,000 men and during the space of three days ravaged the lands of the earl of March'.[23] His service didn't go unnoticed and before the year was out, he'd been appointed warden of both East and West Marches. He and Lord Neville – a formidable partnership when working in harmony – attempted to broker some form of lasting truce. Despite their best efforts the frontier stayed ticklish; in November 1378 Berwick was targeted.

Great border valleys such as those of the Tweed, Teviot, Till, and Eden are deeply fertile, some of the best farming land in Europe. The Tweed marked the border as it had done since that black day of the Northumbrian clergy at Carham in 1018. Later, after Longshanks, Berwick-upon-Tweed became a frontier post, or bastide, guarding the English East March. It used to be Scottish in character, taken and retaken till 1482 when Richard of Gloucester took it back for, up till now, the last time.

Back in 1296 Longshanks easily overcame the tatty palisade during his first attack and the place had a series of makeovers destined to culminate in the construction of the massive Elizabethan Walls in the 1560s, of state-of-the art Italian design and still complete (though never actually completed). At that point, the defences shrank, Edward's, Bruce's, and Henry VIII's walls extended by a good third on the north side where the castle was originally adjacent to the gate. This was a great border fortress but now extraordinarily little except a section of battered curtain wall and lower Watergate survive.[24]

Originally, the castle stood beyond the medieval enceinte on the far bank of the river, very exposed to attack. Though held by the English, Scots constantly desired to repossess the place. The mere sight of the Cross of St George fluttering over battlements was an insult and a goad. It had been English again since Halidon Hill but as the Scots began to gobble up the various enclaves making up the English Pale, Berwick became increasingly vulnerable. Despite the place's signal importance, the walls were sadly neglected and in disrepair. France had taken priority in the old king's time and England's treasury echoed bare.

> About this time, in fact on the Thursday next before the feast of St. Andrew the Apostle [30 November], some brigands from the March of the Scottish King [probably led by John Hogg and Alexander Ramsay] secretly entered the castle of Berwick by night, making use of a door in one of the towers, and coming upon Sir Robert Boynton, the constable of the castle, unawares, they killed that brave soldier on the spot. They did allow his wife and sons and some of their household to leave the castle on condition that they either paid them three thousand marks within three weeks or otherwise gave themselves up to captivity. Then the next day these robbers went out and ravaged the neighbouring countryside . . .[25]

Fordun asserts the original commando was only seven strong, 'desperate fellows' – Leighert, Artwood, Grey, Hog, Hempsede, a Jack de Fordun, and led, inevitably, by Sir John Gordon. Once they'd taken the place, they opened the doors to a larger reinforcement and command devolved onto Alexander Ramsay.[26] While this might seem like a classic case of private enterprise, the prevailing sentiment locally was that the Scottish nobility was behind it, and certainly this behaviour smacked of Dunbar. Percy may well have thought so too as he wasted no time in pulling together a posse 400-strong and laying siege to his pilfered castle.[27]

The earl brought up an array of timber framed siege engines and pelted the walls without respite. Ridpath tells us the siege lasted 8 days and the earl deployed 7,000 archers backed by 3,000 hobilers (suspiciously large numbers that were more than likely much lower). He was supported by lords Neville, Lucy, and Stafford.[28] Hotspur was only 14 but already a knight and we can assume he was more than ready to prove himself worthy. Young Harry raised his banner in front of the main gate, Sir Alan Heron, Sir Thomas Ilderton, and the Heron retinue covered the other flanks, ready for a general assault.

Despite the fury of the bombardment, these hardy Scots weren't in the least cowed, they probably realised their chances of obtaining mercy were limited. For two hours they held their attackers at bay, doggedly defending broken walls. Resistance finally collapsed as Walsingham records; English assault parties all broke through at the same moment. According to the chronicler, the Northumbrians got off very lightly with only two killed and few wounded. Four dozen Scots were accounted for, 'trampled on and finished off with the sword'.[29] Three survivors were spared for 'interrogation' then probably dealt with afterwards. Walsingham waxes quite lyrical over the destruction of these intruders but the fight was clearly a dangerous beginning for Hotspur, crowned with victory and, if the chronicler is credible, one quite cheaply bought.

Harry Percy had had his baptism of fire; he was no longer a trainee but had graduated to fully fledged practitioner in the art of war. It was a good beginning, the start of a reputation that would swell into legend on a frontier where standards were harsh and accolades awfully hard to come by. For his father the earl, this was a good job well done. He'd left any embarrassments in London behind him and smitten the young king's enemies with a flaming rod of iron. From now on though, this was to be a family concern, father and son, ready to act at any time.

Northumberland had written to George Dunbar accusing him of being party to this seizure which the slippery Scot promptly denied. He even appeared before the besieged walls as honest broker demanding the defenders hand the place back. Nobody was surprised when they refused.[30] Later, when Walsingham is writing of a cross–Channel expedition in 1386, he mentions the younger Percy's nickname 'Hotspur' – not as one given to him by his own people but rather from his Scottish opponents:

> . . . a young man who was a shining example of all goodness and military prowess . . . And indeed, previously as governor of the town of Berwick, he had compelled that completely restless race, the Scots to take a rest and had often worn them out by his own eager restlessness. So, in their own language they called this Henry 'Hotspur'.[31]

Catchy, and it would stick, Hotspur would blazon as the very embodiment of chivalry.

Hotspur's youthful triumph in storming Berwick Castle was followed just over a year later, on 10 December 1379, by his marriage to Elizabeth Mortimer. This was an advantageous union, even by expansionist Percy standards, as the girl (she was only 9) was daughter to Edmund Mortimer, English Earl of March. These were great marcher lords from the frontier of Wales, and she was related, on her mother's side, to Edward III's second son Lionel, Duke of Clarence. It was a promising match but ultimately the Mortimer connection would, at least in part, be Hotspur's undoing.[32]

As the new decade of the 1380s opened, the Earl of Northumberland devolved increasing responsibilities onto his eldest son which Hotspur embraced at the gallop. In 1381 young Harry was judge in a trial by combat held at Liliot's Cross (a regular location for days of Truce in Teviotdale) between the Scot John Chattowe and his English opponent William de Badby. This was serious business for a 17-year-old.[33] But his father, the earl, was about to fall out with his old mucker John of Gaunt as well as with his Neville in-laws. That infamous Percy temper would get him into serious trouble, again.

Just before anger erupted into protest, Lancaster had again come north with an army to deal with the Scots. At Berwick late that autumn he met the bishops of Glasgow and Dunkeld, together with the earls of Douglas and Dunbar. It was provided that the duke, as befitting his rank, would meet with the heir to the Scottish throne, the Earl of Carrick (the future Robert III). It rather seems, or so his contemporaries thought, that the wily Scots, surely orchestrated by the very wily Dunbar, rang rings round Gaunt, 'no advantage was gained from this formidable expedition . . . which is said to have cost the public 11,000 marks'.[34] Gaunt's attention had already turned to his proposed Spanish adventure (see below). The talks with Carrick at Ayton in fact produced nothing more substantial than a series of phased extensions to the truce.[35] This was very soon to be the least of John of Gaunt's worries and he'd shortly be seeing the Earl of Carrick again but in vastly different circumstances.

Rebellious Peasants

Walter Bower took a dim view of rebellious commoners: '. . . nothing is more cruel than a poor man when he rises high. And for that reason, as soon as they have risen in revolt, they must be subdued lest they get the upper hand. As Jerome says: Kill your enemy while he is young, so that his villainy is crushed as a seed'.[36] When the explosion occurred, the mob's main fury was directed at Gaunt, 'there was no person among those more hateful to the rabble than the duke of Lancaster whom they regarded as the chief author of their oppression'.[37]

Lancaster and Percy had sheltered together during the backlash following Wyclif's inquisition and the duke was again in everybody's sights. Northumberland was safe in Northumberland but denied Gaunt sanctuary when he begged for it. No doubt he feared being dragged into the mire, but this does seem both petty and spiteful and his refusal would have consequences. At the time disturbances broke out in the south and Gaunt's opulent Savoy Palace was torched the duke himself was also in the north where he'd been negotiating with Dunbar at Berwick, irritating Percy, never used to playing second fiddle.

Shunned by his old friend, he craved asylum across the border and wrote, presumably in desperation, to the Earl of Carrick. Sensing a fortuitous opportunity to win friends, the Scot agreed, 'and sent Sir William earl of Douglas and Archibald de Douglas lord of Galloway with an honourable following to accompany him on his journey from the borders to Scotland . . .'.[38] The duke was safely and comfortably housed in Edinburgh till the storm abated. For the Scots, this generous hospitality was a sound investment, Gaunt would now be in their debt. Cannily, Dunbar refrained from seeking any military advantage from the confusion in southern England, Gaunt's goodwill was a greater prize. Both Carrick and Dunbar showed far more finesse than Northumberland, whose foolish hubris would alienate Lancaster and lead Percy back into dangerous waters.

Increasing the insults, when he tried to return to England through the bastide at Berwick, Gaunt found to his redoubled fury that Percy had one last spiteful trick to play. Northumberland had instructed his castellan, Matthew Redmayne, to deny access to any coming in from Scotland and the governor interpreted this to the letter. Gaunt was shut out.[39] This was foolish and petty, a silly gaffe Percy's subtle brother would never have made.

And like Percy, Gaunt knew how to bear a grudge. He didn't have long to wait. When matters had calmed and he was back in control, the king, at his suggestion, invited Northumberland to a grand feast at Berkhamsted where the duke wasted no time in flinging accusations, accusing Northumberland of overreaching himself in denying him, Lancaster, entry to England. No doubt brother Thomas could have found some oil to pour on these troubled waters, but Henry Percy rose to the bait. More harsh words followed and there was nearly a brawl. Percy had to be restrained and was briefly arrested. The feud festered.[40] Unhappily for Northumberland, Lancaster had the perfect ally to hand in John Neville. Percy's rise had been Neville's eclipse, but he stayed loyal to Lancaster and indeed would remain so right up to and including the Shrewsbury campaign twenty odd years later. This spark of enmity would reach its apogee in the 1450s and climax in the fracas at St Albans in April 1455.

Gaunt now began to favour Neville and their testing ground became a contest for the march wardenry. As has been seen, this means of trying to keep order on the borders had been established as early as 1249, when both monarchies agreed that the border should be divided into districts or marches (two a side at this point).[41] From 1297 these territories were controlled judicially and militarily by the march wardens. It was their duty to see that peace was maintained, to administer justice, and to deal with 'bills' or complaints. Backed up by a staff of deputies, captains, and troopers, they tried with varying degrees of success to administer good law, but in doing so would frequently create personal enemies and further bitterness between already bellicose riding names (some were murdered).[42] In short, they frequently caused more problems than they solved and most certainly did not implement peace and safety for the marchers. For magnates such as Percy or Neville these roles were the principal building blocks for their regional affinities.

In 1381 the existing truce with Scotland still had three years to run but during the previous year Percy, used to having a free hand, was raising a commando of 120 men-at-arms with 200 archers to take revenge for a Scottish raid, pretty much business as usual, truce notwithstanding. Enter Gaunt once again, who had himself nominated as King's Lieutenant on the Marches. This put him directly in charge of Percy who didn't much enjoy having his wings so publicly clipped. The prickly earl saw this as a sneering tap on the shoulder by his former comrade, a personal affront. Hence, the knee-jerk reaction when Gaunt, in desperation, came banging on his door. The rebuff might have felt good, but it was a political blunder of huge magnitude.

After the quarrel at Berkhamsted Percy found himself briefly confined while Neville, as smiling assassin, scooped a major prize, sole wardenship of the East March. The earl still had friends while Gaunt had few and Percy avoided gaol. His reinstatement hadn't made Lancaster any more effective as a politician, nor had the chastening experience of the Peasant's Revolt produced any miraculous conversion to humility. Percy did pick up a consolation prize, wardenry of the emerging Middle March. This brief wasn't yet fully defined, the three-march system wouldn't properly emerge till the next century, but it was better than nothing. In the spring of 1382, Percy and Neville were jointly appointed as wardens for both East and West Marches.

Gaunt might have done best to let the vendetta he was stoking fizzle out, but he wasn't through yet and next year Neville netted both posts endowed with a handsome annuity. Percy was relegated to subordinate and Gaunt kept up his interference in border affairs. As he'd previously undertaken with Carrick, Gaunt met the Scottish prince at Liliot's Cross during the early days of July 1383. It was a cordial meeting, Lancaster had cause to remember his opposite number's kindness and the truce was extended. It was even hoped that a more lasting accord between the kings of both realms could be brokered but again Gaunt was being led. Robert II was already in correspondence with Charles VI of France to launch a second front on the border. There were no free lunches where cross-border politics were concerned.

When the existing truce expired in February 1384, it all kicked off again with the Scots successfully seizing Lochmaben Castle and hi-jacking a fat supply convoy en route to Roxburgh. Naturally, it was Lancaster who insisted on leading the charge. His new chevauchée lasted a fortnight and achieved no more than any of the others. In fairness, he was in a delicate position, he could hardly torch Edinburgh, the city which had earlier offered him such much needed respite: 'About Easter the duke of Lancaster invaded Scotland and embraced the opportunity he had given him of showing his gratitude for the hospitable reception he had met with at Edinburgh three years before by sparing that city when he had it in his power to destroy it'.[43]

Now, Gaunt was back in his saviours' realm with fire and sword. Nonetheless, Bower deals charitably with him at this point, insisting the duke minimised the damage his countrymen inflicted out of respect for the kindness and courtesy shown to him when he was on the run four years before, 'he imposed as little harm as he could'.[43] More, it might be suspected, by good luck than kindness Bower's own Abbey of St Columba of Emonia (Inchcolm in the Firth of Forth) was spared immolation, even though the place was thoroughly looted.[45]

While the duke sojourned in the Scottish capital, Douglas struck back, grabbing most of Teviotdale. As Andrew Boardman points out, once Gaunt had played at being a general, it was left to the wardens to plug the gaps. The pendulum swung back, with Lancaster's farce becoming Northumberland's overture. He recovered governorship of both Berwick and Carlisle, netted £4,000 to charge his war chest, and neatly trumped Neville for control of Roxburgh, surviving key bastion of the shrinking English Pale. To cap it all, Percy managed to recover wardenship of both Marches.[46] Neville was again backfooted. In May 1385 Hotspur took over from his father. This was very much the family business, and he was deemed responsible enough to look after the silver.

Percy and Sons

Happily, the younger Percy had not sullied his ideals by participating in the unseemly squabbling between his father, his mother's tribe, or the Duke of Lancaster. As befitted a noble knight in search of renown, downtime on the border allowed him, in 1383, to contemplate taking part in the Baltic Crusades and then, when a handy cause surfaced nearer home, he switched destinations back to Calais where a putative campaign against the 'anti-pope' Clement VII was brewing.[47] In fact, he missed out drawing a sword in either venture; before the end of the year, he was back in Northumberland, looking to get back to harrying the Scots.

Andrew Boardman sees this crusading urge as evidence of pure chivalric idealism.[48] While this may in part be correct, it is perhaps more an act of conformity with knightly ethos. Many English and Scottish warriors sought experience in the Baltic wars. It was something you needed to your name. Hotspur had earned his sobriquet and bloodied his steel on the border which, useful as it was, didn't necessarily fulfil the cavalier ideal. Border warfare was a dynamic school but strictly down-market. The death of Edward III together with that of his son, the magnetic Black Prince, and the collapse of the English position in France meant that this great arena where so many famous knights such as Knollys or Chandos had won fame (and no small fortune) was effectively closed off. New fields of glory were needed. Scrapping with the Scots over a far flung, dismal, and poverty ridden border line didn't fully count.

Meanwhile, Berwick was more at the forefront as the Scots pulled off a second coup. This time they relied on corruption rather than brute force, but it was equally as embarrassing for Northumberland. Lancaster couldn't believe his luck, here was a mighty big stick to beat Percy with. And he did. The earl was accused of treason, arraigned, and convicted in absentia, his lands and probably his neck forfeit. Luckily for the House of Percy, Northumberland was quick on his feet, swiftly bought off the Scots and recovered the castle. He was immediately pardoned, despite Lancaster's shrill cries of protest.[49] It had to be the young king was beginning to find his overbearing uncle's intermeddling tiresome.

One tricky matter still outstanding was the residue of King David II's ransom. After he'd been captured at Neville's Cross, Scotland was burdened with the huge debt due to England's coffers. Hotspur, together with both his father and Lord Neville, was dispatched to settle the thorny matter of arrears. In 1385, the younger Percy was appointed Governor of Berwick, a more peaceful arrangement than his previous visit. Neville, ever resilient and this time with Roger Clifford, was soon re-appointed as joint warden of both Marches.[50] The Crown was rightfully wary of concentrating too much power in too few hands. Fighting the Scots needed northern satraps but these, as the Percies would so clearly show, could prove dangerous. On 20 May 1385 Hotspur garnered the position of sole East March Warden. His reputation, uncontaminated by his father's spats with Lancaster and boosted by his own restless energy, continued to flourish.

Next season, 1385, Richard II led another chevauchée over the border, accompanied by young Percy and inevitably John of Gaunt. Also, in his retinue rode a Welsh knight named Owain Glyndwr – nobody had heard of him, though many soon would, not least Henry Hotspur: 'indenture, whereby the earl of Northumberland, John, Sire de Neville, Sire de Clifford, Henry Percy warden of Berwick upon Tweed . . . agree to attend the king for 29 days . . . Sir Henry Percy with 100 men at arms and 200 archers beyond his garrison'.[51] In part the expedition was defensive, 2,000 French men-at-arms, commanded by the formidable John de Vienne, Admiral of France, had been shipped in along with a fat war chest containing 50,000 livres in gold.[52] That was a lot of money yet in fact it didn't buy that much and relations between these two allies soon cooled, then froze over.

This raid was, as usual, a costly waste. Scots were masters of guerrilla warfare and under Dunbar's sage counsel had come to appreciate that Fabian tactics produced dividends whereas head-on produced only high body counts. The earls of Fife, Douglas, and Dunbar countered by beating up the English West March, doing a fair amount of profitable damage, yet the French were disappointed that Dunbar avoided confrontation. This wasn't what they'd come for, but the Scots weren't too keen on being used up as expendable allies of easy convenience.

Certainly, Bower wasn't impressed, or cowed by Richard's grand army:

> . . . About the feast of St. Laurance [10 August] Richard . . . sick at heart that the Scots and French were plundering his land so cruelly and were attacking his fortresses and razing them to the ground, assembled a large army and entered Scotland at the age of 19. He advanced in the midst of an arrogant host, destroying everything on all sides and saving nothing. He burned to ashes with consuming flames churches devoted to God and monastic sanctuaries (namely the monasteries of Dryburgh, Melrose and Newbattle), and the noble royal town of Edinburgh with its church of St. Giles.[53]

Despite this orgy of iconoclasm, Gaunt persuaded the king to spare Holyrood (then also an abbey).[54]

Richard was able to pretend the job was done when he occupied Edinburgh but was savvy enough to ignore Gaunt's suggestion the expedition should press on, kind remembrance only stretched so far. It was a modest profile-raising success, and the king was wisely content. The war lasted a fortnight, harvesting some meagre loot but consuming treasure at a far greater rate. Dunbar's next riposte was laying siege to Roxburgh, judging the time ripe to recover this great jewel. The French were keen to help but only on the basis that the castle, once taken, should become property of the King of France as compensation for his outlay. This proved to be a demand too far and the end of a once beneficial friendship. The siege was abandoned, and the French returned home.[55] Soon after Hotspur, probably, or his father possibly, was engaged in inspecting Carlisle's defences, and his report didn't make comforting reading: 'Petition to the King and Council by the Mayor and citizens of Carlisle that he would take note of the report of the lords Percy and Clifford, marchers, and others who were lately there on a March [truce] day, as to the state of their city. Their walls are in part fallen, and great part on the point of falling from weakness . . .'[56]

In March 1386 Ralph Neville and Thomas Clifford replaced their fathers as joint wardens with handsome retainers. Both northern magnatial families were pursuing their ambitions via sons while their fathers, apparently at least, took a back seat. As neither the Earl of Northumberland nor Lord Neville were any longer in the flower of youth, this made sense. This business of policing the line was a young man's game. It was physically taxing, frequently demoralising, and always dangerous. These appointments might be coveted but were never sinecures. The warden always earned his stipend and was frequently out of pocket for his troubles. At best, the Crown was parsimonious and very often forgetful. Richard II, if not his uncle, had realised that campaigning on the borders was both hugely expensive and totally non-effective, so he was happy to leave matters in the north in the hands of surrogates. Hotspur like his fellow officers' sallying out from Berwick with a flying column of a hundred men-at-arms and twice as many archers was happy to oblige. This was his natural element.

Fair Stood the Wind for France

Wider horizons awaited during that summer when alarums buzzed like an upturned hive: 'there were increasing rumours that the French King [Charles VI] planned and intended to lay siege to Calais and that he was gathering a force for this purpose'.[57] Hotspur was sent out with a relief force, but it turned out there was nowhere needing to be relieved. This wasn't at all to young Percy's liking. He'd come out to fight the French: 'So Henry assembled some companions and made raids on Therouanne and into Picardy, making off with booty and performing deeds of war that won him praise'.[58]

Hotspur also gleaned intelligence that King Charles was really planning an attack on England. This was good news.[59] Hotspur, with brother Ralph, was ordered to take station at Yarmouth and be ready. Again, the French disappointed. Charles' invasion fleet waited all summer for favourable winds and didn't weigh anchor till 1 November. They had barely sailed a score of miles till contrary winds drove them back with numerous ships being damaged or lost due to collisions.[60] That was the end of that gambit.

With summer's excitements blown away by autumn winds, Harry Percy found himself, at the end of that October, in London, this time for a question of law as witness in litigation between Lord Scrope, 1st Baron Scrope of Bolton and Sir Robert Grosvenor, a Cheshire gentleman. This was at the behest of his father the Earl of Northumberland, Scrope was of Percy's affinity, a tricky case concerning heraldry, rather akin to a copyright dispute today.[61] Both parties had campaigned in Scotland with the king the previous year where, embarrassingly, each noticed they were bearing the same arms. Scrope claimed precedence but Grosvenor averred his own right stretched back to William I and the Norman Conquest.

A gentleman's brand was important and Scrope was alleging Grosvenor had purloined his ('Azure a bend Or'). A court of chivalry was convened to decide the matter with Thomas of Woodstock, 1st Duke of Gloucester presiding. Hotspur wasn't the only key figure to give evidence, John of Gaunt was called, Henry Bolingbroke his son, then Earl of Derby, Geoffrey Chaucer and even Owain Glyndwr. Despite his links to Scrope, Northumberland still sat on the bench, a fact

Grosvenor's legal team was quick to pounce on. A less thick-skinned individual might have got the hint, but the earl clung to his office; true to character his rather pronounced partiality was far from subtle.

Andrew Boardman intriguingly highlights that Hotspur gives his date of birth as 20 May 1366 and confirms he was born at Alnwick.[62] Now, Boardman favours Spofforth as his place of birth, though I prefer Alnwick, but we both agree he was born two years earlier on 13 June 1364. Boardman suggests the reason for this discrepancy being the Percies' desire to be identified with Alnwick and that Northumberland, no longer Yorkshire, was their principal address. Quite possibly however, Hotspur just got it wrong, birthdays were not the occasions they are today! The legal matter dragged on and judgement wasn't entered till 1389: finally, the court found in favour of Scrope, though Grosvenor was permitted to continue using the same arms though in a modified form, within a 'bordure argent'.[63]

Hotspur probably found the business of extended litigation as tedious as most witnesses find it today, the lengthy arguments of lawyers hungry for their fee scarcely inspiring to one who yearned for martial glory. Happily, further opportunities for mayhem swiftly presented themselves: 'A short time afterwards the members of the king's council advised him that Henry Percy . . . should be sent to sea to repel attacks by the enemy'.[64] The French, stung by recent raids mounted by the Earl of Arundel, were thought to be readying themselves and their boats for some reciprocal action.

'The council neither gave him an adequate force nor provided the proper support, doing this, so it was said, out of envy for the ability of one who had already won a great name for his worth among both English and Scots'.[65] Assuming the chronicler is correct, there were power games afoot and Northumberland's enemies, ever plentiful as tact clearly wasn't the earl's forte, were setting his eldest son up to fail. If so, they were to be disappointed. Hotspur successfully mounted a raid on Brest in September 1387 to relieve the besieged English garrison. He beat up enemy quarters, destroyed their siege towers and ensured the castle was safely in the hands of the castellan John Roches. The expedition had accomplished its objectives. Hotspur, despite the best efforts of his family's enemies, 'fearlessly undertook the commission laid upon him and bravely and vigorously carried it out, and, having finished the term of his command, returned home safe and sound'.[66]

Such swashbuckling was dear to his contemporaries' hearts and Harry Percy found himself a celebrity, the fame and adulation he so craved was his. He was only 23, a good age for heroes, and he was now firmly in the ascendancy. But the Scottish border hadn't gone away. For the Percies, this was their making and their Calvary, for whatever else may be said of them they took their duties seriously. There would be backhanders and eyes turned the other way, affinities fostered or suborned, that's how life was. Theirs was no easy task, a Sisyphean chore that never took a day off. They rode high on the back of cross-border conflict but always earned their keep.

If Harry was looking for a successful role model, he could do no better than follow his uncle Thomas. As demonstrated, Northumberland's younger brother was infinitely more subtle, less cantankerous, smooth tongued and affable. His rise was just as certain as his brother's and with far less gaffes. He wisely stayed clear of the feud between Northumberland and Lancaster, quietly but surely building up an impressive stock of sinecures. His portfolio included command of the northern flotilla and a successful, focused campaign in France where he and the Earl of Buckingham had supported the Bretons. His exploits at sea, proper daring, always played well to the commons, hungry for some desperate glory: 'The noble story of our naval warfare records no exploits more gallant than some of those by which Thomas Percy and Hugh Calveley struggled to maintain English supremacy on the ocean'.[67] He'd crushed Jack Straw's Essex insurrection and seamlessly conducted a series of diplomatic missions.[68]

In 1386, John of Gaunt was 46 but his restless ambition, not blessed with any significant abilities, remained undiminished. He'd got used to being the power behind a young king's throne, but Richard was growing weary of his uncle's constant and damaging dominance. Gaunt probably wasn't bright enough, his self-absorption so total that he failed, as in so many other things, to appreciate his nephew's febrile and often mercurial temperament. Richard too was imbued with a sense of his own importance; of the semi-divine, absolutist nature of his sovereignty. He lacked the worldly perspicacity of his predecessors who though they wanted their own way and meant to have it, perceived there were rules to this game and while English monarchs might be anointed with holy oil, they could never be despots. Richard, had he been less blinkered, could have studied the unfortunate example of his great-grandfather Edward II and learned from his forbear's mistakes. He chose not to, preferring smooth sycophants to robust advisors.

In 1387, the king was 20 and had ruled for a decade. By medieval standards he was easily old enough to rule but also to be accountable. A powerful triumvirate of magnates, the Duke of Gloucester (his younger uncle), with the earls of Warwick and Arundel, together badged as 'the lords Appellant', 'appealed' to Richard to seek wiser guidance, ideally theirs. Their offer was not well received and matters quickly escalated till swords were drawn and the king humiliated in a fracas at Radcot Bridge on the Thames. These Lords Appellant had ample support, Gaunt's son Bolingbroke was with them as, possibly, was Hotspur, though not at the forefront. Richard's exalted ideas of monarchy were deeply outraged. He forgot nothing and learnt nothing. Those who'd conspired against him were now marked men.

Gaunt, more by accident than design, escaped the fallout. He had found a new project to occupy his ambition and no doubt his nephew encouraged him in this. Thomas Percy accompanied the duke on his expedition to Spain where in right of his second wife, Constance, he had a claim to rule Castile and Leon. Ultimately, like all his other grand schemes this one would end in expensive failure but at least it kept him out of the firing line while his own younger sibling Gloucester took the king in hand.

It was a harsh process. These Lords Appellant, through the medium of the 'Merciless' Parliament, ruthlessly cleared out all advisors they deemed unsuitable, and they didn't spare the axe. Robert de Vere, Duke of Ireland was a prime target. A son of the Earl of Oxford, de Vere's rapid rise and salacious rumours of his sexual involvement with the king had goaded his rising chorus of detractors. Worse, he'd abandoned his wife, a granddaughter of Edward III, and taken up with one of Anne of Bohemia's women, who Walsingham snobbishly decries as 'a foul creature of ignoble birth whose father was a saddler'.[69] Worse, the jilted wife was Gloucester's niece. De Vere had led Richard's ramshackle force in the rout at Radcot and was sentenced to death, happily for him, in absentia (he lived long enough to die from injuries suffered in the hunting field in 1392).

De Vere's loss was Hotspur's gain. In fact, 1388 opened quite well for the Percies. John Neville had died which neatly removed the main competition and Hotspur had been reappointed both as East March Warden and Governor of Berwick with a handsome wage of £3,000 per annum in peacetime, quadrupled in war (over £3 million today).[70] An indenture dated 3 April reads: 'Henry Percy eldest son of the earl of Northumberland, undertakes the keeping of the east march of Scotland [i.e., adjoining Scotland] and the town of Berwick upon Tweed for three years from 19th June at £12,000 per annum, reduced to £3,000 during a truce or peace'.[71]

Furthermore, with the disreputable Duke of Ireland demoted, there was a vacancy within the elite ranks of the Order of the Garter and Hotspur was nominated.[72] Victorious on land and sea, hero of the commons, idol of chivalry, plenipotentiary in the north, this was all heady stuff, but Hotspur's fame was only just beginning, and that year would produce his greatest test to date. He'd be the loser, but immortality his gleaming compensation.

Act 4

Death on St Oswin's Eve –
The Battle of Otterburn, 5 (or 19) August 1388

The old song of 'Chevy-Chase' is the favourite ballad of the common people of England, and Ben Jonson used to say he had rather have been the author of it than of all his works. Sir Philip Sidney, in his discourse of Poetry [*The Defence of Poesie*], speaks of it in the following words: 'I never heard the old song of Percy and Douglas that I found not my heart more moved than with a trumpet; and yet it is sung by some blind crowder with no rougher voice than rude style, which being so evil apparelled in the dust and cobweb of that uncivil age, what would it work trimmed in the gorgeous eloquence of Pindar?' For my own part, I am so professed an admirer of this antiquated song, that I shall give my reader a critique upon it without any further apology for so doing.
—Joseph Addison[1]

The Ballad of Chevy Chase (see Appendix 1) and the Battle of Otterburn, far more so than his other fights, were what really gave his legend its first major boost. Losing doesn't necessarily damage your mythic status, but a big part of the Hotspur saga rests on this minor and otherwise unimportant fight. What is it about Otterburn? Thanks to Froissart and poetic tradition, the battle has become synonymous with chivalry, Douglas dies a hero's death, most definitely *Kalos thanatos*; Leonidas couldn't have done it better and Hotspur, as even his enemies acknowledged, fought like Hector. To lose the fight in such circumstances was no disgrace, half of history's enduring legends champion the losers – Thermopylae, Watling Street, Hastings, Roncesvalles and all the way to the Alamo and Gloucester Hill.

On a rather wild and windy day in August 1988 and on the actual site (depending on whose account you believe), I was part of a team who'd organised a 600th anniversary re-enactment of the Battle of Otterburn. No high summer heat for us. To add spice, and highly likely real bloodshed, the MoD had furnished the day with a company each of English and Scottish junior leaders, trainee NCOs with a cadre of instructors. Thank goodness the weapons were wooden, as the

Scots took the whole business very seriously and if anyone doubted they'd won first time around, now it would be definite. It wasn't any wild melee but well-drilled and coordinated fury, with proper NCOs bellowing themselves hoarse and urging their charges on to closer drill and even more focused blood lust. In both they succeeded admirably and we *actual* reenactors in proper harness with nearly real weapons were glad of our armour.

Ground

One day somebody will write a definitive account of the battle and much good work is being done, at the time of writing, by the Northumberland National Park Authority, Revitalising Redesdale, and the UK Battlefields Trust.[2] Otterburn field poses several problems which historians have struggled with and generally failed to resolve. Our main primary source is Jean Froissart, one of our leading authorities for the 'chivalric revival' of the fourteenth century, and he travelled widely across both England and Scotland. That said, he's a dreadful gossip and serial name dropper. Nonetheless, Hotspur owes him a good deal even if a lot of it is spin.

Of Otterburn Froissart says: 'Of all the battles and encounterings that I have made mention of heretofore in all this history, great or small, this battle that I treat of now was one of the sorest and best foughten without cowardice or faint hearts'.[3] Yet, the various descriptions are often sketchy and regularly contradict each other. These will be investigated thoroughly and conclusions offered. At first glance the ground appears straightforward though at least one credible writer, Charles Wesencraft, believes the battle was fought not at Otterburn but Elsdon and that the error is due to Froissart's confusion and cavalier approach to detail.[4] In terms of modern sources, Andrew Boardman and Pete Armstrong are broadly in agreement with the views presented here.[5] What can be added is an attempt to reconcile several of the anomalies in a way which may make sense.

George Ridpath, a comprehensive and redoubtable early complier (1787), gives extraordinarily little detail and relies on Percy's *Reliques*.[6] He affirms the fighting began at evening, continued under moonlight and lists casualties on both sides. Irritatingly, he says nothing about ground.[7] White (1857) gives a far fuller account of the terrain. He describes the Scottish force as passing the 'tower' (Otterburn Castle, now the Towers Hotel), and taking up position on 'the eminence north-west of Hott-Wood above Greenchesters – this forms a kind of promontory, jutting out to the south-west from the high land behind'. He goes on to suggest that 'Hott' comes from 'Holt' indicating that the rise was previously wooded.[8]

There is no compelling reason to argue with this and the 1:25,000 OS Map clearly supports White – the high ground is called the Holt still and Greenchesters Camp crowns the crest. He gives the distance from the Tower as a 1½ miles

THE BATTLE OF
OTTERBURN
5th August 1388

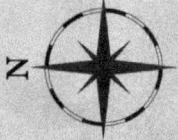

N

Deadground

Greenchesters

Marshy areas

Battle
Stone

Road

River Rede

Otterburn
Tower

0   500

YARDS

① Hotspur 1st position
② Redmayne and Ogle 1st position
③ Scottish lower camp
④ Scottish higher camp
⑤ Redmayne and Ogle 2nd position
⑥ Hotspur 2nd position
⑦ Douglas' flank attack

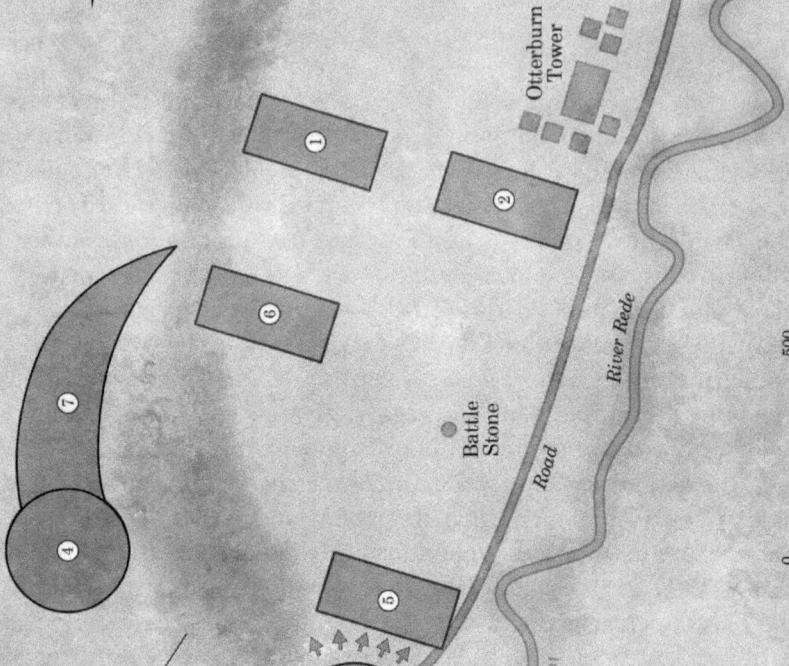

(2.4km) and this is also correct. He goes on to say the Scots made camp here on this commanding rise which gave them the necessary 'long view' to warn of any approach by English forces. Based on Inherent Military Probability (IMP) this makes sound sense.[9] The Scots wouldn't establish their main position on the low-lying, wet ground directly below them towards the Rede. They would see that as a natural trap if they were attacked (as indeed it became for those stuck there). White does confirm that pilfered beasts with the *bouches inutiles* ('useless mouths') were sent into the wet bottom.[10]

White also argues that the vicinity was dotted with scrubby trees and bushes, birch, alder, and hazel. This seems not unreasonable given botanical evidence from nearby Chattlehope Spout which he alludes to. He gives the date of the battle as 19 August and goes on to state that having failed in their efforts against the Tower the Scots dug in, throwing up earthworks on the north flank of the higher camp (this is unlikely as the ditches belong to the Iron Age site) and creating field defences, *abbatis*, to secure the lower enclosure, which is much more likely. White then goes on to assert that the Scots would have had few if any wheeled carts, relying instead on their hardy ponies, 'hobbyies' – this ties in with established principles of hobiler warfare, avoiding slow-moving baggage trains and using lances to prod recalcitrant beasts. Cattle were valuable booty, the profit element, and this was important.

White does suggest that this minor or lower camp extended across both sides of the Newcastle road, from where Greenchesters farm now stands down to the river.[112] Again, this conforms to Inherent Military Probability, no commander would want to leave a handy gap through which an enemy might infiltrate and turn his flank. He makes the point that the 'servants' would be hardy skirmishers, able to hold their ground at least for a while against men-at-arms until they could be reinforced. This turned out to be wrong, but the principle was sound.

Next, White covers the English approach to contact, coming over from Elsdon, swinging down past Davyshiels to reach Otterburn. He gives a highly accurate estimation of the view from the Scottish camp on the Holt and he's confident both sides fought on foot. However, he's also adamant that Hotspur told off a detachment led by Umfraville and Redmayne to skirt around the north flank to cut off any line of retreat.[12] The main body would then barrel along the road to attack the Scottish camp.

Owing to the existing scrub and woodland, together with fading light, White suggests it would be unlikely that Hotspur had seen Greenchesters but had assumed the Scots were all encamped on the lower ground. Clearly, he was determined to attack and hadn't spent time in reconnaissance. Then, he has Percy attacking the camp defended by the auxiliaries.[13] For a while the defenders, protected by their improvised field works, hold out as Douglas feeds in infantry support to bolster the line. Meanwhile, the Scottish earl leads his main strike force north-east, making full use of the contours and masking woods to deliver his own flank manoeuvre.

White credits Umfraville with a rather tortuous route, effectively passing Douglas by moving further north and attacking the newly dug entrenchments. Realising he's missed the bus, he abandons scrapping with those few reservists guarding the main Scottish camp and attempts to re-join the fight below but ends up colliding with the right flank of Percy's Brigade, just adding to the confusion. This account, as detailed as it is and correct in its analysis of ground, has influenced many if not most who've written about the battle since (including the author in my publication *Battle for Northumbria* (Newcastle upon Tyne, Bridge Studios, 1988)). Ramsay (1892) places the whole battle 1½ miles (2.4km) east of the (now) agreed site: Burne, Boardman, Armstrong, and I all disagree with this.[14]

Bates (1895) gives a fairly sketchy account, describes the Scottish camp as surrounded by marshes with an entrance facing east along the line of the Newcastle road; armed camp followers form a first line of defence. He says nothing about any English flanking attack.[15] Sitwell (1925) just says: 'The Scots made themselves bowers of trees and branches in a strong position surrounded by marshes, the entrance towards Newcastle was occupied by varlets & foragers . . . the cattle could graze between the two camps'.[16] Sitwell, who'd been a serving soldier, maintains the English battered their way into the camp which exposed them even more to Douglas' flank assault. He has Redmayne running from the fight pursued and captured by Lindsay, who is himself taken by the Prince Bishop.[17]

Redoubtable Colonel A.H. Burne (1952) was the first since White to have a serious look.[18] He points out that the present road, the turnpike (A696) follows the line of the old medieval way. He rightly points out that the Scots defensive position covers the 'pass' between the river and rising ground north. He identifies two key problems: 1. Location of the Scottish camp; and 2. Flank marches by both armies. Burne argues that the English flank attack struck out northwards from the right of Hotspur's army in a wide flanking movement which today would take Umfraville past Otterburn Hall as far as Hopefoot (the way they'd just come), westwards, skirting Blakeman's Law to attack along a north–south axis, hitting the north flank of the higher camp. Burne projects the line of Douglas' own flank attack as an inside track, west to east around Greenchesters, parallel with Otterburn Hall.

The colonel had walked the ground and is confident Douglas was able to strike, initially undetected, against the right flank of Hotspur's main brigade at a point close to the current marker. Burne admits he struggled to work out what then happened to Umfraville, or how these two flanking manoeuvres failed to collide.[19] He rejects any notion that Umfraville attacked on the left and not on the right – he feels the river prevents this.

This is a touch of *deus ex machine* and might be suspected that Burne was adapting the possibilities to suit his own hypothesis. He rejects Greenchesters as any site for a second camp on the basis it's too ancient, but this is not a reasonable hypothesis. It is difficult to disagree with so respected an authority, but Burne's vision is wrong. The idea of two large bodies of armoured men passing each other without noticing, even allowing for poor light and scrub/tree cover just doesn't add up. If Umfraville had to march back up the Davyshiels Road then strike out cross country, that's over 3 miles (4.8km) in distance. Yet, if he'd tried a tighter angle, he'd have smacked into Douglas.

Macdonald (2000) specifies the date as 5 August and he says that Percy sent Redmayne and Ogle off on a flanking manoeuvre but omits to specify which flank, the implication being this was a northwards move and the camp they attacked being that at Greenchesters.[20] He airily dismisses the idea of night fighting. He does credit Redmayne and Ogle with 'success on another part of the field' and of capturing Lindsay. This really doesn't add much. Nor does Moffatt's account (2002) which contains a rather bare and vague summary.

Boardman considers the battle in considerable detail and carefully analyses both ground and sources; he gives the date as 19 August. He points out that the area generally agreed upon was known on early maps as Battle Riggs.[21] He further observes that the line of the river is an important constraint and narrows the area available to the combatants. Now he says, quite rightly, that Froissart asserts the castle 'stood in the marsh'.[22] This is a different marsh to that at Greenchesters or, more likely at the time, a continuous belt of low–lying alluvial bog. Boardman asserts, and Colonel Burne would have approved, that it was this very marsh which had partly frustrated Douglas' attempts to take the Tower which is after all built close to the confluence of the Otter Burn and Rede and none of this can be criticised. He confidently accepts the idea of two Scottish encampments one on higher, another on lower and that the defence of one could be supported by reserves from the other.

Boardman cites Oman and his analysis of Scottish fourteenth-century tactics, based on 'King Robert's Testament'.[23] This is important because it strongly implies, as the accounts seem to support, that the Scots were not relying just on defence. This was a clever diversion to pin the English while Douglas circled their flank. Boardman is adamant that Redmayne and Ogle attacked the lower camp by the river. He goes on to suggest that light from cooking fires would have alerted Hotspur to the reality of two enemy camps and he intended to strike at the upper base with the bulk of his forces, having divined that the lower camp was not his prime target.[24]

Boardman is confident (and the author concurs) that Redmayne's success outpaced Hotspur's own advance. Bearing in mind the scrubby, wooded nature of the ground and failing light, this is understandable ('time spent in reconnaissance is never wasted'). He didn't know, could not see, exactly where the main camp stood. Despite being taken by surprise, Douglas' men formed up, as they'd been schooled to do and carried out their own flanking tactics, knowing exactly the ground over which they'd advance. He does say Redmayne's force remained mounted, but this unlikely. He dismisses the idea of a separate flanking move to the north led by Umfraville, which seems correct.[25]

The author's previous account in *Border Fury* (Cambridge, Pearsons, 2004) is broadly consistent with Boardman, except it being more likely that Redmayne's Brigade attacked dismounted; wet ground and field obstacles would have frustrated any attempt at a mounted charge. Whether, having beaten up the camp, the English on this flank mounted up for the pursuit could, however, be a strong possibility. Armstrong (2006) takes a similar line.

If you approach Elsdon from the south along the straight-as-a-die road past Harwood, coming up from Cambo, you reach the high ground of Steng's Cross, the tarmac then winding and curving down towards the settlement. Directly in front you, angular and uncompromising against a grey winter's sky, is the sinister shape of the gibbet. This significantly postdates the bad old days of the reivers and was erected as late as 1791, built to cage the mortal remains of William Winter who'd been hanged at the Westgate in Newcastle.

By this date Elsdon was already ancient, the traditional town of turbulent Redesdale – the name derived from the old English 'Elli's Valley'. Below the castle is a well-restored Vicar Pele, an impressive tower house, deluxe by border standards, much extended and given a less military makeover in the nineteenth century. St Cuthbert's is a charming and surprisingly large church, an early foundation and one of the resting places for St Cuthbert's coffin on its extended travels. It was rebuilt in the later medieval period and there's some suggestion it might have been trashed by the Scottish army prior to the Battle of Otterburn in 1388.

What most would say about Otterburn itself is that a road and, if they notice, a river run through it. It has a distinctly unloved look with the MoD camp lying behind. Nonetheless, the current Otterburn Towers Hotel, mainly *c.* 1830, stands on the site of the original Umfraville castle, though no visible traces endure. The later Otterburn Hall (*c.* 1870) was built for Lord James Douglas who was apparently gifted the site in recompense for the death of his ancestor in 1388 (see Map 2).[26] For a detailed examination of the primary sources, please refer to Appendix 3.

The Battle

Though not a major fight, the very intensity of the battle and the balladry this inspired guaranteed its lasting fame (see Appendix 1). And though he lost, Hotspur's legend began to flourish. Froissart lets us know that while Harry might have been beaten, his ransom (7,000 marks) was soon raised and paid over. Hotspur suffered no fallout from the defeat. How then do we summarise the facts as they appear to us and reconcile the various anomalies? We can accept the facts of the Scottish invasion as the sources broadly agree and that there was some skirmishing outside the walls of Newcastle near the extended timber outer barbican or barrier; whether knightly pennons changed hands is open to speculation. What we can accept is that Percy, realising he was facing far fewer numbers than he anticipated, decided to seize the initiative, which the Scots had so far monopolised, and go after them.

That Percy's force at about 6,000–7,000 was substantively larger seems reasonable. On that afternoon, to cover 32 miles (51km) given that most would be mounted on hobbies and travelling at about 7 to 8mph probably means they could have covered the distance in perhaps five to six hours. If they marched at noon that means they could be approaching Otterburn by late afternoon/early evening, the hour of Vespers, plenty of time to deliver a knockout blow in daylight given dusk would have been at about 2100 hours.

To risk an immediate assault and avoid leaguering for the night made tactical sense. The Scots, being outnumbered, would, in all probability, have used the cover of darkness to clear off, content with keeping their loot intact. Given how far the beasts had been driven and at a rapid pace, they had probably needed to rest before going on to make that long climb to the border, so hanging on at Otterburn and pummelling the Tower didn't appear to entail much risk as the speed of Hotspur's reaction was partly unanticipated.

Let's also assume Douglas and March were, in part, surprised to find themselves under attack, their dispositions were still sound. The livestock was guarded by the ad hoc defences of the lower camp and the watchers could be relied upon to give a decent account of themselves; holding out long enough to be reinforced. Douglas had clearly trained his men-at-arms in the flanking manoeuvre they'd execute if attacked frontally. Walking the ground confirms the feasibility of this and we know the scrub and tree cover was denser at the time. Hotspur was relying on speed and dash rather than careful reconnaissance and he'd be aware of the risk that entailed.

Hotspur's plan to divide his forces does make sense if we accept he knew the location of the Scots' lower camp but not that of their main fighting base. What developed were almost two separate battles. Redmayne and Ogle performed their allotted task admirably and beat up the Scots guarding the camp; even reinforcements of men-at-arms couldn't finally stem the rot. Fatally, however, the flank attack developed into a wild pursuit, and they were unable to come to Hotspur's aid. As Percy hesitated, and this would be necessary to marshal his men for the second prong of his assault, Douglas gained the respite he needed. If, as has been suggested, Hotspur commanded up to 7,000 men and that these were mounted, his column in line of march would have stretched back for up to 8 miles (13km) and taken a deal of time and sweat to deploy for the attack. We are ready to surmise that a large part of his strength never in fact engaged.

As the column came north from Elsdon, they'd know the enemy was close, both sides would. Much has been said of the Scots being surprised but both sides would have had their prickers ranging. What the English would notice would be the absence of livestock and only the mournful dirge of curlews punctuating the summer's evening. The Scots would have lifted whatever they could and whatever locals had failed to spirit away or conceal and that creates a feeling of unnatural calm. This was experienced in Northumberland again as recently as 2001 when foot and mouth disease resulted in mass culling and emptied fields. A rural landscape suddenly cleared of livestock is uncanny, and the extent of this is not realised until it happens. It feels like a harbinger.

At what point did the fighters dismount? We think Hotspur dismounted his men as he prepared to deploy. This would take time. We don't think Douglas mounted for his flank attack; the Scots tradition was to fight on foot in dense, packed spear phalanxes – the schlitron. That short distance over difficult ground must imply the Scots came down on foot, already marshalled into battalions so they could deliver their own counterattack while maintaining an element of surprise and with it tactical initiative.

At first the English were caught off guard but soon rallied and were able to hold their ground. The fight degenerated into stalemate in which the English possibly still had an advantage in numbers, though they'd be bone-weary after their exhausting yomp while Douglas' men were fit and rested. Both sides had reason to feel confident in their officers and neither at this stage could claim any morale advantage.

If the Earl of Douglas had been following Robert the Bruce's example he'd have done what the great man did at Bannockburn and kept one battalion in reserve to deal a decisive blow. We're thinking that is what Douglas did in fact do; his attack was no berserker rush but a sound and well-executed strike against Percy's extreme right flank which was effectively in the air. Clearly, the earl led from the front, and it cost him his life, but he died unrecognised, so his men didn't lose heart. This whole tactic was a well-rehearsed manoeuvre and his charge the signal for a renewed effort along the line with serial bruisers like Swinton showing the way. It worked.

We look at plans of troop deployments and moves on maps, but we must always bear in mind that while careful cartography and writer's hindsight appear to make sense of the whole thing, it was never like that on the day. Medieval commanders had no means of controlling a fight once it began other than by flags or messenger. 'No plan ever survives contact with the enemy' is a sound military maxim and the face of battle changes everything. It's also very ugly and confused.

Finally, after much hard fighting, Percy's line faltered and then broke, knots of fighters spilling untidily in the gathering dusk. If we assume the English reached the battlefield at about 1800 hours and were attacking on their left by 1830 with Douglas' counter punch ramming home at about 1900–1930 hours that's over an hour of decent daylight to win the day. We don't think the battle was, at any salient point, fought by moonlight but the pursuit would have been.

So, on the English left, Redmayne and Ogle pelted after their beaten opponents, losing all contact with Hotspur on their right and playing no further significant role in the overall decision. They cheered after the fleeing Scots, jubilantly relieving them of anything that was worth nicking or perhaps re-nicking. On Hotspur's right it is presumed there was no rout and that while many men were captured, a large part of Percy's 'tail' would have got off in good order and retreated towards Elsdon, harried all the way but still in fighting trim.

How do we explain the apparent interment of so many, presumably English dead, at Elsdon? Bodies were buried where they fell not carted for several miles. We're going to get even more heroic in our assumptions and suggest that this came about because of a negotiated truce. These were not uncommon and while it cannot be proved, it is a tantalising possibility. After the battle, the Scots remained in possession of the field, but they may have agreed to allow English survivors access to the ground to remove their dead and inter them elsewhere. Now, we don't even know who the dead of Elsdon are. It was thought at the time they had to be casualties and while this makes every good sense, we'll know nothing more until, or indeed if, further forensic archaeological work is undertaken to open and investigate the supposed mass grave.

What does the Battle of Otterburn tell us about Hotspur as a commander? Winners are usually labelled as decisive; losers are plain impetuous. Harry Percy lost and is invariably described as rash and impetuous. His decision to attack at night or at least evening is routinely cited as evidence of folly. This isn't necessarily so. Having tracked the Scots and regained, for the first time in that campaign, a measure of tactical initiative, he really had no choice but to press this advantage or see it vanish. Besides, if he did attack at Vespers, he had well over two hours of daylight, medieval battles rarely lasted that long.

Hotspur had never led a sizeable field force into battle, medieval commanders didn't like battles, they were too unpredictable, impossible to control, and failure meant catastrophe. Percy had made his formidable reputation as a leader of light cavalry, hobiler warfare, now perfected by both sides on the Border Marches. Success, as he'd demonstrated, demanded dash and vigour. He had plenty of both. It took nerve. He had that, and it took fine judgement, luck helped as well. Trying to translate hobiler tactics onto a larger battlefield was tricky, different dynamics applied as command and control was far, far more difficult.

A key element in conventional combat was, as ever, intelligence gleaned through sound reconnaissance. This was lacking and proved a serious flaw; he would be attacking while not knowing exactly where his main enemy was stationed and the clear potential of dead ground which Douglas had previously spotted. We could say the Scots won because their close knowledge of the ground was superior.

Another serious failing on Percy's part was his inability to coordinate the two pincers of his assault. Redmayne and Ogle did well at the outset, achieved their key tactical objectives but seemingly had no orders or possibly just couldn't control their men when it came to reforming. Whatever the reason, he lost perhaps a third or more of his force who, had they been able to support his wing, might well have tilted the balance and it does seem to have been a fine balance. What we can say is that Hotspur gambled, he took a significant risk and he lost. History tends to be hard on losers. Yet, his contemporaries didn't seem to blame him.

An even more famous loser, American Confederate General Robert E. Lee, noted that: 'there is always hazard in military movements, but we must decide between the *positive* loss of inaction and the risk of action'. James Wolfe, a posthumous winner, said very much the same: 'In war something must be left to chance and fortune, seeing that it is in its nature hazardous and an option of difficulties'. Hotspur, had he left us any written testimonial, would doubtless have concurred.

The Elsdon Burials

One of the most tantalizing aspects of the battle, which I referred to earlier, are the presumed remains of those found beneath the floors of St Cuthbert's Church in Elsdon in the nineteenth century. These interments were known about by 1810 but no full excavation took place until 1877 when floor levels within the nave and transepts were being dug out and re-laid. A local doctor, E.C. Robertson, attended the site after remains had been discovered and wrote up his findings.[27] Workmen confirmed they'd uncovered a total of 996 bodies from what appeared to be a single mass burial, overlaid with many others from a mix of later periods. Robertson noted that the wall of the nave (*c*. 1400) had been built *over* part of the mass grave and therefore, he guessed, had to predate re-building – the fifteenth–century church replaced a smaller predecessor.

Robertson judged that the remains were all male and relatively young. On one skull he found evidence of healed battle injury. On the basis of this he came to the conclusion that these were English casualties from the Battle of Otterburn. This was supported but the fact that no females seemed to lie among them and the presumed age range ruled out plague or any other natural cause, besides no record of an outbreak of disease exists. How fascinating it would be to exhume some of these bones and have them analysed using modern scientific methods.

Act 5

Ill-weaved Ambition – Kingmakers up North

There is a tide in the affairs of men
Which, taken at the flood, leads on to fortune
Omitted, all the voyage of their life
Is bound in shallows and in miseries
On such a full sea are we now afloat
And we must take the current when it serves
Or lose our ventures.

William Shakespeare,
Julius Caesar, Act IV, sc. iii

All in all, Hotspur didn't suffer any serious fallout from his defeat at Otterburn, even though it sent shock waves through the English polity. It had been a long time since an English army had been soundly beaten by Scots. But like Hector, Harry Percy rose untarnished from the ashes; his ransom soon paid off. The king contributed a hefty purse towards the cost.[1] Brother Ralph had suffered serious injuries but Harry himself, despite the fierceness of the fight, was left with few scars. He received a further tranche of 1,200 livres for services at Berwick and another 500 livres as extended, part payment of his ransom in mid-July 1389.[2]

King Robert II of Scotland died in 1390, to be succeeded by his son John, Earl of Carrick, Lancaster's old sparring partner who adopted the name Robert, thus becoming king Robert III ('John' had unfortunate connotations of John Baliol, 'Toom Tabard', who nobody wished to be reminded of). The new king suffered from an old malady, leading to degrees of incapacity, not helped by having been kicked in the head by his brother's horse. That brother, the Earl of Fife, effectively ruled as quasi-regent. But a weak king means internal troubles, or as Bower puts it, 'under a slack shepherd the wolf fouls the wool, and the flock is torn to pieces'.[3] The border and borderers would still be in a foment of anarchy.

His star status undimmed, Hotspur was soon appointed Governor of Carlisle and West March Warden, sweetened further with a hefty annuity of £6,000. The family business was flourishing with as yet no revived competition from the Nevilles. Percies, father and son, were enjoying a virtual monopoly. John Neville's convenient demise pretty much cleared out the field for now, though his son Ralph (1st Earl of Westmoreland from 1397) would mature into a formidable player. In 1391 Ralph was granted a warrant along with a clutch of English knights to perform 'feats of arms' after being challenged by Alexander Lindsay, a Scottish opponent, a form of proxy war in peacetime, but with no fear of swords being beaten into ploughshares.[4]

A Right Royal Revenge

King Richard's febrile temperament had chafed under the yoke of the Lords Appellant and boiled from the humiliation they'd inflicted. In May 1389, now aged 22, the king declared himself fit to rule personally and be free of those detested 'tutors' who had cloaked their own hunger for power as concern for the young king's inexperience and vulnerability.

As a piece of political theatre this was impressive, Richard had neatly turned the tables on his oppressors. One of the casualties whose head had rolled during the Lords Appellants' purge had been Simon Burley, a rather disreputable favourite of the young king who seems to have been willing to sell off Dover Castle to the French.[5] Yet, Henry Bolingbroke had interceded in an unsuccessful effort to secure clemency for Burley and had rowed mightily with Gloucester. Still, this wasn't enough to extricate Bolingbroke from the king's hit-list, though vengeance, for the moment, could wait.

For a while all was amity, Arundel, Gloucester, and Bolingbroke kept their offices and their heads. Richard loved kingship, its pomp and ceremony, the sacred aura of his crown. He was partly obsessed by an attempt to have his predecessor Edward II canonised, commissioning a compendium of miracles associated with the dead king's tomb. Papal authorities remained unimpressed. When his disgraced paladin and possible lover Robert de Vere died, the king had his coffin opened so he could have a final longing gaze.[6] This did not play well.

Hotspur, meanwhile, uninvolved in and untainted by central politics, had added wardenship of the East March to his portfolio. He was the king's champion with a further, guaranteed annuity of £100 to his account. As 1389 ended the king spent Christmas at Eltham with Queen Anne. Things were looking up generally, it had been a year of 'abundant grain and fruit harvests . . . a gloomy year for traitors . . . a ruinous year for the French' (who'd lost heavily due to Arundel's cutting out raids).[7] Next year the king responded presumably to Hotspur's request to introduce measures aimed at boosting Berwick's declining local economy, 'losses and *depauperation* of the town'. He obliged by granting a licence to the burgesses to export wool and hides at favourable customs rates.[8]

Richard, capitalising on the moment, had thrown out peace feelers toward France. Negotiations were both protracted and tortuous, the French insisted their Scottish and Spanish allies be included but Richard's commissioners argued as he was rightful King of Scotland, they were merely disobedient vassals needing a spot of chastisement. To underline this point, the Scots raided Northumberland again 'inflicting great slaughter'.[9] It wasn't until 24 June (the feast of John the Baptist) next year that terms were finally hammered out and Scots were given the option to either concur or be dumped by their French allies. Wisely, the lords and Council responded that while they might consent, the commons were too incensed, fresh forces had been raised for another crack on the border.[10] This was all bluster, and those 'wicked Scots' finally agreed to the truce.

Northumberland, happily distracted by his judicial responsibilities in the Scrope v Grosvenor trial, had avoided direct involvement in the Lords Appellants' coup, though he had supported their ascendancy while nicely avoiding any consequences once the king had recovered the reins. By 1390, he'd netted the prestigious job as Governor of Calais, England's continental entrepôt, shuttling back and forwards between diplomatic missions in France and the usual turmoil on his northern patch. While Harry Percy too was abroad, the king allowed him to appoint brother Ralph as proxy.[11] Otterburn had boosted Scottish confidence, and truces notwithstanding, there were numerous and costly incursions.

Boldly, the earl opened a dialogue directly with King Robert III (though Fife, now Duke of Albany, was de facto ruler) with a view to arranging a royal marriage following the death of Queen Anne. This was in 1394 but failed to bear fruit and the next year Northumberland tried his marriage-brokering skills in France, part of the team trying to fix a union between King Richard and Isabel of France (even though she was only 7) and this time, he and they were successful.[12]

Five years previously, Hotspur had been busily earning his annuity, leading a further expedition to Calais tasked with lifting the siege of Brest in the company of his uncle Thomas. Back on the frontier, Ralph Percy, seemingly recovered from his wounds, saw off a Scottish raid against the west and subsequently took part in diplomatic activity. De Fonblanque tells us little more about Ralph, stating he died in the Holy Land in 1399 in a fight against Saracens.[13] Hotspur was certainly back in charge by 1393 when he presided over a judicial duel between Richard Redmayne and William Haliburton.[14] Very soon, and in that same year, King Richard dispatched him on a state mission to Cyprus – he was certainly earning his fee.

Hotspur's spree of shuttle diplomacy wasn't done. Richard II had made his uncle Old Gaunt Prince of Aquitaine and Gascony, jewel in the overseas crown. As ever, Lancaster managed to antagonise his new subjects who resented this imposition and argued the king did not have the right to transfer their ostensible allegiance without consensus. Hotspur had also acquired a plum role as Governor of Bordeaux, hub of the wine trade. Normally a pleasant sinecure but Hotspur had to negotiate just to get through the gates. Gascons were so incensed over Lancaster's appointment Percy had to provided assurances he was indeed King Richard's representative not that of Gaunt (in fact he held the post for three years). His negotiating skills prevailed. A year later and he was back on the border as Governor of Berwick, rather more familiar territory, and he next served as part of Thomas Percy's retinue dispatched to escort young Isabel back to England with her new husband.

In all of this, young Harry Percy shines as a rising star and this surely tells us something of his abilities. His noble birth obviously facilitated career progression, but he would not be entrusted with such a demanding list of diplomatic and military tasks if he wasn't competent at carrying them out. His more sensitive missions show a man who can negotiate and finesse as much as bluster. The empty-headed bruiser of unenviable legend simply wouldn't be up to the job. Like his uncle Thomas, almost certainly an accomplished mentor, he displays a positive gift for sensitive assignments. He combines real talent with his bewildering reserves of energy, shuttling back and forth with what appears to be consummate ease. This shows us a Hotspur who's far removed from the caricature. Barely into his thirties and he has a most impressive pedigree.

Returning to the Borders, he was soon in talks with his old adversary George Dunbar whose life and career were to prove so closely interwoven with his own. This time it's rather mundane and clearly amicable. Hotspur petitions the king to grant Dunbar's wife and sister grazing rights over a substantial tract of ground near Caldsbrandspeth for 2 flocks of 1,600 ewes.[15] On 3 February 1394, Hotspur's wife had given birth to a healthy son destined, despite his father and grandfather's spectacular falls, to become 2nd Earl of Northumberland and live long enough to die in St Albans in spring 1455, fighting, ironically, for the House of Lancaster. Backing the right horse would always prove problematic.

Next year, his various offices were re-affirmed:

> Indenture whereby Henry Percy *le fils* undertakes the wardenship of the east march of Scotland and the town of Berwick-on-Tweed for ten years from 2nd June next for 3,000 *l* per annum in time of peace or truce, viz, 2,000 *l* for the town and 1,000 *l* for the march and in time of war 12,000 *l* sterling for both per annum, he shall make forays in Scotland in time of war and if the French arrive in force on the march he shall reinforce his garrison with 80 men at arms and 160 archers in the king's pay.[16]

Nonetheless, in June 1396, Richard had to remind the Earl of Northumberland to release any Scottish merchants together with their accumulated goods who'd been 'captured' or shipwrecked and were being held in violation of the truce.[17] Such providential opportunities for lucrative salvage or ransom were always an attraction for both sides.

Regime Change

Any lingering hopes that Richard II might turn out all right after all soon vanished, though his uncle Old Gaunt had one last surprise up his sleeve, having fathered a child by his long-time mistress Katherine Swynford. Parliament, sitting after Christmas in 1397, legitimised this love child who was elevated to the earldom of Somerset. These Beauforts, though debarred from ever attaining the throne, would come into their own during the minority of Henry VI when their avarice would push England into a generation of internecine dynastic war. Rumours were also rife that Richard might be about to be elected Holy Roman Emperor.[18] He wasn't but Walsingham and others thought the mere prospect so turned the mercurial monarch's head that 'he began to have higher thoughts than before, to impoverish the commons and to borrow large sums of money from anybody he could'.[19]

Despite this, the omens seemed favourable; the king was to be married, sealing a thirty-year truce with France, sweetened by a handsome dowry. Yet, on 12 January Richard struck, arresting his uncle Gloucester who was bundled off to Calais, a prisoner. The Earl of Warwick found he was out of favour when he was immediately gaoled. Arundel was persuaded to come quietly. At a stroke he had neutralised his previous opponents. This was decidedly authoritarian, as the lords had been exonerated from any guilt and Richard had to invent trumped up charges in an attempt to justify these incarcerations.

Parliament, which convened on 15 September, was stuffed with the king's placemen who shouted loudly that any earlier pardons should be rescinded. The bishops tamely concurred, with the lords happy to acquiesce. These were proper show trials, Arundel pleaded the earlier charters as his defence, but these had already been set aside. On 21 September he was convicted and sentenced to a traitor's hideous death. Richard, in a perverse gesture of magnanimity, commuted this to straightforward execution. But just to reinforce the message, the earl was dragged to his murder by the king's Cheshire praetorians, 'wild roughs armed with axes, swords, bows and arrows'.[20] Arundel met his end with better grace than those around him could muster and, or so Walsingham tells us, prophesied they would soon be marvelling at 'their own misfortunes'.[21] If so, his prophecy would come true.

Thomas Beauchamp, Earl of Warwick, was next to appear in the dock but lacked Arundel's backbone, tearfully confessing his guilt. His remorse didn't affect the sentence, but Richard commuted this to life imprisonment on the Isle of Man. Gloucester's end was the most shameful:

> . . . because it did not seem safe to the king that the duke of Gloucester should take his stand in public to answer the charges against him

because of the support of the people who had a deep affection for him, he ordered the earl marshal [Thomas Mowbray, Earl of Nottingham] to kill him in secret, and the earl marshal dispatched his ministers of iniquity and had him suffocated.[22]

By this act of base murder Richard set the seal on his vengeful triumph.

He had won nonetheless, and fully turned the tables on those who'd humiliated him more than a decade earlier but at a higher cost that he appeared capable of recognising. The countercoup had been swift and admittedly surgical, far less bloody than the Lords Appellants' own clean sweep. But kings of England should never allow themselves to be perceived as tyrants. He would have done better to have let sleeping dogs lie but these show-trials and quasi-judicial murders would, like Arundel's ghost, come back to haunt him. Walsingham asserts that Richard's nights were plagued by unearthly visitations from his noble victim, 'that woke him in terror in the middle of the night'.[23]

At the beginning of 1398, Richard had ruled for twenty-one years and now seemed inexpungible master of his realm. Parliament continued into the new year, sitting at Shrewsbury and the king maximised his advantage to ensure any unfinished business could be delegated to his own nominees, a 'pernicious precedent'.[24] Richard created himself as Prince of Chester, while Henry Bolingbroke, seemingly immune from the fallout and still protected by Old Gaunt, was raised from Earl of Derby to Duke of Hereford. Thomas Mowbray, Gloucester's murderer, moved up to Duke of Norfolk. There was a slew of other promotions, Thomas Percy did well too, becoming the king's steward and Earl of Worcester. Lands taken from the convicted peers were liberally distributed to cement allegiances.

Any semblance of restored harmony didn't prevail for long. Bolingbroke and Mowbray quarrelled, with the former accusing the latter of what amounted to sedition. Details of this remain unclear but it seems Mowbray had warned Bolingbroke he was still on a list of the king's enemies to be disposed of and that his vast Lancastrian patrimony, the envy of so many other peers, was at risk. The king, Mowbray implied, was fully backing the scheme. It is by no means impossible Richard had set Mowbray up just to flush Bolingbroke out so he could be disposed of. A judicial duel with all the panoply of chivalry was arranged for Coventry but, literally as their lances were about to clash, the king ordered a halt. He proclaimed that Bolingbroke had acted honourably but very soon after ordered a ten-year banishment. Mowbray was exiled for life. Tidily, as Walsingham acidly highlights, Norfolk's sentence was handed down exactly a year after he'd arranged Gloucester's murder.[25]

Richard seemed secure but resentment against his arbitrary rule, the blatant thuggery of his Cheshire Varangians, and constant extortions was building, '[a] vast amount of hatred which had piled up for him from his own subjects and to the bitter feelings which the common people had against him'.[26] In 1399 more bother flared up in Ireland where Roger Mortimer, Earl of March was killed in battle against Irish rebels. Blind to the swelling tide of discontent, Richard decided upon a retaliatory strike, an expedition that would certainly cost much and deliver little. Lent that year was wholly taken up with preparations, most of which involved seizure of supplies, equipment, and further ruthless extortion. This was all blatant theft as the king had no means of repayment, Ireland like Scotland seldom yielded any spoils, and as a consequence 'he became an object of hate and loathing for his subjects'.[27]

Finally, Old Gaunt died during the time his nephew was blindly amassing pilfered stores for his Irish adventure. No sooner was his uncle cold than Richard moved to extend Bolingbroke's exile to a life sentence, 'revoking his public letters patent which he had formerly granted to Henry [Bolingbroke]'.[28] This was a first step in enabling the king to grab the vast Lancastrian inheritance, a stroke that would solve or certainly ease his money troubles. It also indicated quite clearly to his subjects that no man's lands were safe from the greedy tyrant Richard had become. It was equally obvious that the whole theatre of Bolingbroke's banishment was mere pretence.

Richard wasn't done. To finance his expedition across the Irish Sea he stepped up his borrowing and sequestering, raising dazzling sums from unwilling lenders, intimidated into acquiescence. Even though he was lining his pockets at his cousin's expense, he could never hope to repay any of this colossal indebtedness. Richard was acting more like a gang leader than king. He attempted to cast a veneer of legitimacy on this gangsterism by extorting 'new unheard-of oaths' from his subjects, swearing blind obedience with fearful reprisals upon any who demurred.[29] Richard reminds us of Shakespeare's Macbeth:

> I am in blood
> Stepped in so far that should I wade no more,
> Returning were as tedious as go o'er.[30]

Richard's iron grip seemed complete, but the day of reckoning was fast approaching. Even some limited successes in Ireland did little to raise his stock at home.

We should recall those three youths who had kneeled before the aged King Edward III – Richard, Henry Bolingbroke, and Harry Percy. Their lives remained intertwined and would continue so till Hotspur fell at Shrewsbury. That connection would never be more intense or far reaching than now, in 1399, when two would combine to bring down the other.

The Coup

'Henry of Bolingbroke . . . could now see the king was being unjust to all his subjects . . . so he seized the opportunity of the king's absence and decided to return to England to seek his inheritance.'[31] With only a handful of supporters but including Lord Thomas Arundel, former Archbishop of Canterbury and son of the murdered earl, Bolingbroke finally landed at Ravenspur. Richard had appointed the Duke of York, his uncle, to act as regent while he campaigned in Ireland. York dutifully summoned a muster at St Albans, but the rally fell flat. Bolingbroke had timed his move well, support for the absent king evaporated. Soon, he was joined by Northumberland, Hotspur, and Sir Ralph Neville, Earl of Westmorland. At a stroke, the northern lords had abandoned Richard and thrown in with the challenger.

This was somewhat unexpected, for just the previous year the king had relied on Northumberland, designated by the Shrewsbury parliament, to enforce his edicts. While Thomas Percy, now Earl of Worcester, still appeared a staunch supporter. Yet, Northumberland and his eldest son appeared to be having doubts. The elder Percy had pleaded on behalf of Arundel and, according to De Fonblanque, was sent by the king to the church of the Augustine Friars in Moorgate Street to check that Arundel's severed head had not been miraculously re-united with the trunk, as he'd seen in his nightmare.

This peremptory alienation of Bolingbroke from his huge patrimony was a step too far, both for the magnates in general and Percies in particular. If Lancaster wasn't safe from grasping dictatorship, then no lord was secure, and the rule of law no longer counted for anything. Both Percies (as De Fonblanque suggests), or possibly the more bellicose Hotspur, spoke out publicly and were instantly summoned by the king. Wisely, they hurried north and replied that the state of their Marches prevented any early return to court.[32]

Brother Thomas was already shifting his allegiance and it was seemingly he who alerted Northumberland and Hotspur to the very real dangers of remaining within the king's lethal grasp. The consequences of their no-show were banishment and confiscation. The Scots, spotting an opportunity, offered both Percies sanctuary but they preferred to stay in Northumberland. In real terms Richard couldn't touch them in their northern lair and he was soon distracted by his Irish escapade. It does seem astonishing that the king had become so distanced from looming reality, or so blinded by the success of his own coup, that he would feel secure enough to leave the country at such a time.

As the props of his regime began to splinter and fall, Richard suddenly realised the mess he was in and hurried back across the Irish Sea, making landfall at Milford Haven. But it was too late, support was haemorrhaging. His summonses remained unanswered. Bizarrely, he'd included the Earl of Northumberland as one of the 'faithful lieges' he appealed to.[33] Needless to say, he received no comfort there and finally holed up in Conway Castle. At this point Thomas Percy was still ostensibly supporting the king but Richard dismissed most of his household and attempted to negotiate.

The whole grand, puffed-up vision of his undimmed kingship had come crashing down. The house of cards he'd created tumbled, his sycophants fled with his enemies closing in. The king, clearly in desperation, called on Thomas Arundel, whose father he'd killed and whose archbishopric he'd stripped, together with Northumberland whom he'd just tried to destroy. All he now sought were assurances that if he abdicated, he would be given 'a livelihood suitable to his position and the sure promise of safety of life for eight persons whom he wished to name'.[34]

Walsingham may have massaged realities here, allowing his pro–Lancastrian sentiment too much licence. The facts may be more tortuous; Richard dispatched envoys to prepare the ground, Bolingbroke being now at Chester. These were interned and Northumberland was sent back on Henry's behalf, reaching Conway by 12 August. It's unclear if Arundel was even involved at this stage. Bolingbroke demanded Parliament be convened to restore his Lancastrian inheritance while Richard's intimates faced trial for treason. The king prevaricated for three days but, on the 15th, bowed to the inevitable and handed himself over. At this point he remained king, at least in name, though he cannot have imagined he'd be allowed to continue. We cannot say at which point Henry of Lancaster decided on regime change and that he would, indeed must, take the crown. The thought must have been there from the start. Giving Richard a second chance had proved fatal for the Lords Appellant and Bolingbroke, given how he'd been treated, was far too smart to make the same error.

Richard moved to Flint Castle, where he and Lancaster met, but was hustled on to Chester where he formally surrendered. The size of the duke's army was impressive, a real show of strength and Richard was soon on his way to the Tower of London.[35] To what extent were the Percies aware that Lancaster meant to seize the crown? Surely the answer is that they were aware of it from the outset. Richard's track record for murderous cruelty effectively sealed his fate. To allow him to continue and permit his rancour to fester was obviously most unwise.

Conversely, the Percies had a family interest in the Mortimer succession. In 1395, prior to his death in Ireland, Roger Mortimer, Earl of March had been recognised as the childless king's heir and De Fonblanque is adamant this would argue against allowing Bolingbroke to seize the throne and effect a dynastic shift.[36] However, the Percies, like the rump of the magnatial class, had come to appreciate that Richard had to go and that fears of present survival would outweigh any longer term considerations. The Percies weren't duped, they were fully complicit.

De Fonblanque goes on to assert the seeds of further discord and civil broil were sown by Henry of Lancaster's duplicity, but this is too simplistic, and the chronicler is too keen to absolve the Percies of their own slipperiness. Richard was condemned by his own actions, he had to go; Henry of Lancaster had now to be crowned in his place. Other chroniclers have accused Northumberland of a fair measure of dissembling, promising on oath that Lancaster came only to recover what was rightfully his, but this is the land of realpolitik – what Lancaster and Northumberland desired was Richard's tame submission and whatever ruses were needed to persuade the mercurial and distraught king to come quietly were means to an end and nothing more.

Hotspur meanwhile appears to have been in command of the duke's sizeable army, mustered at Chester.[37] His part, if any, in the negotiations for the king's surrender seems muted. Andrew Boardman sees him as the dupe of his father's cynicism, craftily excluded from any decision-making.[38] This seems naïve; old Henry, young Harry, and Uncle Thomas were a triumvirate, the family firm and it appears inconceivable Hotspur was left in the dark. Nobody in his right mind would have trusted Richard again, the precedents were too stark and too bloody. Both father and son were already under a substantial cloud just for daring to criticise the king's arbitrariness. If, as he had done before, he recovered his grip on power they were marked men, just as the Lords Appellant had been. Boardman cites both John Hardyng and the Dieulacres chronicler (see below). The latter asserts that Hotspur while complicit was not a prime mover like his father and uncle but was led into believing Bolingbroke sought only restitution not usurpation.

After landing in Yorkshire on 4 July, Bolingbroke had swept up Pickering and Knaresborough, garrisoning both before moving up to occupy Doncaster. It was here he met up with the Percies, Ralph Neville, Earl of Westmorland, Lords Willoughby, Roos and Greystoke, a real northern mafia. Andrew Boardman suggests Westmorland's presence would lead Northumberland into rash decision-making, not wishing to share any spoils with his in-laws. Certainly, he saw them as serious rivals, but the elder Percy knew exactly what he was getting into and Boardman rightly cites the subsequent grant dated 2 August where Bolingbroke styles himself 'Henry by the grace of God, King of England and of France and Lord of Ireland'.[39] This same deed confirms that Percy's expenses acting as Governor of Carlisle and Warden of the West March should be met from the public purse.

Boardman suggests Northumberland was just being pragmatic and keeping a check on Neville aspirations, but we can all agree that he accepted Henry as rightful king while ensuring his own position remained secure. Once he was crowned king, Henry IV, as he'd become, paid out a grand total of £4,900 in back wages distributed among all of his supporters. Of this total, the lion's share went to the two Percies, father and son: Northumberland garnered £1,333 and Hotspur £666.[40]

At the same time as styling himself monarch, Bolingbroke swore a very public oath that he had returned with the sole purpose of recovering what was rightfully his. Hardyng makes much of this, the duke swearing solemnly that he would claim 'no more than his mother's inheritance, his father's lands and those of his wife'.[41] Hardyng then maintains that all three Percies were duly taken in but this doesn't ring true and Hardyng, it must be remembered, was very much a Percy hagiographer.

Hardyng's accounts were only written down after the failures of the Percy risings of 1403 and 1408 and it can be argued that these had, in reality, nothing to do with the usurpation. As Andrew Boardman correctly points out, the *Dieulacres Chronicle* supports Hardyng's claim that Henry did swear the oath at Doncaster and Hotspur subsequently flaunts this as a major contention in his rebellious manifesto four years later. This can, of course, all be put down to expediency, and much of what occurred in that frantic summer of 1399 was dictated by expediency.

Was Hotspur disingenuous before Shrewsbury, bearing in mind his own strong Mortimer connection and the fact that the infant Edmund, Earl of March had inherited his dead father's claim? Most probably. The lesson is Radcot Bridge. Richard had been corralled by the Lords Appellant and his coterie of sycophants eliminated. Nonetheless, he had shown himself both patient and cunning with a deep reservoir of vindictiveness. If he remained king, the rebels of 1399 could, at some point, expect the same treatment.

It was one thing to rule as king but trying to keep the actual king a puppet would not work. Richard's grandfather had got rid of his mother's paramour Roger Mortimer; the Lords Appellant had gone the same way. If Richard was left as king, he would be king, and his day would come round again. Nobody could take that risk. Hotspur wasn't fooled by Bolingbroke or manipulated by this father; he knew exactly what he was about. The oath at Doncaster, as solemn as these matters were, was window-dressing, a pardoner's promise, and a wholly false manifesto. That Henry Bolingbroke should swear his ambition was limited to recovery of his duchy gave his cause full legal legitimacy, if the lords chose later to force the throne upon him, well that was a completely different situation.

Though King Richard's forces had splintered and scattered, he could still hope for some support in Chester, but Bolingbroke occupied the place by 8 or 9 August with an army large enough to dissuade even the most ardent Ricardian. Adam of Usk tells us the Lancastrians came down hard on any embers of resistance while pillaging at will, true medieval frightfulness. Hotspur, as the chroniclers (almost) universally agree, remained in Chester while his father departed to negotiate with the king.

This made good sense, one envoy was enough and, as a senior statesman, Northumberland had sufficient gravitas to impress the desperate monarch. At the same time, Bolingbroke needed a proven leader, loyal to his cause, to keep a firm hand on the Cheshire men, still frothing with resentment. And who better? Harry Percy was an experienced captain with an impressive track record of keeping down fractious marchers. This was just the kind of aggressive policing he'd cut his teeth on. He knew all about stick and carrot and he knew even more about frightfulness. Nonetheless, the Monk of Evesham insists that Lord Henry Percy accompanied his father to meet with King Richard, however, as Chris Given-Wilson points out, the Evesham chronicler confuses Conway with Flint and may be unreliable here too.[42]

Harry Percy's appointment was a sound move and he didn't disappoint, proving his capacity to deal with random guerrilla attacks, launched by opportunistic marchers rooting for Richard who '. . . continued to launch furtive attacks on the duke [of Lancaster], assaulting his baggage train and plundering the local residents, until through the valour of the younger Henry Percy, their presumption was punished, and their boldness repaid in kind'.[43] None of this need imply Hotspur was unaware of his father's mission. He'd also know that Sir Thomas Erpingham had a brigade of Bolingbroke's men stationed between Conway and Rhuddlan castles, effectively an ambush party.[44]

What did Northumberland and Arundel (if indeed the ex-archbishop was present) promise Richard, swearing to the same on the host? De Fonblanque quotes a couple of French sources, knights who were in Richard's service during his Irish adventure, though the Percy historian takes a view that both were rather pro-Ricardian. In their description of the interview between king and earl, Northumberland promised that Lancaster desired only the restoration of his estates, a promise of good governance from the king and the handing over of a handful of advisors for trial before Parliament.

Richard was perfectly willing to sacrifice a few intimates to keep his throne but insisted Northumberland swear an oath that Lancaster would abide by these terms. De Fonblanque is convinced Northumberland, at this point, was sincere but it rings rather hollow. Erpingham's force was already in place, ready to spring the trap once Richard could be drawn from his lair. De Fonblanque goes on to say the king, for his part, was equally false and saw these present negotiations as little more than an enforced truce. As he had with the Lords Appellant, he'd find ways to deal with Bolingbroke and the Percies.[45]

Richard allowed himself to be drawn out of the castle with an escort of only twenty-one riders.[46] He soon realised, when he saw the men-at-arms Erpingham had deployed, that the game was up, and he'd been conned. Percy had to have been in on this, the whole thing is a concert party. It seems quite obvious that Richard had been tricked into surrender and that once Lancastrian forces had him in their unbreakable grip all bets were off. This can hardly have come as too much of a surprise, Richard knew all about false assurances and double-dealing, his own perfidy had come full circle to bite him. In his precious uncertainty he may have allowed himself to believe he could still play a winning hand despite the odds. Now, he knew different. Northumberland, still playing the diplomat, blandly assures Richard, these men-at-arms are only there for his protection.

For Henry Bolingbroke, it's more or less a certainty, 'then the king was led to London, to be kept in the Tower until the next parliament was held'. That Parliament duly assembled on 29 September with Northumberland and Neville both in attendance. Richard publicly renounced his throne and broadcast that Lancaster should succeed him, '. . . And he at once added that he wished the duke of Lancaster to succeed him in the kingdom'.[47] So, it was done, out with the old and in with the new. Richard wouldn't be missed (other than by those who'd lose out) and it was all constitutionally valid. To all intents and purposes, the king had willing abdicated, naming Lancaster as his legitimate successor. Parliament obliged and Henry Bolingbroke's claim to succeed was not disputed. Once Richard, returned to captivity in the Tower, was informed that his successor was now recognised and a date for his coronation fixed, he remarked, 'Well, after all this, I hope my kinsman is willing to be a good lord and friend for me'.[48]

Hardyng persists in the assertion that the Percies were against Henry's taking the throne, though quite what the alternative was, other than a Mortimer minor, is unclear; 'The earls of Northumberland and Worcester, Sir Henry Percy and the Earl of Westmorland all advised him [Lancaster] not to do anything contrary to his oath and although he listened to their request in the evening, on the following day he took private counsel and decided he would undoubtedly be crowned king'.[49] *Alea iacta erat* – in fact, the die had been cast when Henry Bolingbroke set sail, he knew it and the Percies knew it too.

On or before 14 February Richard, then incarcerated in Pontefract Castle, was dead, probably the result of deliberate starvation. The ostensible excuse, not that any was given, was a conspiracy, the so called 'Epiphany Rising', plotted by some of Richard's attainted adherents. Whatever the nominal justification, two kings were always going to be one too many. John Hardyng paints a picture of the Percies being shocked by Henry breaking his earlier oath. Yet, technically he had not, he had never personally laid claim to the throne. Richard had voluntarily abdicated, and it was Parliament who foisted the crown onto Henry. Moreover, all three Percies willingly participated in Lancaster's subsequent coronation, old Northumberland acted as the new king's sword-bearer with Hotspur being made a Knight of the Bath.[50]

Andrew Boardman cites the *Dieulacres Chronicle*, compiled at Dieulacres Abbey in Staffordshire, as providing evidence of Hotspur's rising disaffection with Lancaster, now King Henry IV.[51] This chronicle is in three parts: 1. A description of England compiled from Bede, Ranulf Higden, and Gerald of Wales; 2. A history of the earls of Chester and Dieulacres Abbey in the thirteenth century; and 3. A history of England from 1337–1403. Initially, the compiler seems to have been pro-Richard, but the text was altered, presumably on the new king's instruction, to adopt a more pro-Lancastrian stance. Hotspur's biographer singles out the sentence that he repaid 'their [the Cheshire Ricardians] boldness in kind' as a suggestion of empathy. But it wasn't. Hotspur used an iron fist to corral the Cheshire men. These were marchers, who came with a dangerous reputation; he knew how to deal with such people.

Perhaps the core of the differing interpretations is that Hotspur was a far more subtle character than he gets credit for. He's not the bonehead brawler with more scar tissue than brain cells. He has made his career and vast reputation serving on the world's toughest frontier and now, here on the fringes of Wales, he's on another. The experience translates effectively. This is probably why Bolingbroke gives him local command, a proven marcher lord to contain troublesome marchers. Percy quells armed resistance but otherwise soothes troubled waters. After all, he can say Henry of Lancaster has not come to depose Richard but merely to right evident wrongs and that overall these Cheshire men won't lose out.

For the moment, Hotspur could argue Lancaster never did break his oath, that when Northumberland represented restitution as the prime objective, not regime change, he was correct. That Richard should, for the common weal, resign his throne and Parliament should choose a successor was perfectly legitimate. Overreaching the Mortimer inheritance was Parliament's prerogative. Hotspur, with his father and uncle, could say he'd done perfectly right. He clearly did amass some credit in Cheshire as the events of 1403 would show.

Percy support had been crucial to Lancaster's success and now he'd reaped his full reward, all constitutionally sound or sound enough. Henry IV was naturally aware that the Percy family firm of father, son, and uncle wasn't a charitable institution. Partly, they had been motivated by self-preservation, already on King Richard's hit-list and would be fully aware of how the fractious monarch might subsequently decide to act even if they came fully back into the fold. For the Percies, regime change was necessary, and their collaboration had been both total and effective. Hotspur had kept Richard's former praetorians in check while his father had talked the desperate king into surrendering.

And to the victors their spoils. On 21 October 1399, the king confirmed Hotspur's offices as East March Warden plus governorships of both Berwick and Roxburgh. These jobs came with hefty salaries, £3,000 in peacetime, four times that when at war. Hotspur was also given control of mighty Bamburgh for life. Henry had already confirmed Northumberland's grip on Carlisle and the west while still ostensibly Duke of Lancaster. The earl was also elevated to Constable of England, though Ralph Neville, Earl of Westmorland wasn't overlooked, he was appointed Marshal of England with a life interest in the lordship of Richmond.[52] Worcester too did well enough, a life annuity of 500 marks, steward of the king's household, Admiral of England, Treasurer and Keeper of the Privy Seal.

Thomas Percy had switched adroitly from being a loyal devotee of Richard II to an enthusiastic Lancastrian. For the Percies overall, this regime change was a job well done, the main trouble being it could get to be a habit.

Welsh Wizards

> So shaken as we are, so wan with care
> Find we a time for frighted peace to pant
> And breathe short-winded accents of new broils
> To be commenced in strands afar remote.[53]

Owain ap Gruffydd, lord of Glyndyfrdwy, was born in about 1349 and therefore more than a decade older than Hotspur.[54] Almost certainly they would have met as the Welshman, who could claim descent from those ancient princes of Powys, served Richard II at Berwick in 1384, then as part of Gaunt's affinity again on the border, two years later. He had also fought for England under luckless Arundel. Furthermore, he'd been a witness in the Scrope v Grosvenor matter. An Anglo-Welsh landowner of some standing, he had trained for the law besides military service. Next, he'd been 'out' with Bolingbroke at Radcot Bridge and wisely retired to his Welsh estates once Richard II was back in full control.

That might have been that; a man who figured as no more than a footnote in history, but his neighbour was Baron Reginald Grey of Ruthyn, and a local land dispute turned nasty. Glyndwr, relying on the law, appealed his case to Parliament but was ignored. Grey was an intimate of Bolingbroke and in 1400 deliberately failed to send the royal summons for service against Scotland to his neighbour. This gave him the pretext to strut and denounce Owain as a coward and traitor. From then on matters escalated in a way neither Ruthyn nor indeed Henry IV could have envisaged. On 16 September that year, Owain Glyndwr announced he was now Prince of Powys and a Welsh icon was born. The King of England would rue the day he listened to his malicious crony.

> . . . A dispute arose between him and Grey over lands which Owain claimed belonged to him by hereditary right, and when Owain saw that Sir Reginald paid no attention to his reasonable claims, he began by leading a force against him, destroying his possessions by fire, and putting to the sword in an exceptionally cruel and barbaric manner several members of his household.[55]

As he'd started Owain kept going, attacking Denbigh, Rhuddlan, Flint, Hawarden, and Holt before marching on Oswestry and Welshpool. His wild career through Wales was finally stopped by an ad hoc English force, commanded by

Sir Hugh Burnell, on the banks of the Severn. Beaten in the field, he still kept his force together and withdrew into the wilds of Snowdonia, switching to a highly effective form of asymmetric warfare. The very act of his defiance ignited anti-English sentiment throughout the principality, and copycat risings sparked like brushfire.

King Henry responded vigorously. Though he may already have been troubled by the stirrings of that mystery illness that would, in time, enfeeble and then eventually kill him, he never lacked dash or decision. Forces he'd deployed in Scotland were now shunted westwards into Wales for a massive retaliatory strike:

> And so the king decided to attack Owain as a disturber of the peace of the land and entered Wales with an army. But the Welsh with their leader occupied the mountains . . . and at once put themselves beyond the reach of the threatened punishment [26 September–15 October]. The king set fire to the area and killed some men who chance then put in the way of their unscabbarded swords.[56]

Andrew Boardman makes the valid point that had Henry paused to consider the nature of Owain's and his countrymen's grievances, he could have saved everyone a deal of blood and treasure, but he allowed a wave of rabid anti-Welsh sentiment to blind him. His expedition, like its predecessor against Scotland, cost much but delivered little. The Percies had spent half a century learning the wiles of guerrilla tactics and there were no quick fixes. This torrent of racist abuse simply persuaded many Welsh in England from university students to farm labourers they had had no future in such a hostile land and decamped back to Wales, ready to enlist; 'I heard debated many very harsh things to be put in force against the Welsh, to wit: that they should not marry with the English, nor get them wealth nor dwell in England and many other grievous things'.[57]

This kind of inflammatory approach pretty much guaranteed that the insurrection which had, after all, begun as a purely local affair, would swiftly kindle into a full-blown rebellion. Marcher lords such as Grey, together with Edmund Mortimer, were spoiling for a fight, motivated by the twin lures of threat and opportunity. King Henry was, to a degree, hamstrung by this popular sentiment and he had reason to fear Mortimer's dynastic pretensions, Richard's fall had been the marcher lord's very tangible loss. Appointing one of these frontier magnates was bound to be unsatisfactory, neither had proved himself and both were tainted by personal interest.

Who better then to champion the king's cause in Wales than the nation's universal paladin, Henry Percy? Hotspur had to be a sound choice. He was related by marriage to Mortimer and had probably almost certainly encountered Glyndwr. Percy had years of experience in fighting bush-fire wars. He had proven he could talk the talk as well as fight the fight. His loyalty to the house of Lancaster was untarnished. That aside, the mission was, from the start, a poisoned chalice.

Hotspur cannot have entertained any illusions as to the tricky and frustrating nature of his new command. Royal paymasters had a long track record of being infuriatingly stingy, yet counter-insurgency campaigns such as this were typically long, drawn out, and expensive. They very rarely delivered any dramatic results, a big win that would resonate in publicity terms. In reality, this was a job nobody wanted. On paper his remit was impressive: justiciar of Chester, North Wales and Flintshire, constable of Chester, Flint, Conway, and Caernarvon castles, together with a life interest in the island of Anglesey. All he had to do now was beat Glyndwr on his own turf with an unpaid army.

At the same time, he was mentor to the king's eldest son, Henry, 'Prince Hal', another life that would be so intricately linked to his. Prince Henry could not have had a finer teacher, nobody in England had more experience of war than Harry Percy. He was every inch the perfect chivalric hero, and the prince would mature into one of England's most successful even glamorous kings who would work wonders in reviving the English cause in France, win the field of Agincourt, and die young enough for his legend to flourish. He was also as dedicated to war as Hotspur but even more utterly ruthless, cold, cynical, and calculating. The pupil would come to far outshine his master, yet we must think they liked each other, even if they'd end up trying their absolute best to kill one another.

A hint of that steely resolve, not to mention more than a hint of cruelty, emerges after Harry and Hal laid siege to Conway seized by the opportunistic Tudor brothers (see Act 6) in spring 1401. The slippery siblings bargained their way out of retribution but were happy to dump their associates who paid the full price of princely vindictiveness. Hotspur paid out £200 to cover the costs of the leaguer which tied down a contingent of 120 men-at-arms plus 300 archers. The king thanked both son and lieutenant for 'their great pain and diligence'.[58] Henry was big on words but rather less forthcoming with cash, though, as Boardman points out that Hotspur, in April 1402, was granted £200 worth of assignments from royal revenues, to cover his costs.[59]

It is from his time in Wales that we finally hear from Hotspur himself, the text of his several missives sent, with mounting frustration, to the Council and all focused on his unpaid, rising expenses. While these aren't personal, and they don't give us a direct window into his soul, they do intimate something of the style of the man. We sense the restlessness of one used to rapid and fluid action, balked by that petty parsimony of the officials in London.

Written in Anglo-Norman, the court language of the day, the letters date from a three-month period in 1401 when Hotspur was besieging Conway but was subsequently paid less than half his expenses.[60] The first letter is written from Denbigh on 10 April 1401, in which Hotspur answers his doubters at court, who had told him to guard well the castles in his charge in Wales, on pain of forfeiture. Hotspur replied that he only had two castles in his care and that he had done as much his loyal duty as any of the king's liegemen, and trusted that if anything should go wrong, he could count on the Council's assistance (rather than punishment).

The next letter, written at Caernarvon, 3 May, becomes more insistent:

> . . . And for the other part, do you wish to call to mind how many times I have pursued you for the payment of the soldiers of the King in the town of Berwick, and on the East March of England, who are in such great poverty that they will not be able to bear it nor endure for lack of payment; and on account of this I implore you to order that they will be able to be paid in the manner that was agreed between the Treasurer and me at our last meeting . . . because otherwise they desire me to come before you for the said payment, leaving all other things aside.
>
> Signed Henry Percy, Warden of the East March of England towards Scotland.[61]

Two weeks later, Hotspur gives the Council a deadline for payment: '. . . for the great need and necessity that I see in the country, which in good faith are so unbearable to me that beyond the end of this month or in three or four days following I can in no way endure it'. Four days after the end of May, Hotspur reiterates that he cannot remain in Wales without further funding:

> . . . nor was he receiving the help promised to him that if good and hasty remedy be not forthcoming both by land and sea, all the country is in grave peril of being destroyed without doubt by the rebels, if I leave forth from this country before the ordinance has arrived for these; the which I will be forced to do out of necessity, because I cannot bear the costs which I face here without another order from you.[62]

In the final letter, dated 3 July and written from Swynshede in Lincolnshire, Hotspur has clearly lost all patience and includes some thinly veiled threats. The Lords of the Council had convinced Parliament that during time of war the Marches and other troubled areas such as Calais and Ireland should have an allowance of £37,000 per annum, and yet the truce time payment of £5,000 owing to him and his father could not be paid. Hotspur had this to say:

> . . . in good faith it is a great marvel to me, and it appears to me that you are too neglectful of the said Marches, which will be found the most powerful enemies that you have, or otherwise that you are not satisfied

with our service in the said Marches . . . I have written to the king, my sovereign Lord aforesaid, in supplication that if anything bad should happen to his towns, castles or the March, which I have in governance, because of the default of payment (God prevent), that no blame will attach to me, but instead the blame will lie with those who we who would not pay me, according to his honourable mandate and will.[63]

Hotspur signs off by half apologizing for the abrupt and forthright nature of his letter, labelling it 'ignorant, rude and 'feble' (which we might translate as 'inferior in style' rather than 'feeble' as in weak):

Very reverend fathers in God and my very honoured Lords, be not displeased that I have written ignorantly in my rude and inferior manner on these matters, because necessity made me do it, not only for me, but also on behalf of my soldiers, who are in very great mischief, without remedy for which I neither can nor dare to go to the Marches, for which you supply and require to be ordered such measures as you deem fit. Pray God that you may be in his most holy keeping.[64]

By the end of June Percy had left Wales for his own Marches, equally troublesome, leaving his protégé, Hal in charge or, fiscally speaking, in the lurch. It's not long before the prince is writing in a similar despairing vein which at least shows Henry's parsimony wasn't personal, was not a slight directed at Hotspur or the Percies; he just didn't have the cash and left his own son in the same impasse. This also shows that Hotspur's written complaints weren't mere whining, his concerns were real. Henry was intending to mount another campaign personally and, for the meantime, replaced Hotspur with Hugh Despenser. Henry did indeed mount another major attack that October. Adam of Usk paints a despairing picture of savage depredations and reprisals, mainly visited on civilians.[65] The campaign was murderous but largely pointless, Glyndwr was neither beaten nor intimidated. The war went on.

These frustrations aside, destiny would soon present Hotspur with his defining triumph. His legend, fostered by Otterburn, that earlier glorious defeat, was about to be supercharged by Homildon, his most dazzling victory.

Act 6

At Holmedon Met – The Battle of Homildon, 14 September 1402

The proper strategy consists in the first place in inflicting as telling blows as possible upon the enemy's army, and then in causing the inhabitants so much suffering that they must long for peace and force their government to demand it. The people must be left with nothing but their eyes to weep with over the war.

Kaiser Wilhelm II

A lot of myths surround the Battle of Homildon and even some modern writers fall into the old trap (see Map 3). Those who've never seen the ground, assume that the Scots drew up on the summit of the hill which stands at just under 1,000ft (298m), while the English faced them across from another rise, Harehope, standing due north. This is a virtual impossibility. Deploying medieval forces on such steep-sided terrain would have been a mammoth task and to no purpose, as the distance between would be far more than even the most powerful archer's best shot.

A Defection

For the Scots, dawn of a new century brought a severe blow. Canny George Dunbar defected to England and brought his vast experience and many talents with him. Losing so resourceful a commander was both damaging and, in the circumstances, foolhardy. Marriage alliances were at the root of it. March had contracted to marry his daughter to David, Duke of Rothesay, King Robert III's eldest son, a mercurial and rather unstable character, at odds with his authoritarian uncle Albany. So far so good. But the duke changed his mind, or Dunbar was outbid, and Rothesay opted for a Douglas bride instead. Bad enough, but he refused to hand back the advance on the proposed dowry he'd already pocketed to seal the bargain. You could see Douglas' hand in this as well, but any triumph turned sour when March, understandably peeved, embarked on treasonous correspondence with Henry IV.[1]

It was around Christmas 1400 when, on the death of the 3rd Earl, Archibald, Master of Douglas, and Lord of Threave, swept the pot.[2] March's sequestered lands boosted his rent roll and the marriage alliance with an heir to the Scottish

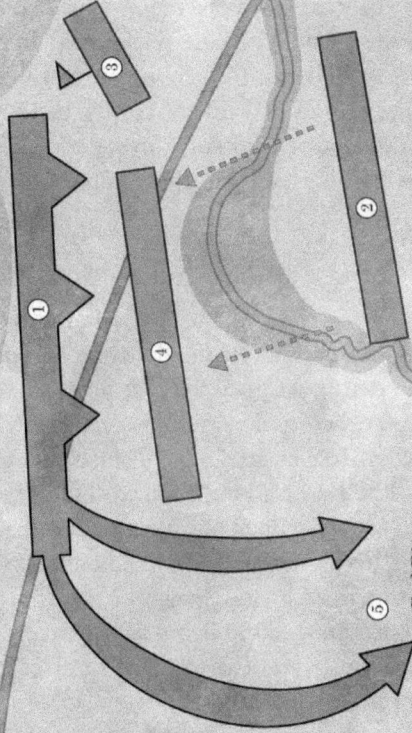

Humbleton Hill

Havehope Hill

To Wooler

Red Riggs

River Glen

To Millfield

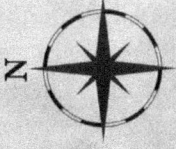

YARDS

0   500

① Scottish 1st position
② English 1st position
③ Hotspur and English cavalry
④ English 2nd position
⑤ Line of Scottish rout

**THE BATTLE OF
HOMILDON HILL**
14th September 1402

throne set the seal on what looked very much like a Douglas hegemony in southern Scotland. Despite such an apparently auspicious beginning, the 4th Earl only ever earned the unfortunate cognomen 'Tineman', or 'loser'. He'd earn it, fighting numerous battles and invariably coming second. His last was Verneuil in 1424 where he went down championing France against John, Duke of Bedford.

March was a useful turncoat and Henry IV appreciated his worth. The earl signed an indenture at Newcastle to serve the King of England and was rewarded by a grant of the Manor of Clippeston (Clipstone) in Sherwood Forest.[3] This was boosted in spring 1402 with a handsome annuity of £400 for as long as hostilities lasted, though he was contracted to provide a dozen men-at-arms plus a score of mounted archers. His son Gavin was similarly retained at £40 per annum.[4]

Despite Dunbar's defection, his eclipse was only partial. He kept control of Lochmaben, Cockburnspath, and wild Fast Castle, his own fortified dowry. England still held on to Jedburgh and Roxburgh. Taken together, these were the keys that could yet unlock the Marches. This provided Henry IV with an opportunity. If he could march into Scotland and use these stepping stones to resurrect the English Pale, he'd score a major success, one that had, like so many others, eluded his predecessor. The king was already in negotiation with the Lord of the Isles to open a second front in the north and west of Scotland.[5] This was bold talk indeed for a monarch with an empty bank account, but it gave him the chance to carve out rewards for such loyal supporters as the Percies. To give the 1st Earl of Northumberland his due, nobody ever called him charitable. Kingmakers expect payback.

Another Chevauchée

Henry may have led a force up to 13,000-strong, supported by a powerful fleet which cruised up the east coast, nabbing any Scottish vessels which couldn't sail fast enough.[6] Still, the expedition came to nothing. Henry found out, as Richard had before him, the wily Scots preferred Fabian tactics; inglorious, frustrating, and highly effective. The English king ravaged the borderland during the last two weeks in August and then gave up, his stores exhausted and his wallet thinner than ever. His navy might have enjoyed some profitable raids, but his captains were soundly beaten off Strangford by the Scots.[7]

Had March still been on side the Scots might have landed an effective riposte, but Douglas was no Dunbar and the Council fumbled. What might have been a masterly counterstroke turned into a series of feeble probes, all easily seen off. Umfraville drove off raiders trespassing on his turf in Redesdale, capturing Richard Rutherford, their commander, and a move against Bamburgh fared no better. There was perhaps now a real chance to coordinate operations with Glyndwr in Wales, but this too was frittered away.

It didn't take Dunbar long to illustrate the cost of his defection. In February 1401, accompanied by Hotspur, the pair launched a big raid into the Lothians, though Douglas, to his credit, chased them back to the line. The 4th earl was a significant player, but it was the king's ably unscrupulous brother Albany who was in effective control of the Scottish polity and at odds with the rebarbative Rothesay. Albany who was de facto regent owing to his brother's incapacity was not inclined to continue war with England, so Douglas and Northumberland brokered a fresh truce which was to endure for a further year once the current term expired that November.[8]

Rothesay too, as his thin power base shrank, veered towards conciliation. He might be the king's son and heir, but his uncle held the reins of power and had no intention of letting go (he would hang on into his eighties). Besides, the troublesome duke lacked any solid affinity. Douglas, uninterested in peace, neatly switched to Albany's faction, side-lining Rothesay but at the same time drawing Albany himself in with the hawks. Not that he wanted war but that was the price of Douglas' support.

A Rumbling of Hawks

Douglas prevaricated over the proposed truce and was already having another go at dominating the country around Bamburgh before negotiations finally foundered on 23 October. From the next month onwards, English border officials were paid at 'war' rates. Nobody was placing much reliance on truces.[9] Henry IV had problems too aside from cash-poverty. It was now that trouble in Wales flared up again and Glyndwr captured Sir Edmund Mortimer who also appeared to be on the verge of defecting (see Act 7). The Scots were seeking, through aggressive diplomacy, to secure French aid, the 'Auld Alliance' once again and the piratical Earl of Crawford was planning joint naval operations in the Channel.

During the early months of 1402, Rothesay continued to stumble but then he died (in circumstances never properly explained but his uncle's hand was suspected), and the gloves were off.[10] Douglas, in February, had written complainingly, if disingenuously, to King Henry that Northumberland and Hotspur were violating the truce. In late May, the king ordered a general muster against the Scots, but all available resources had to be shifted to Wales where the situation continued to deteriorate.

On the Borders both sides were riding hard. That outwardly unlikely partnership between March and the Percies, father and son, offered tremendous potential. Northumberland had clout and guile, Harry had dash, elan, energy, and affinity, while March brought wisdom and strategic nous, he effectively filled the perceived gaps in Hotspur's character (though these may have been overstated). Meanwhile, Douglas must have thought he'd properly got one over on his rival March, but that glee would soon turn to ashes.

Thomas Haliburton, Lord of Dirleton, had another crack at Bamburgh while Patrick Hepburn of Hailes struck deeper into the English East March. Dunbar had Hepburn in his sights, however. On 22 June, and leading 200 soldiers from the Berwick garrison, he and Hotspur tracked them back over the line and sprung their trap at Nesbit Muir (Moor) in the Merse. Despite odds of 2 to 1, the duo won their fight. Hepburn with 'the flower of the youth of Lothian' went down.[11] Haliburton, who'd attacked Bamburgh, was captured along with his brother John, Robert Lauder, William, and John Cockburn.[12] Winning was always made perfect by a nice cash crop of ransoms.

Subsequent correspondence (see below) suggests Northumberland was present but this is unlikely, as West March Warden he is more likely to have been keeping an eye on Carlisle. De Fonblanque asserts he was yet doesn't mention March, he also alleges Hepburn had blitzed down as far south as Durham (which seems unlikely).[13] Hotspur was warden in the east and Dunbar, as Andrew Boardman points out, had proprietorial scores to settle with both Douglas and Hepburn.[14] The fight is classic Hotspur, even if advised by March, a lightning dash and surgical strike. Not a big scrap by any means but a definite win for Harry Percy and one that shouldn't be overlooked. There's no sign of recklessness here and, as warden he'd no compelling need to listen to March unless he chose to do so.

This fortuitous if eccentric partnership between Dunbar and Percy is an anomaly. Previously they were enemies, both key players on their respective sides and now they were working together in a handy if essentially uneasy alliance. Both would have understood that March's present defection wasn't likely to be permanent and his overriding interest lay in recovering and retrenching his own position. Thereafter, they'd be foes again. For the moment, whatever damaged Douglas suited both admirably and that common aim was about to bear fruit and perhaps far more so than anyone could, at that time, have foreseen.

In his capacity as Warden of the West March, Northumberland wrote a dispatch to which King Henry refers in a letter to his Council:

[Percy] has informed the King that he and his son with the garrison of Berwick upon Tweed to the number of 200 have defeated 400 Scots. John Haliburton, Robert Lewedre [Lauder], John Cokbourne and Thomas Haliburton, Scottish knights were captured, and Sir Patrick Hepburn and other Scots killed and taken to the number of 240. There is also news from the letters of the Earl of Northumberland and reports from the bearer of these that 12,000 Scots have been near Carlisle but have done little damage. The earl says that the Scots are proposing to enter the kingdom with so great a power that it appears that they wish to give battle and the King urges that reinforcements be sent.[15]

Rubicon

Undeterred by this ill-omen (which oddly presages Lord Home's defeat, the Ill-Rode, before the disaster at Flodden in 1513), Douglas went ahead to plan a bold stroke for late summer. English sinews were stiffening for this inevitable onslaught all through July and August. Yet, the army Douglas mustered was formidable, between 10,000 and 12,000-strong.[16] With him, under his symbolic banner of the 'bludy hert', rode the regent's son Murdoch, the earls of Moray, Angus, and Orkney, lords Montgomery, Graham, and Erskine, John Edmonton and William Stewart, together with those two tough fighters Adam Gordon and Sir John Swinton (the latter of Otterburn fame).[17] Present also was Patrick of Biel, George Dunbar's brother. Rank and file were made up of Gallowegians, marchers and Clydesdale men, bolstered by a detachment of thirty French knights eager to win renown. As Alistair Macdonald points out, while Douglas enjoyed high status as a public official, an agent of the Scottish polity, his army was raised primarily on the back of more traditional, personal, and feudal obligation, rather than on any concept of 'national service'.[18]

Meanwhile, March and both Percies were gathering their own forces at Bamburgh. They'd be in no doubt as to the magnitude of their task. They scraped together every fighting man they could from the Marches and co-opted a detachment of those renowned Cheshire archers (see Act 7), initially recruited to fight Glyndwr. Northern gentry, as ever, were ready to ride alongside them; Ralph, Baron Greystoke, Sir Henry Fitzhugh, Sir Ralph Eure, William Lord Hylton, those hardy Umfravilles, the Lieutenant of Roxburgh plus the Constable of Dunstanburgh.[19] In addition were some Lincolnshire levies, a smattering of Welsh marchers, and Newcastle's militia.[20] At best, however, they might be half as strong as their opponents. Who commanded overall? It had to be Northumberland himself with Hotspur as his deputy. March's exact status was uncertain probably as much then as now. Temporary ally he might be, but his reputation was extremely high and his advice always worth heeding.

Battleground

Walsingham, no friend to the Scots, recounts:

> At that time the Scots, made restless by their usual arrogance, entered England in hostile fashion; for they thought that all the northern lords had been kept in Wales by royal command; but the earl of Northumberland the Lord Henry Percy, and Henry his son, and the Earl of Dunbar . . . with an armed band and a force of archers suddenly flung themselves across the path of the Scots who, after burning and plundering, wanted

to return to their own country, so that the Scots had no choice but to stop and choose a place of battle. They therefore chose a hill near the town of Wooler, called Halweden [Homildon] Hill . . .[21]

At the outset, Douglas had it all his own way. Marchers hid what they could and just got out of the way – at least they'd had a whole century to practise. The Scots penetrated fully down into Northumberland, possibly as far south as Newcastle and were retreating, or rather returning, roughly along the line of the current A697, passing Wooler and marching north when they discovered a most unwelcome surprise.

If you're following their footsteps and once you pass the market town, land on your left begins to rise while the Glen flows to your right, quite a narrow alluvial belt before the higher ground swells up. Homildon (Humbleton) and Harehope rising beyond are outriders of the Cheviot Massif which dominates the central borderland and is almost impassable for large armies. Most of the battlefield terrain is presently cultivated and not accessible, though there are good views of the ancient Bendor Stone (said to mark the field but it is prehistoric and happens to be in the right place) from the roadside and a track to your right leading down to a modern sewage works gives a good appreciation of the field. Both Humbleton and Harehope Hills can be climbed via public footpaths, steep going but the views repay the effort. The UK Battlefields Trust website has some helpful maps, although the deployment of both armies as shown is still incorrect.[22]

This rather leisurely withdrawal (obviously the Scots were slowed by their four-footed booty) suggests that Douglas may have been overconfident and/ or misled by his spies in assuming, as Walsingham asserts, the border had been stripped of fighting men to bolster a precarious situation in Wales. In any event he had blundered. His scouting had to have been faulty, he shouldn't have failed to detect such a large body of troops approaching nor, as it seems he did, should he have assumed his enemies would be cowed merely by superior numbers. He had grossly underestimated both Dunbar and the Percies. His followers were now about to reap that whirlwind and it would be a bitter harvest.

Having checked the Scots retreat by establishing a block across the road home, the English most likely deployed on flat ground with the line of the Glen on their right flank which was effectively refused and the Till some distance behind. Ground generally would have been wetter by far than now, but this was mid-September (the 14th) so would have dried out after summer's warmth. The English were now the cork in a narrow-necked bottle. Whether the archers were massed in front, billmen and men-at-arms behind or whether detached wings of archers stood ready to enfilade, it is impossible to say. Walsingham's account of English bowmen taking ground in the re-entrant between the two hills suggests this may have been the case. Both Armstrong and Boardman seem to show the

Scots' initial deployment too far up the hillside, any infantryman would say so. Colonel Burne's axiom of Inherent Military Probability seems more applicable here and one assumes the Scots deployed at the very base of the hill where ground forms a natural shelf sitting above the plain. Armstrong has them occupying the hillfort itself which was unlikely.[23]

Andrew Boardman quite rightly notes that Walsingham describes the English leaving the road and ascending 'another hill facing the Scots' – clearly Harehope. It's easy to see how this confusion arises but it's simply not a practical proposition. The chronicler is probably referring to a move by the English away from the alluvial plain to bring the Scots, deployed at the base of Homildon, within range. It seems certain that a detachment of English, Hotspur's cavalry, and maybe a body of commanded archers did occupy the gap between the two hills and this is likely what Walsingham is talking about. This also assumes that the men of the grey goose feather began shooting at about 200yd (183m). Boardman is confident that greater ranges were perfectly possible and while this is reasonable, it is unlikely that volleys would be shot at extreme range – the arrow supply was always finite, so it made sound tactical sense to ensure causing maximum damage.

A Perfect Storm

Was the Earl of Northumberland present, in which case he would surely have been in charge? Opinion varies, though John Hardyng who claims he took part in the fight is emphatic that he was:

> To Homildon, where on Holy Rode Daye, the earl them met in
> good and strong array
>   His son also, Henry Percy, was there.[24]

This is not entirely convincing. It may well be Northumberland had directed operations and the overall muster beforehand but it is doubtful he was present on the field. Hardyng also gives Douglas a huge army of 40,000, a wild exaggeration.[25] It's a shame he barely mentions the battle itself at all.

Bower, our most informative, chronicle source, is as biased towards the Scots as Hardyng to the English:

> The new Earl of Douglas, (the second Archibald), who had custody
> then of the castles of Edinburgh and Dunbar and who was the king's
> son-in-law wished to seek revenge on the English for the slaughter of
> the Scots at Nisbet. He approached the Governor of Scotland, the Duke
> of Albany, for his help in strengthening his army, because he said it was
> [only] with the duke's advice [and backing] that he would be willing to

go to England. The duke gave him his eldest son Sir Murdoch with an augmented force of knights and brave men.

He therefore assembled a large army in the same year to the number of 10,000 fighting men, including the earls of Angus and Moray as well as the Master of Fife (the governor's son), and entering England they plundered it as far as Newcastle. As they returned Sir Henry Percy the younger (otherwise Hotspur) with Sir George de Dunbar Earl of March and a large army reached Millfield before them. [The master of Fife and] the earl of Douglas climbed to some rising ground called Homildon where they waited for the arrival of the English. As they stood on the plain facing the Scots, the English were impatient to attack them on Percy's order; but the Earl of March reined Percy back, saying that he should not move, but should send archers who could easily penetrate the Scots as targets for their arrows and defeat and capture them.[26]

Hotspur, leading the *arme blanche* (cavalry), was positioned on the English right, ready to exploit any crumbling of the dense-packed Scottish schlitron now massing to face the impending storm. Douglas had been neatly out-generalled and appeared to have no idea what to do next. His men had to just stand there and take it. Seldom had the men of the grey goose feather been offered such an obliging target. They nocked, drew, and loosed, deluging the exposed ranks. Knights, encased in fine plate, had some measure of protection, spearmen in jacks had virtually none and down they went in droves.[27]

Walsingham says that the Scots did have archers and that these tried to compete but failed and gave way beneath the English barrage.[28] Bower doesn't mention these, and Walsingham goes on, gloatingly:

The Earl of Douglas, who was the leader of the Scots, saw their flight, and did not want to seem to desert the battlefield; so he seized a lance and rode down the hill with a troop of his horse, trusting too much in his equipment and that of his men, who had been improving their armour for three years, and strove to rush on the archers. When the archers saw this, they retreated, but still shooting, so vigorously, so resolutely, so effectively, that they pierced the armour, perforated the helmets, pitted the swords, split the lances, and pierced all the equipment with ease.

The Earl of Douglas was pierced with five wounds, notwithstanding his elaborate armour. The rest of the Scots who had not descended the hill turned tail and fled from the flight of arrows. But flight did not avail them, for the archers followed them, so that the Scots were forced to give themselves up, for fear of the death-dealing arrows. The Earl of Douglas was captured; many of those who fled were captured, but many were drowned in the river Tweed [in fact the Glen], so that the waters devoured, so it was said, 500 men. In this fight no lord or knight received a blow from the enemy; but God Almighty gave the victory miraculously to the English archers alone, and the magnates and men–at–arms remained idle spectators of the battle.[29]

It was slaughter, and Douglas stayed supine, poetically imagined by A.G. Bradley in his *The Romance of Northumberland*:

> In blind red clouds the sun arose
> Which saw that fatal day
> where breathless on the green hill side
> fu' mony a braw Scot lay
> For sair the English bowmen gall'd
> the van that ungeared stood
> nae thirsty shafts 'een reached the earth
> unstained in Scottish blood.[30]

March kept Hotspur's riders in check until their charge could achieve maximum effect while Douglas did his best to help the English. Galling for him, his rival was guiding the opposing army, satisfying for Dunbar he was wreaking his revenge, even if the victims were his own countrymen.

At one point the Scots were either ordered to advance by Douglas and Murdoch or those erstwhile rivals Gordon and Swinton just charged anyway. It made no difference. Their initiative was a stillborn thing, the arrow storm beat too hard, that rain of death incessant, neither of the paladins survived. Bower gives them a glorious send-off:

> . . . [Swinton] shouted out in a harsh voice as if he were a crier saying: 'Illustrious comrades! Who has bewitched you today that you do not behave in your usual worthy manner? Why do you not join in hand-to-hand battle nor as men take heart to attack enemies who are in a hurry to destroy you with their flying arrows as if you were little fallow-deer or young mules in pens? Those who are willing should go down with me and we shall move among our enemies in the Lord's name, either to save our lives in so doing or at least to fall as knights with honour.'
>
> On hearing this the most famous and valiant Adam de Gordon of that Ilk who indeed for a long time had cultivated mortal enmity against the said lord of Swinton following the death of stalwart men-at-arms from both sides in various fights, knelt down before him to ask pardon from him in particular (as the worthiest knight in arms in the whole of Britain, as he claimed) so that he might be girded as a knight by the hands of the same Sir John. This was done, and a band of a hundred respected knights

followed these leaders who had thus been reconciled. They contended intrepidly with a thousand Englishmen; and that whole Scottish group fell dead, though not without a great slaughter of English. It was assuredly believed, and it was sworn on oath by some Englishmen, as I have heard, that if the other Scots who had stood on Humbleton Hill had fallen on them with like vigour, either the English would have fled, or the Scots would have achieved victory over them.[31]

As has been seen, Walsingham credits Douglas with leading this doomed charge (or perhaps another). With a company of mounted knights, he spurred forward – this clearly shows the Scots were nowhere near the top of the hill, no downhill charge would have been possible. Obviously, in good quality harness, these Scottish horsemen stood a better chance than their workaday comrades, falling in such disheartening numbers around them but Walsingham brags gleefully of their fate and the comprehensive havoc and destruction wreaked by those terrible English bowmen.

As the great mass began to shiver and splinter, the English line advanced, Hotspur's riders finally touched spurs, but they barged into a rout not a battle. If March was responsible (as might be assumed), for timing, he got it exactly right. Scottish morale had collapsed, perhaps 700 had already died and as many if not more drowned in the mad scramble to get over the Till.[32]

Douglas, minus one eye, was taken as were Murdoch, Angus, Moray, Orkney, Montgomery, Erskine, Stewart of Innernethy, Sir Patrick Graham, Sir Robert Logan, and Sir Adam Forster. In addition to Gordon and Swinton, the butcher's bill featured Sir John Livingstone of Callendar, Alexander Ramsay of Dalhousie, and 'about 80 other knights'. The same correspondence refers to only five dead on the English side.[33] While this may be disingenuous, casualties had clearly been exceptionally light. After all, the English didn't come to contact until the enemy was already running, more a fox hunt than a fight. Walsingham states that 500 Scots drowned trying to cross the Glen and/or Till but the *Chronicle of Evesham* suggests twice as many.[34]

To swell the cash value of the bag of prisoners, several notable French knights, come to slake their ardour, were also netted. These included Sir Jacques d'Heilly and Pierre de Essarts. Charles VI laid out 3,000 francs towards the former's ransom and the Duke of Burgundy provided another 600 towards the latter's.[35] The path of the Scottish rout, where so many casualties would have been sustained, as they pelted towards the Till, is today sombrely known as Red Riggs, an innocuous looking field but a proper slaughterhouse on the day. Hardyng pens their epitaph:

> Six earls taken and XL, thousand plainly
> some fled, some died, some maimed there for ever
> that to Scotland again then came they never.[36]

Losers clearly tend to get short shrift from chroniclers.

This Scots defeat was a major turning point. By supreme irony it was the founder of the Scots resurgence and increased military hegemony, George Dunbar, who helped undo the situation. Hotspur too must get significant credit; their partnership had already produced a neat victory at Nesbit Muir and there is no reason to suppose that March was the sole presiding genius. Victory at Homildon was the zenith of a remarkably effective partnership. Macdonald, rightly, is in no doubt as to the resonances:

> Defeats like . . . Humbleton deprived the Scots of leadership and brought a collapse of resistance in their wake, especially in the south. The English were given an opportunity to capture strongholds and force the submission of local men to the English King. They also gained prisoners . . . as a source of ransoms and, more importantly, a means to exert political leverage on Scotland.[37]

Homildon might have been the destruction of a largely magnatial force but Macdonald goes on to assert '. . . Humbleton was the annihilation of the Scottish nation in arms'.[38] It's difficult to disagree with this.

Wyntoun brushes over the whole debacle as rapidly as he decently can. He tells us Douglas, as Lord of Galloway, invaded England with a great power but was stopped at 'Homyldoune in to Glendaille' where Sir Henry Percy defeated him, 'Scottis men mony slayn war there'.[39] This was more than just a Percy/ Dunbar victory. It was validation of the entire system of borderland defence originally instituted by Edward III. Now Henry IV was the inheritor not an innovator. From the outset of the Scottish wars, Percies had been major players. They might have done very well out of their service, but they had fought, steadfastly, conscientiously, and well.

Despite the increased tempo of Scottish aggression since 1370, these northern lords had held their own and now, with little or no assistance from the king, they'd trounced the Scots and trashed their chances for a generation. Hotspur and his father, albeit ably abetted by March, had forged a strong and successful partnership. Otterburn ranks as a defeat, but Homildon had washed that stain away and now they'd won the most complete and, from an English perspective, near bloodless victory, the most perfect and effective use ever of the English warbow. And their success opened up the Scottish border like a magic wand.

Two of the captives proved of special interest to Hotspur; Sir Walter Stewart of Forest and Thomas Ker, both knights of Teviotdale and both had been Percy adherents who'd since reverted. Yet, a jury on the day of truce had acquitted the pair of March Treason on account of their alleged oath-breaking. But this wasn't enough for Harry Percy, who had both men killed without trial. This rather nasty bout of vindictiveness seems to have been a Percy characteristic, allied to a casual contempt for due process which must have raised more than a few eyebrows, and not just on the Scottish side. In this hour of his greatest triumph, Hotspur's blindness and hubris marred his success. Nonetheless, he was the man of the hour and his star was firmly in the ascendant: 'In faith it is a conquest for a prince to boast of'.[40] And it would be the death of him.

Act 7

Overmighty Subjects – The Path to Calamity

My liege, I did deny no prisoners
But I remember, when the fight was done
When I was dry with rage and extreme toil
Breathless and faint, leaning upon my sword
    Came there a certain lord, neat, and trimly dress'd
Fresh as a bridegroom; and his chin new reap'd
Show'd like a stubble-land at harvest-home
He was perfumed like a milliner . . .

William Shakespeare,
The First Part of King Henry IV, Act I, sc. iii

'Henry in the congratulatory letters he wrote to the Percies and the rest of his leaders in this battle [Homildon], strictly charged them not to ransom, nor dismiss on whatever security, any of their prisoners without his express allowance. This prohibition is said to have provoked in old Northumberland and his son, a resentment, which not long after broke out to their own destruction'.[1] Shakespeare and others make much of this quarrel, a sour footnote to Hotspur's great victory. Yet, while the king's peremptory and unchivalrous demands did cause pricks of resentment, this wasn't what finally prompted that fatal rift.

'Hero to Zero'

This about sums up Hotspur's fate in 1403. Everything he, his father and uncle had tried to build would come crashing down around them. The zenith of his knightly career at Homildon would end in the dusty stubble of Shrewsbury. It's generally accepted that his final military failure would be partly brought about by his father's failure to support him together with his inability to rendezvous with Glyndwr's Welsh rebels. He'd come to be seen as rash, impetuous, and reckless, the foolish dupe of his Machiavellian parent. Walsingham, no friend to the Percies, certainly thought so: 'They placed their hopes, *so it was thought* [author's italics], in the help of Owain Glyndwr and Sir Edmund Mortimer and other men of Cheshire and Wales'.[2]

Nonetheless, this view may be unduly slanted, and the reality may show that Hotspur was nobody's fool and that he hoped to achieve his tactical objectives on the Welsh Marches without assistance from either the Earl of Northumberland or Glyndwr and Mortimer. This is the view put forward by Peter McNiven.[3] He points out that, at the outset, the Percies appear to have held all the aces, so the question is not so much how they failed so catastrophically but why they failed at all. This approach casts Hotspur in a wholly different light, one that is most persuasive and when the sources are thoroughly interrogated a compelling 'fit' can be discerned.

Victory at Homildon had led to what amounted to a Percy hegemony on the border, they held the wardenships of both English Marches (each for a term of ten years) and the captaincy of Roxburgh.[4] Hotspur was also constable of Flint, Conway, Caernarvon, and Beaumaris, another rising hegemony in North Wales. Moreover, he held Chester Castle and the post of chief justiciar. His nephew, the Earl of March, being a minor, Harry Percy controlled two-thirds of the vast Mortimer patrimony, the bulk of which was centred on the Welsh Marches.[5] Thomas Percy, Earl of Worcester did very well too, he retained his title, granted in 1397, was appointed Admiral of England for life and headed up the team negotiating for Queen Isabella's return.[6]

These plums were the fruit of their support for Bolingbroke in 1399 and subsequent service against the Scots, including this major win at Homildon. It did mean, significantly, Hotspur had a second reservoir of power in Wales and his offices at Chester allowed him to tap into latent hostility towards Henry IV from the rump of King Richard's old Cheshire affinity. This would bring forth dangerous consequences when Percy disaffection seethed to boiling point and triggered rebellion. What is significant in unravelling these complex threads in the of summer 1403 is that Hotspur wasn't just a northern magnate with his base in Northumberland, he had equal status on the Welsh Marches.

Meanwhile, as far as the Scots were concerned, King Richard was alive and well, not dead at all:

> In this way King Richard was deprived of his kingdom and was speedily removed and condemned to perpetual imprisonment. [But] he was cleverly removed from there and taken to the islands of Scotland, where he was recognized and discovered in the kitchen of Donald, Lord of the Isles by a certain jester who had been trained at the court of King Richard while he was in power.[7]

Some accounts say it was a woman who had met the exiled king in Ireland who recognised him. This shattering revelation, arising during the winter of 1401–2 that Richard II was still alive and well, working in Clan Donald's kitchens, proved most helpful to the Scots. In due course it would also help boost Hotspur's manifesto, as there were many in England, growing uneasy under the usurper's rod, who might also want to believe King Richard was still alive.

North of the border, Regent Albany was no admirer of Henry Bolingbroke and, with some cause, feared the king's possible ambitions on the border, spurred by a need to keep his powerful Percy sponsors on side. This unlikely imposter he'd found, often dubbed the 'Mammet' (puppet), in fact one Thomas Ward of Trumpington, could prove useful. When he was paraded at court a real exile, William Serle, formerly esquire of the bedchamber to Richard II, spotted an opportunity. Soon, Serle was forging the royal signet and rushing off correspondence to all and sundry promising the late king's imminent reappearance.[8]

Both Scots and French were happy to chime with this convenient fiction and even though Charles VI wisely sent one of Richard's former household men to check, he kept believing even though his agent, Jean Creton, had reported back that the Mammet was clearly a fake. Imposters still have their uses and Ward was a handy stick with which to beat King Henry. Hotspur would be another who, for his own purposes at Chester, would choose to resurrect Richard. And while the whole charade of the Mammet would seem laughable, there were plenty in England prepared to think twice. Henry's rule was not going well; the Welsh rebels could not be tamed, the treasury was bare, there was unrest and disorder.

No Prince but a Percy

One precious perk which had landed in the Earl of Northumberland's lap was his office of Constable of England. This was every bit as grand as it sounds and effectively made the elder Percy commander in chief of all royal armies. Given their existing pre-eminence on the border and the likelihood of further conflict with Scotland, this simply confirmed the earl's hegemony, but as Peter McNiven points out, 'they could hardly have been better placed to stage a successful military coup'.[9] Most of our conventional understanding of these events of 1403 assumes that the Percies intended to ignite a overwhelming flow of rebellion when their differences with the king had reached boiling point during that previous autumn.

Chief among these was this thorny matter of ransoms and Hotspur's refusal to hand over his prize captive, the Earl of Douglas. Yet, despite the highly contentious nature of the argument, Percy didn't come out against the king till July 1403, eight months after. In the meantime, both Worcester and Northumberland were much at court. Hotspur was the one in the saddle, sword ever at the ready, but the older generation remained close to the seat of power acting as sage senior statesmen. This was not mere posturing, both men had proven track records of success in high office. Further prizes came their way in March 1401 when Thomas Percy was appointed steward of the royal household and seven months later made Prince Henry's governor. This reflects not only the unrivalled power of the Percy clan, but the level of trust King Henry felt able to place in them.

In April that year, as mentioned earlier, Hotspur himself was in action with the prince, laying siege to Conway castle which the opportunistic Tudor brothers had grabbed in a daring *coup de main*. After a month's hard leaguer, a deal was struck. The rebellious siblings escaped with their necks but shamelessly handed over nine of their accomplices who got short shrift from Prince Hal, the future victor of Agincourt showing his colours early. Glyndwr played no part in this episode, and it seems the Tudors were no friends, but it does seem their boldness inspired Owain to stir himself and flaunt his rebel banner with redoubled energy.

The king was probably not pleased to see these ruffians get away with it, but Hotspur was already critical both of Henry's anti-Welsh ordinances and by his failure to furnish him with enough cash to fund operations.[10] Henry would be well aware the Percies were bankrolling much of the substantial cost of supplying garrisons in Wales, this was more a case of poverty than exploitation. Henry was locked into a costly and protracted asymmetric war, with no exit route in sight. Hotspur's fears that repression wasn't the answer were proved right, as trouble flared up across the principality once again, both the king and his son were obliged to resume campaigning. Glyndwr showed himself a master of guerrilla warfare, yet he was willing to submit, sending a message to Hotspur he'd be prepared to lay down his arms if, like the slippery Tudors, he'd be offered a full pardon. This was a tempting offer, and it may be speculated that Hotspur was in favour but, in November, the Council at Westminster said no.[11] Such literal-mindedness would have consequences.

This doesn't seem to have been discussed by any of the secondary sources but perhaps Hotspur's experience of border warfare can be seen coming through. He, far better than King Henry, knew how difficult indigenous irregular forces, living off the land and plunder, aided and abetted by sympathic locals, were to trap. He could see how the deployment of large-scale conventional forces was an unsuitable response, using a hammer to crack a walnut you couldn't find. His attitude therefore reflected a degree of realpolitik based on lessons from the school of hard knocks. Henry, as king and as a usurper-king, naturally felt he had to make his point and not concede to rebels. For Hotspur, a negotiated settlement appeared the best way out of a costly impasse but for the king it would imply a massive loss of face. He needed to win.

Any doubts Harry Percy might have felt were fully vindicated when it all flared up again in 1402. This time Glyndwr fought both his old enemy Reginald Grey together with the new one, Edmund Mortimer, beating and capturing both. Ugly rumours quickly began to circulate that Mortimer was somehow a willing party in his own capture. The king seems to have thought so, hence his animosity

The bronze statue of Hotspur in Alnwick, created by Elsdon-based sculptor Keith Maddison: 'the attention to detail is eye-watering, with the statue capturing the essence of the medieval warlord right down to the rivets in his armour'. (*Photograph by Gerry Tomlinson*)

'Arms of Sir Henry Percy, called "Hotspur" . . . Arms: Quarterly, first and fourth, Louvaine, Or, a lion rampant Azure, second and third, Lucy, Gules, three luces hauriant Argent'. (*Drawing by Chloe Rodham*)

Alnwick Castle, one of the Percies' main fortresses since they acquired the barony in 1309 from Prince-Bishop Anthony Bek. It was much rebuilt in subsequent centuries, by Robert Adam in the eighteenth century then again by Anthony Salvin in the nineteenth. Much of its recent fame derives from being featured in the *Harry Potter* films. (*Wiki-commons*)

Warkworth Castle, for a while held by the Scots but much improved by the 1st Earl Percy in the fourteenth century. It was rather unfairly derided by Shakespeare as 'that worm-eaten hold of ragged stone'. It avoided later makeovers and is today in the care of English Heritage. (*Photographs by B.A. Palin*)

Bamburgh Castle, one of the great border fortresses and a constant redoubt against the Scots, held by the Crown and then the Forsters before being bought by Lord Armstrong in the last decade of the nineteenth century and undergoing a fabulous restoration. (*Photograph by Adam Barr*)

The walls of Berwick-upon-Tweed, what remains of the medieval enceinte much altered by Henry VIII before the grand state-of-the-art circuit, commissioned by Elizabeth I. The town Hotspur knew was encircled by a longer set of walls than the Elizabethan which contracted the defensible area. (*Photograph by B.A. Palin*)

What remains of the castle at Berwick, once the key to the East Marches but literally blown up to make way for the railway in the nineteenth century. This act of industrial age vandalism accomplished what three centuries of border warfare failed to achieve – in all the place changed hands thirteen times between 1296 and 1482, Hotspur's first official posting. (*Photograph by B.A. Palin*)

Dunstanburgh Castle, 'the Fortress of Earl Thomas', belonging to the House of Lancaster and another of the great English coastal defence chain. Most of what is seen today is original and the site is currently in the care of English Heritage. (*Tim Simpson, CC BY-SA 2.0*)

Facsimile armour of the fourteenth century such as Hotspur would have worn, showing the distinctive 'pig-face' bascinet. By this stage full plate armour with mail additions was becoming the norm, weighing about 60lb (27kg). (*Photograph by kind courtesy of D.A.E. Fairey*)

Newcastle Keep, a great Norman fortress much beleaguered by nineteenth-century railway development but saved and restored by John Dobson. The nearby Black Gate would have been the fourteenth-century barbican with a timber framed 'barrier' beyond. This is where the clash between Hotspur and Douglas would have taken place. (*Photograph by Adam Barr*)

The Otterburn battlefield memorial, which is currently located just off the A696 north of Otterburn township, though this is not the original location. The Redesdale Project will provide refreshed and improved interpretation for the site. (*Author's photograph*)

A general view of Otterburn battlefield looking west from the monument showing Greenchesters on the left edging towards the river – likely site of the Scottish baggage and lower camp, attacked by Redmayne and Ogle. (*Author's photograph*)

Looking east at Otterburn from the likely location of the higher Scottish camp and showing the re-entrant along which Douglas funnelled his flank attack on Hotspur's division. The ground would have been far more wooded at the time. (*Author's photograph*)

The Silloans Sword unearthed at Silloans on the MoD Ranges in the 1980s. The overall condition, although poor, does give some hints as to how it might have looked in 1388 (assuming it did feature in the battle, which is purely conjecture). (*Photograph by Jo Scott*)

The replica Silloans Sword which was installed at Elsdon church by the author and the Revd Elaine Ryder in August 2020. The church is a fitting location for the new facsimile crafted by Ulfric Douglas, thanks also to Karen Collins of NNPA and Geoffrey Carter of the UK Battlefields Trust. (*Photograph by Defence Photography*)

Elsdon church where it may be the English dead of Otterburn or most of them lie interred. The structure is larger now than it was in 1388 and the mass grave would have lain outside the walls. Following excavations and construction work in the nineteenth century the bones were re-interred in an external mass grave – a treasure trove for future archaeologists. (*Peter McDermott, CC BY-SA 2.0*)

The Neville effigies in Staindrop church. Despite being related by marriage, both Neville and Percy maintained a keen rivalry which would fester into the fifteenth century and come to the fore under Henry VI's weak rule, igniting the Wars of the Roses. (*Photograph by the Revd Ken Steventon*)

A medieval spur, recovered from the vicinity of Albright Hussey and while of older design may have featured in the Battle of Shrewsbury. Such survivors from an actual field of battle are rare and it is difficult to establish their provenance. (*Reproduced by permission of Shropshire Council, Shropshire Museums*)

On 26 August 2021 the Battlefields Trust organised a battlefield walk conducted by the author accompanied by the Dukes of Northumberland and Buccleuch – the first time Percy and Douglas had met on the field since 1388. (*Reproduced by permission of Geoffrey Carter and the Battlefields Trust*)

An aerial view of Battlefield church and its environs in Shrewsbury which shows where the heart of the melee occurred. Bones uncovered in the nineteenth century may well have been, probably are the remains of fallen combatants interred immediately after the fight in 1403. (*Reproduced by permission of Shropshire Council, Shropshire Museums*)

Battlefield church. This nineteenth-century image probably shows the church as it was at the time of antiquarian and battlefield historian Richard Brooke's visit in the 1850s. (*Reproduced by permission of Shropshire Council, Shropshire Museums*)

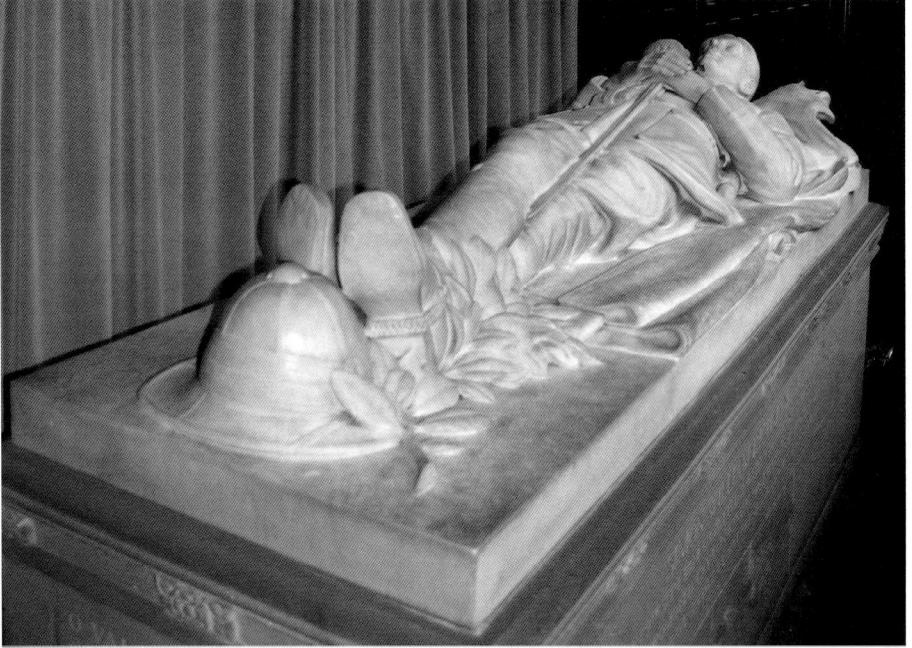

The effigy of Simon Mewburn from west Northumberland in the Church of St John of Beverley, St John's Lee. A casualty of the First World War, his pose here is nonetheless reminiscent of that of a medieval knight laid to rest. (*Photograph by Alan Grint*)

to notions of ransom. Meanwhile, Grey could buy his own liberty for £6,666.00. On 30 November Mortimer married Owain's daughter Catherine and wrote to his people he'd thrown in with his father-in-law, which could explain the king's reluctance.[12]

This was worrying for Henry in that he could perhaps begin to discern threads of collusion between Glyndwr, Mortimer, and Percy beginning to emerge (though at this stage he was probably wrong). Percy was married to Mortimer's sister so they were aunt and uncle to the 10-year-old Mortimer, Earl of March whose dynastic claim to the throne could, it might be argued, trump that of Henry Bolingbroke. The captive Mortimer had, as he renounced his allegiance to Henry, issued a public call to put the lad on the throne in his place (with the delicate assumption King Richard was no longer alive). Hotspur, at odds with the king over his repressive policy, smarting over his unpaid expenses, and Henry's refusal to either ransom the elder Mortimer or permit the Percies to do so, was clearly feeling aggrieved.

In fairness Prince Henry too was soon much vexed by his father's enforced parsimony. The plain truth was the king was forced to fund a costly domestic war in Wales which had no allure for Parliament or the taxpayer, a messy internecine struggle where Henry's hard-line approach was failing to win any friends or, more tellingly, any battles. His castles were constantly under threat, his proxies routed and humiliated with the chief of them now having defected. Even worse, it was all about to blow up again on the northern marches, until Hotspur's ringing triumph at Homildon created a new paradigm. Henry would be less than human if his grateful thanks to the Percies weren't tinged with more than a dash of jealousy. They'd succeeded on their marches; he'd failed on his. The contrast was bound to be noted.

J.M.W. Bean, in his excellent article on these expanding disagreements between Crown and ever so mighty subjects, doesn't specify what he believes the flashpoint to have been.[13] What was raging during the spring months of 1403 was growing Percy exasperation with the king's failure to remit their expenses (even if they knew he couldn't pay). As seen and before King Richard was even formally deposed, Henry had given Earl Percy the West March wardenship. This might have been Northumberland's fee for joining the revolt, and it certainly cemented the family's hegemony along the English borderland.

While Henry was fulsome in his praises once he received news of the great victory at Homildon, it might indeed be wondered if secretly he felt humiliated as his own Welsh expedition had gobbled up so much money he didn't have and had achieved nothing. Why then on 20 September did he send that letter to Hotspur cautioning him against ransoming his captives without prior royal acquiescence, instead ordering him to bring them down to London where Parliament was due to assemble? Worse, by the late autumn of 1402, Hotspur had lost his role as captain of Roxburgh and that post had gone to the Neville Earl of Westmorland, a double blow in terms of prestige. Was King Henry now setting up a system of checks and balances to curb the sweep of his overmighty subjects' power?[14] And he wasn't interested in their proposals to settle terms with Glyndwr, no more than he was willing to ransom Edmund Mortimer.[15] The Percies might be mighty but it did seem the king was more than aware of the risks in allowing them to become arbiters of royal policy. It was a tricky balancing act. Henry was insecure and impecunious, his weakness exacerbated, in December 1402, by Mortimer's defection. He was of course Hotspur's brother-in-law, and this must have sharpened the king's worries. Kings always must fear kingmakers, as their role could become a habit.

Meanwhile, the French were being very troublesome. Chris Given-Wilson brilliantly describes Duke Louis of Orleans as 'the self-appointed archpriest of Anglophobia'.[16] He'd soon, in the run up to the Homildon campaign, be stirring up the Auld Alliance and liaising with the Earl of Crawford (as seen in Act 6) for a joint naval offensive against English shipping in the Channel. He also stimulated the fashion for sending out chivalric challenges. King Henry, who could easily have ignored his taunting, chose to get testy. As did the Earl of Northumberland, who was challenged by Guillaume de Chastel. Percy responded crushingly to the Frenchman's presumption, suggesting that if de Chastel was serious, he could come to England's northern frontier 'where you will behold the quivering sword of our office, which we wield against your execrable vow and your accomplices'.[17]

On 20 October, the northerners' Scottish prisoners were paraded before Parliament with the notable exception of Douglas, Percy's greatest prize, who Hotspur disobediently kept to himself. The remaining quartet of Scots nobles with three French knights were duly displayed before lords and commons before they bowed to the king and entreated him to accord them the usual courtesies of war. Even if Douglas wasn't present, Albany's son Murdoch Stewart was, a captive of equally high rank. Nonetheless, it was Sir Adam Forrester, a smooth trimmer, with whom Henry had previous dealings, who acted as mouthpiece. The king grew angry, and Sir Adam needed his silver tongue to calm royal passions. In fairness, Henry accepted his grovelling apology and fed the prisoners at his own table.[18]

Henry undertook a smart move in March 1403 when he granted to the Percies the best part of captive Douglas' vast holdings on the border, Eskdale, Liddesdale, Lauderdale, Selkirk, Ettrick Forest, and Teviotdale (at the same time, these were annexed to the English Crown, the Scottish interest was to be permanently alienated).[19] This was a brilliant gambit in that it appeared to offer much but conferred rather less. Douglas might be behind bars but the Scots were not simply going to allow the Percies to march into the void. If they wanted to extend their northern empire into Scotland, they'd have to fight for it. Henry was hoping he'd not only keep the Percies on side but, through their efforts, he could revive the old English Pale and create a buffer zone on the Scottish side. McNiven points out tellingly that another three months passed between the grant and the Percy rebellion.[20] He assumes they took him seriously and this seems correct. This was after all precisely what they'd been hoping for.

As the matter of outstanding ransoms still rankled and wasn't likely to just go away, the king established a royal commission to settle all claims. Neither Hotspur or his father was asked to participate but given their pecuniary interest in the outcome this isn't surprising, nor indeed was the Neville Earl of Westmorland appointed. There was clearly no slight intended here and the king's territorial grant was, outwardly, a huge mark of approbation. He had obviously decided he could not risk a deepening rift with the House of Percy. At the same time, it was a clever move, his kingdom could expand, and his popularity be correspondingly increased but it would be the Percies who did the hard work.

George Dunbar, acute as ever, had seen both opportunity and threat in this grant and swiftly got his claim in, 'if you or other lords of the realm on your behalf, should conquer all or part of the realm of Scotland . . . the said supplicant can have and enjoy all his castles, lordships and lands which are in the aforesaid realm of Scotland, should you or any other person whatsoever conquer the said castles, lordships and lands, or any of them'.[21] Henry was quick to provide the necessary assurances. Dunbar would come back into his own, the king might offer the Percies much but not quite all. Dunbar was the perfect counterweight. No friend to Albany, even less to Douglas and perhaps the one man those Percies, father and son, might be sufficiently wary of, a great Scottish magnate in his own right but also an active and pliant collaborator.

McNiven cites four factors in support of the seriousness of this grant: 1. It was effectively a declaration of war on Scotland, either directly by the Crown or through its most powerful surrogates; 2. It now appeared the dispute over Douglas' ransom had gone away (or at least been shelved); old Northumberland might have been the grantee, but Hotspur would be doing the fighting; 3. It was a kick in the teeth for the Nevilles, now totally relegated, even though their own prior claims to parts of Annandale and Roxburgh were suitably ring-fenced; and 4. It was also a demotion of sorts for George Dunbar, despite any assurances.[22] Even if the wily earl could, on the swing of English broadswords, claw back his own estates, he too would now be a relatively minor player hemmed about by this shining Percy empire. King Henry appeared to have moved greatly to accommodate the Percies and written off his previous grievances while also reversing his apparent policy of imposing checks and balances. He was conceding he could not manage without the Percies. No small wonder the earl and Hotspur took him at face value. This had the makings of a major coup. Each generation of Percies had added to their wealth, holdings and prestige and had achieved this by loyal, conscientious service to the Crown. Now, the 1st Earl and his eldest son looked set to round off these achievements with a golden coronet. What could prevent this happening?

In pursuance of the grant, Hotspur crossed the border and laid siege to Cocklaw (or Cocklaws or even Ormiston) Tower which lay about a mile south-east of Hawick.[23] Disobligingly, the defenders refused to capitulate and Harry was constrained to agree terms – the place would be surrendered if not relieved by August. McNiven argues that this incident has not been correctly interpreted, it's written off as just another Anglo–Scots fracas, or that it was partly a smokescreen to veil the Percies' treasonous plans which were already in hand. Specifically, some fear it was a clandestine recruiting campaign and/or an attempt to inveigle Scots lords into the plot. Walsingham doesn't help, he asserts Hotspur crossed the line and attacked areas in Scotland without meeting any significant resistance.[24] This was not the case; Percy had stirred a hornet's nest.

It was unclear to some contemporary writers exactly where Cocklaw was or the confusion of names with Ormiston suggest two different castles were involved – Northumberland himself, in his letter to the king dated 30 May 1403, calls the place Ormiston.[25] Correct identification clarifies any doubt that the Percies were bent on destroying wherever was nearest to conceal their evil intentions. Given that the actual location lies in the heart of the very territory Hotspur was seeking to annex, indeed Cocklaw had been a Douglas hold, surely shows he was behaving in accordance with his instructions. Albany definitely considered Cocklaw worth fighting for, he didn't have much choice as its capture would unlock the whole of Teviotdale to Percy expansionism.

> . . . Hotspur wanted to provoke Scotland and England into a pitched battle more disastrous than Homildon, thereby stretching Henry to his limits and leaving him vulnerable to attack. The first step in rallying support for the Percy family was to besiege Innerwick Castle, near Dunbar, with the help of new ally Archibald Douglas. Although the castle was badly burned, the siege was short and sweet; the allied forces soon withdrew, and repairs were made. Their next target was Cocklaw Tower, more ideally placed in the heart of the Borderlands, and in early May 1403 the tower was attacked while its owner James Gledstane [Gladstone] was absent.
>
> Hotspur's men were expected to meet with little or no resistance but were instead drawn into attrition warfare that lasted nearly two months. Gledstane's esquire John de Grymslaw (Greenlaw), likely a young attendant to his master, stoutly defended Cocklaw. Siege engines i.e., battering rams and catapults, were brought north to break the garrison's resistance, without success. After a few weeks, Percy agreed to suspend the assault on condition that Cocklaw would surrender if no Scottish relief force arrived before 1 August. News of Hotspur's agreement

reached London in early June, by which time Robert Stewart, Duke of Albany, was contemplating an official state response. The Scots were divided on whether to send aid to Cocklaw as it was deemed an insignificant peel tower, while there were reservations about starting a fresh conflict with England. This indecision did much to damage the Duke's reputation and prestige.[26]

That Hotspur was ready to agree a truce and allow the Scots a crack at relieving the siege followed custom. It might not be a large fortress but was certainly strong enough to resist timber framed siege engines.[27] It is known that the castellan, James Gladstone, immediately petitioned Albany for relief and received an equally swift assurance.[28] This showed how seriously the Scottish regent took the threat posed by Percy. By promising aid, he was committing his available forces to battle, a bold move given the unhappy precedent from the year before. It may be Albany's resolve wrongfooted Hotspur who might have thought his enemies so cowed they'd not be able to fight back. This was tricky. Powerful as they were, could the Percies take on Scotland single-handed?

Presumably, when King Henry issued the grant he must have been aware the Scots wouldn't take such rampant Percy aggrandisement lying down. Northumberland, in his letter to the king of 30 May, asked for financial support, the remittance of cash already owed by the Crown and he'd need this by 24 June.[29] It must be stressed that with this Percy wasn't complaining or pressing. These monies would empower the Percies to hire in or build up a force equal to whatever Albany might be about to throw at them and avoid the need for wider English intervention on their behalf.

Walsingham tells us that the Percies had distributed details of their conditional truce with the Scots throughout England in the hope knights would flock northward to get in on the action. At the same time this was also an attempt to discourage the king himself from becoming embroiled. Clearly the arrears they claimed were indeed owing, some £20,000 or more (rather more than £12 million in today's money). If Henry came up with the money this would have been enough to fund their private war and take on Albany without 'official' support.

Some would say this was just a ruse to win supporters for the coming coup and yet none of these men subsequently came out, so perhaps the attempt was wholly genuine at that time.[30] Hardyng, however, claims to have had sight of letters from several lords expressing a level of complicity in the Percies' plan 'to overthrow the king'.[31] This assertion must be taken seriously and yet Hardyng may just have seen correspondence supporting the Scottish venture, it's unlikely, as a relative junior, he'd by privy to any such inflammatory texts.[32]

Then the king wrote back. He made it quite clear in this correspondence that if the Percies wanted to win lands in Scotland it was down to them how they did so.

He wouldn't be paying for it. This was not the anticipated response and must have made sour reading. Henry must have been aware that this was about far more than just about taking a single border castle, and that Hotspur without a large army at his back couldn't fight a whole Scots' levy. Perhaps now and only now, it dawned on both father and son that the grant apparently wasn't worth the paper it had been written on. There'd be no funds, and therefore no army and no showdown with Albany. They'd have to give up on taking Cocklaw and they'd no chance of winning as much as an acre in Teviotdale. Worse, everyone would know it, all those who'd oiled their swords in happy anticipation would be disappointed and the Percies would look like idiots. It was both insult and humiliation.

In fairness Henry did send some money, enough to meet the core necessities of border defence, to maintain the status quo. It might be he wasn't looking to abandon Northumberland and his bellicose son at all. He was simply pointing out that their fight to acquire Douglas lands was theirs, not England's. Henry clearly wasn't looking for, certainly he could not afford, a full-scale war with Scotland, especially if the Percies were the only likely beneficiaries. Needless to say, the northerners took it differently and that 'their campaign in Scotland was an altruistic labour undertaken for the benefit of the kingdom of England'.[33] After all, he had provided that Douglas' lands would be annexed directly by the Crown so Percy would hold only as tenant in chief. Henry and his heirs would also be beneficiaries.

What Henry was now saying was that he had indeed given the Percies free rein in the north but for their increase not the country's. This was a fundamental difference and clearly showed Northumberland he'd read the king's earlier grant all wrong. What they did over the line was their crusade and at their cost. This was an impasse, and Peter McNiven is of the view that this was the real tipping point.[34] I concur. Up till now, the Percies had been conducting themselves as loyal subjects fully in harmony with the king's intentions. Only now did they perceive a fundamental difference. As far as they were concerned Henry had left them in the lurch and the whole of England would know it.

The author of *An English Chronicle* writes:

> The earl of Northumberland prayed the king might pay him the monies due to him for defending the marches and said, 'my son and I have expended our gold in keeping the said marches'. The king answered, 'I have no money, nor shall you have any'. The earl said, 'when you came into this country you made promises to be guided by our advice, you've taken much money but paid none in return and so you break your word'.[35]

The chronicler goes on to recount a tense meeting between Hotspur and the king where the former rebukes his sovereign over the contentious matter of

Mortimer's ransom. Henry continued to refuse, citing the fact Mortimer had gone over to the enemy so why should he pay to fill rebel coffers? Percy, true to his nature, couldn't let it go, to the extent matters became so heated Henry called Harry a traitor which Hotspur angrily refuted. Neither man was built for compromise and both inclined to hot-headedness. King Henry became so incensed he drew his dagger. Hotspur with classic sangfroid replied, 'not here but in the field'.[36] This sounds a little melodramatic but there is no reason to believe it didn't take place. Both may well have regretted their respective outbursts once tempers had cooled, and the drink worn off.

Northumberland's reply, dated 26 June, accuses the king of firstly 'jeopardizing the good name of English chivalry' and secondly that he'd failed to provide sufficient funds to defend the border anyway. It rather depends on how 'the border' is defined at this juncture. Both Percies clearly thought it should now encompass those Douglas lands which the king had awarded by his earlier grant and that wresting these from Albany was for the common weal – the obvious precedent being Edward III's earlier extended frontier zone, the Pale. Henry was now saying he'd not meant that at all and that the actual border meant the line of the Tweed.

Was Henry being disingenuous? Perhaps he was, he had issued this grant to patch up a potential split with his powerful subjects and sponsors. He'd not thought he'd now have to wage war on their behalf, as blindly supporting Percy ambitions could not by any means be seen as being in the wider national interest. Henry intended this strictly as a private, not a public sector venture. Or that's what he was saying now. It does seem unlikely Henry could have expected the Percies to carry the whole burden – after all those Douglas lands were being annexed to the English Crown and the Percies were subjects. It is easy to see how they would have seen themselves as the cutting edge of Crown policy. Of course, they would be major beneficiaries, but this was still very much in the national interest.

The Quarrel

It does, at one level, seem rather naïve of Percy to imagine Henry would fund their expansion with taxpayers' money but this ignores the fact that the precedent established by Edward III would loom large in their thinking and, if the king was simply giving back what he owed them anyway, then, in reality, they *were* paying themselves. But no cash meant no war. In a single blow, the whole grand Percy scheme to annex huge tracts of the Scottish border fell flat. Albany wouldn't need to raise an army and Cocklaw was safe. It was, as Peter McNiven points out, clear that, for as long as Henry stayed on his shaky throne, the Percies were thwarted. Lesser men might be content with the huge bounty they'd harvested from their support but to be truly kings in the north, they'd need regime change, again.

Any such attempt was already and in no small part hamstrung by their Scottish adventure. They had set the Marches on fire hoping to stoke a furnace but, just because they were forced to step back, wouldn't put that fire out. Even if they had sufficient military clout to brush the usurper aside, they could not deplete their forces on the border to make the effort. Whatever they did now, they still had to hold the line. The Scots were famously resilient, the lustre of Homildon would soon fade and they would be back for more. If they were to deal with Henry, they'd need to find ready reserves of manpower elsewhere. Happily, there were of course those Cheshire men, truculent, disgruntled, and waiting in the wings. It was time to offer them their cue.

By tapping into this resource Hotspur was playing for huge stakes: 'in the light of this self-inflicted predicament . . . we should consider Hotspur's remarkable decision to make the men of Cheshire the nucleus of his insurrection'.[37] Just because the king was unpopular in Cheshire did not, of necessity, imply Hotspur was likely to be welcomed with open arms. Up to now he was Henry's loyal adherent, he'd stamped hard on the county in 1399 and as justice had enforced the usurper's will. Only three years before, he had headed up the inquisition after an abortive rising.[38] He was banking on the fact Henry was still the perceived enemy and it must be accepted this wasn't mere wishful thinking. Hotspur knew the county gentry and judged them shrewdly, any resentment towards him would be outweighed by hatred of the usurper. In the event, he wasn't wrong.

When looked at in this light, Hotspur's rebellion, while breathtakingly bold, appears far from reckless and shows him as a very astute political operator, not the headstrong youth as depicted by Shakespeare. If he could raise forces in Cheshire then he'd not need to deplete the earl's northern army, the status quo could be maintained along this vital frontier. Secondly, Henry would not expect an attack from the Welsh Marches, so much closer to the heart of his realm. By neat synchronicity, raising the standard of deposed Richard II in the heart of his devoted affinity added a strong moral compunction – Henry was a base usurper and regicide. Equally important, these Cheshire knights and yeomen, their much-feared archers, were first-class fighting men, ideal material.[39] This could be said to be, as Peter McNiven trumpets, a 'stroke of outrageous genius'.[40]

This is sufficient to dispose of any idea the Scots were party to the plot. If they had been Hotspur could have used the Percies' northern army, augmented by any number of willing Scottish adventurers. To any red-blooded borderer the lure of loot easily outweighed any notion of national loyalty, insofar as any ever existed. One only needs to consider the grand chevauchée Margaret of Anjou was able to muster after her victory over the Duke of York at Wakefield in December 1460. She had many borderers in her vast army which lumbered south, consuming all in its path to the shrill, demented choirs of southern chroniclers, lamenting the savagery of these *boreales bobinantes* ('roaring northerners') and their light-fingered ways. The mere fact the Percies had to maintain the bulk of their domestic reserves up north clearly showed they'd truly stirred the hornet's nest. Possibly Henry was relying on this, that they would be tied to their project and unable to contemplate mischief elsewhere. It's fair to say, at this stage, he'd not contemplated they might use Cheshire as their springboard, outrageous genius indeed and a masterpiece of improvisation.

If so, the king badly underestimated Hotspur who hurried towards Chester with only a handful of his household men, including his esquires Thomas Knayton and Roger Salvayn, who'd be his emissaries in the parley before battle at Shrewsbury.[41] His plans for the border had to be put on hold, not abandoned. That was the whole point behind the rising. He needed to remove Henry so he could put himself in a position to confront Albany when the time came. The Percies were playing for exceedingly high stakes indeed.

De Fonblanque tells us of the Tripartite Indenture, a pact entered into jointly by the Percies, Mortimer, and Glyndwr. In this, the parties agreed to divide the kingdom into three zones of influence. The Welshman got Wales, Mortimer, all England south of the Trent. Everything north of that and whatever Hotspur might slice off Scotland would belong to him, his father, and uncle.[42] This is preposterous and represents either the total cynicism of temporary expediency or arrogant folly. The Percies weren't short of hubris, but this does seem far-fetched. Even as devout a hagiographer as De Fonblanque thinks it's rich and would only have laid the grounds for further civil strife.

It is known that the Earl of Northumberland was in Yorkshire on 26 June, as it was from there he wrote his frosty reply to the king's earlier letter. Might Hotspur have expected some reinforcement from that county? This was, after all, Percy heartland where they still retained substantial holdings. Yet, there seems to be no real suggestion he *was* expecting forces from there either. It was early July when Harry Percy, with just a small company of retainers, slipped southwards towards Cheshire. Of itself, there was nothing suspicious in this, his appointments and offices there conferred every valid reason why he should need to do so. With him travelled his old adversary Douglas and a select cadre of Scottish knights. Edward Hall, writing much later, asserts he commanded a considerable number of Scottish adherents or mercenaries but this seems unlikely.[43]

Douglas to a degree remains the anomaly in this. Clearly, he was a prisoner and might have expected teaming up with Hotspur would cancel out any ransom obligations. Yet, he must have been acutely aware that the Percies' long game entailed acquiring all his lands. For him to be set at liberty and return to Scotland would not have been in Hotspur's longer term interest, so quite what final deal the two may have hammered out can only be guessed at. Douglas might have been ready to cede ground to gain liberty, no doubt reckoning he could win it back later. Besides, he had that his old adversary Dunbar, now advising King Henry, to contend with.

Insurrection

It is known that Hotspur's party travelled through Lancashire. The *Dieulacres Chronicle* tells us he recruited several prominent knights from that county; Sir Gilbert Halsall of Halsall, close to Southport, Thomas Bradshaw of Haigh, near Wigan, and Geoffrey Bold from the Eccles area.[44] He reached Cheshire on about 9 July and immediately set about recruiting.[45] McNiven considers that as it took him a week to complete his initial muster, he can't have had time to lay down many foundations beforehand, lending weight to the view the whole plan was very recent in concept. He then moved along the line of the Welsh Marches; now, had he been expecting Percy's retainers from York to rendezvous, he'd have instead made straight for Derby, the obvious junction. Equally obvious is the implication he was looking to find Glyndwr. There can't be much doubt Hotspur had a line of communication direct to the rebel Welsh hero, there were the negotiations over Edmund's ransom after all.

> Henry Percy marched to Cheshire where he had earlier been appointed as justice by Henry IV. He hoped to augment his retinue by drawing on the latent loyalty to Richard II still present in the palatinate. Hotspur was not disappointed as Cheshire men flocked to his banner and followed him to his ill-fated encounter with the usurper at Shrewsbury.[46]

Up till now Hotspur had not shown himself as any friend to the disaffected men of Cheshire, quite the reverse. As the usurper's loyal accomplice, he could easily be perceived as their mortal foe, but he was in a handy position if he wanted to tap into that simmering layer of dissent. Generally, Richard's Cheshire archers, his elite bodyguard, were universally detested but their military potential, as they had shown at Homildon, was indeed considerable.

The King's Praetorians

When the time came, Hotspur had valid reasons to assume he'd soon win friends in Cheshire, despite his own role as the usurper's proxy. The county had formed the backbone of Richard's personal affinity: '. . . Richard began to build his own retinue centred on his palatinate earldom of Chester. In this vein, he granted a general royal pardon to the inhabitants of the earldom as a token of his affection. Richard II was favouring the interests of his earldom, which he raised to a principality, over those of the kingdom'.[47]

King Richard II, as discussed earlier, was a man obsessed by the trappings of royalty without ever necessarily understanding the balances that went with it, as Machiavelli might have cautioned: 'Since men love at their own pleasure and fear at the pleasure of the prince, the wise prince should build his foundation upon that which is his own, not upon that which belongs to others; only he must seek to avoid being hated'. No more obvious example of this was his recruitment of a cadre of Cheshire archers: 'Richard II has been condemned by both his contemporaries and modern historians for his utilization of a bodyguard of Cheshire archers in the final years of his reign. Richard has been seen as the tyrant who attempted to impose his will with the support of a praetorian guard composed of the dregs of Cheshire society'.[48]

What the king achieved by this overt favouritism was, by so relying on men recruited from his own palatinate earldom, that he further alienated his other magnates. He was asserting himself not so much as ruler of the whole but as a *primus inter pares*, enforcing his writ with a brigade of locally recruited storm troopers and failing to curb their arrogance and excess:

> It is ironic and even tragic that a king who was so sensitive to his Regality and so advanced in his conceptions of royal prerogative should have been so limited in both his material resources and social vision that the very measures which he chose to adopt in defence of his position were, in fact, counterproductive of their intended goal.[49]

On 13 July 1397 Richard dispatched a writ to the Sheriff of Chester instructing him to raise a force of 2,000 archers to serve the Crown. This was intended to be exclusive; none could enter the service of any other lord till the king had recruited his full complement. In fact, he raised a force 2,300-strong. He used this private army to bully the Parliament summoned to Westminster for 17 September that year: 'Employing a form of strong-armed maintenance, the king assured himself that Parliament would yield itself to his personal direction. The merits of the king's case against his baronial rivals, and merits there were, were overshadowed by this manifestly unjust method of procedure'.[50]

Even when this immediate need to put the 'frighteners' on Parliament receded, not all the Cheshire men were furloughed, he retained a hardcore as his personal praetorians. Their special status induced an insufferable degree of hubris and the king's bodyguard became a law to themselves. They followed him on his expedition to Ireland and their wages were paid direct through his chamberlain for Cheshire, side-stepping the normal route via the Keeper of the Wardrobe:

> The above king [Richard II] had seven brave and noble esquires of the county of Chester and around eighty selected household retainers

specially assigned to each of them standing guard with great axes outside
the king's chamber. The names of these men were John de Legh del
Bothes, Thomas Ghelemeley, Ralph Davenport, Adam Bostok, John
Downe, Thomas Bestone, Thomas Halford.[51]

The king's bodyguard was the subject of many complaints, as Walsingham
indignantly noted: 'These Cheshire men were ready to commit every sort of crime
and their shamelessness soon increased to the point where they regarded only the
king as their equal, treating everybody else, however powerful of noble he was, with
contempt'.[52] It's not surprising that they'd not only resent their sudden demotion
but doubly resent the rough treatment they'd had from Henry IV. The king was
moved to issue a general amnesty but only because he needed their specialist
skills to facilitate his crack at the Scots. In 1403, they remained rebels in waiting.

So, what about Glyndwr and the Welsh rebels, was Hotspur contemplating some
form of alliance? It is known that one of his retainers, William Lloyd, a gentleman
from Denbigh, was acting as go-between.[53] Furthermore, Shropshire knight John
Kynaston was later charged with soliciting aid from Glyndwr.[54] Hardyng backs
this up, suggesting an agreed rendezvous on the banks of the Severn.[55] Obviously
this never happened, and writers ever since have offered up a list of reasons why
not. Peter McNiven believes these are all based on incorrect assumptions and
this seems reasonable. Hotspur was playing an altogether more subtle game.

During those early days of July, Glyndwr marched first into the south-
west of Wales, surprised Carmarthen and Newcastle Emlyn Castles, before
continuing on into hitherto untouched Pembrokeshire.[56] As Hotspur moved
towards Shrewsbury in mid-July, Glyndwr was moving ever further away from
him. This wasn't bad luck or worse planning, quite the reverse.[57] Both Lloyd and
McNiven argue persuasively this was clever coordination, very much a planned
joint strategy. The tactical reality was that Glyndwr's irregulars would be outclassed
by English men-at-arms in a conventional fight so why take the risk?

But, as raiders, as masters of manoeuvre, they were a different prospect and
by launching a major opportunistic attack in the south-west of Wales, they could
contribute significantly to Hotspur's overall strategy. Glyndwr's raid would
draw onto himself any available English forces who'd therefore not be around to
fight Percy. The fact that Hotspur and the Welshman moved their forces at the
same time and given the known lines of communication, it is certainly possible
this was the fruit of a previously agreed and concerted strategy. Glyndwr
was indeed fighting with Hotspur, just nowhere near Shrewsbury.[58]

The Road to Shrewsbury

Next question then is why, if there was not planned link-up, was Hotspur heading
for Shrewsbury? As suggested by McNiven, this is simple, the town itself was

his tactical objective. Prince Henry was there with a royalist garrison. It was Hal's headquarters and his forces there had not been drawn into the fight against Glyndwr's sudden initiative. This garrison was the king's most northerly outpost. If Hal and his men there could be eliminated or forced to capitulate, then the whole of England was open wide, and the northern rebels' strategic initiative could only gather momentum. Clearly, by showing his colours in Cheshire, Hotspur could move rapidly and deal with Prince Henry before the king could reinforce his son.[59]

Shrewsbury, as Peter McNiven nimbly highlights, was important for another reason.[60] Hotspur's thus far esteemed uncle Thomas Percy, Earl of Worcester was there. Among his wide estates he held Newcastle Emlyn Castle in Carmarthenshire, together with the lordship of Haverford in Pembrokeshire, which paid him a decent annuity, and he was the king's lieutenant for South Wales.[61] Worcester was also Prince Hal's governor and guardian.[62] There's a hint he'd absconded beforehand, after embezzling royal funds to help fund his nephew's rebellion.[63] McNiven thinks it more likely he'd accompanied the prince to Shrewsbury and prepared to decamp from there.[64]

With all this now in mind, we can begin to discern Hotspur's overall plan. And while this may have been worked out at the gallop, it does make sense. It's plain he could not dilute the northern frontier defence, this would be an open invitation to the Scots, who were very evidently not involved in any concert party. Only a handful of his household men and Douglas' small contingent joined Harry Percy in his dash to Chester. Following McNiven, it can be asserted that lines of communication were open with both Glyndwr and Worcester and that the Welsh rebels' unexpected move against the south-west of Wales was part of Hotspur's overall strategy as was a move against Prince Harry at Shrewsbury. This, if successful, would not only enable Worcester to slip safely between the lines but, once the garrison was overcome, prize open the heart of England and allow Hotspur's rebel banners to spill southwards on a swelling tide of resentment against the usurper. This was boldness indeed but not recklessness. Had it succeeded, bold would have been re-branded as genius.

Once Shrewsbury had fallen, some juncture with the Welsh rebels could have been possible, attracting many more local recruits as well as disgruntled Englishmen, seduced by the Percy manifesto together with Mortimer adherents over whom Percy already had significant influence. What is equally obvious is that Hotspur could not hope just with his Cheshire insurgents to defeat the whole of Henry's power if he could move fast enough to support his son at Shrewsbury. Speed and timing, as ever, were of the absolute essence. Speed was what Harry Percy was incredibly good at; dash and daring were his trademarks.

Controversy still arises over the role of old Northumberland and whether Hotspur ever expected him either to join forces, or at least send a contingent. The earl plainly did neither, and Hardyng is extremely critical of his performance.[65] Northumberland himself, after he submitted in August, blandly claimed he was innocent of any involvement in his son's actions and that the whole venture was Hotspur's alone. It is impossible to say if he really thought anyone would believe him.

Nonetheless, on 22 July, Westmorland was given a commission to act against the earl who was then, it seems, in Northumberland. Chroniclers agree that old Percy marched a sizeable force south at about this time.[66] Next year he was tried, ostensibly for treason, during the Westminster Parliament but escaped conviction, though found guilty on the lesser count of 'trespass'. This has all the hallmarks of a cover up, a compromise designed to rap Northumberland's knuckles rather than result in an appointment with the headsman. It implies he had illegally raised forces but glosses over the issue of what he intended to do with them. The prosecution might have noted but chose not to press the point that the earl's castellans had consistently refused to hand over their keys to the king's officers. This was of itself treasonous and surely can only have been because of a direct order from their feudal lord.[67]

What is most difficult is to work out exactly what game the earl was playing and whether it was ever intended he'd reinforce his son on the Welsh Marches. Details are very sparse indeed, but it seems generally agreed, as Walsingham states, that he did come some distance south but was halted and turned back by Westmorland (who would be relishing the chance).[68] However, Walsingham says this occurred towards the end of July, over a month after Shrewsbury. This ties in with the date of Neville's orders. On the other hand, the author of the *Northern Chronicle* claims this confrontation happened *before* the battle. This would appear a more logical chronology and yet there would hardly have been time for Westmorland to muster such a decent-sized force prior to Shrewsbury as, at best, he could only have had a few days' notice. If looking at the July assumption, he'd have had a week after the issue of his commission and might already have set matters in motion beforehand.

What may well be the case is that, even by 30 July, Northumberland had still not had credible news of the disaster which had overtaken his brother and son. Walsingham makes it clear that the earl, bested by Westmorland, lost his nerve, and decamped to Newcastle.[69] That clearly implies the confrontation took place south of there either in County Durham or North Yorkshire. Northumberland owned wide acres in Cleveland which would yield a fair crop of recruits during his next abortive rising in 1405 and when Hardyng tells us he didn't stir from Northumberland prior to the battle, he must be right. As Neville saw him off with only a muster of his own affinity, this argues Northumberland's force was not a large one and we can surmise that he hadn't stripped the border garrisons any more than his son had done before him. That strategic line still had to be held. It therefore appears that by 30 July he'd only just marched south from Northumberland and hadn't yet been able to raise that many recruits.[70]

It does appear clear that the Earl of Northumberland could not have brought armed support to aid Hotspur and Worcester before the Battle of Shrewsbury. Did he simply fail through faint-heartedness or perhaps illness to make the planned rendezvous or had it in fact never been the intention that they'd fight united? Hotspur had certainly instigated the Cheshire rising on his own, he took a calculated risk and it paid off, his assessment of the prevailing sentiment there proved highly accurate. This all made sense, Hotspur could and did tap into the Cheshire men's hatred of Henry IV, we can safely assume his campaign was coordinated with Glyndwr's strike into South and West Wales.

Hotspur had an ace, his uncle, seeded in the enemy camp and he controlled a large part of the vast Mortimer patrimony. But once Worcester had defected, once he crept out of Shrewsbury to join his nephew all was revealed. Had all gone to plan thereafter Harry Percy could, by the end of July, have controlled almost all of Wales and the Marches. While he might be the junior statesman compared with his father, he was the royal appointee in Cheshire, a warlord of immensely high standing, still possessing sufficient youth and dynamism to get the job done.

Winning control of Wales and dealing with Prince Henry's garrison at Shrewsbury was a tactical gambit not the strategic goal. That was the unseating of Henry IV. With Wales and the northern frontier in rebel hands, what was the king to do? How might he respond, given that his son and heir would highly likely be a prisoner of his erstwhile mentor? He could march north to meet Northumberland or west to meet Hotspur. Whichever path he chose, his enemies could close in and take him in a pincer movement. Northumberland only prepared to move when he did, he wasn't setting off to reinforce brother and son but to be able to confront the king or to sandwich him between the jaws of a Percy trap. Either way King Henry was in trouble, except of course, Hotspur and Worcester were dead, their army smashed, their cause in ruins. It was Northumberland who was now trapped.

Up to 20 July the rebels' prospects appeared bright. All Hotspur had to do was march rapidly on Shrewsbury then beat or just overawe the prince's modest force. All his father had to do was hang on in the north to give continuity of leadership and keep the Percy lion flying. It could be argued the Percies *should* have colluded with the Scots, which could have freed up many more northerners. Yet, it was their desire to win and hold lands in Scotland which had set the whole business of rebellion in being. Their endgame wasn't just regime change it was regime change which facilitated their ambitions on the Scottish side, Albany had no incentive whatsoever to collude, quite the reverse, any defeat of the Percies was a clear win for him.

McNiven speculates further that Northumberland's seemingly belated move south towards North Yorkshire during that week following the battle may have been triggered by the realisation that the king had been able to move much faster and with greater numbers than the Percies had anticipated. Perhaps he didn't fully grasp or was only partly informed of the catastrophe which had overtaken his son and brother, still thinking he might be able to intervene effectively. His rude awakening, when confronted by Westmorland, must have been a crushing wake-up call and explains his apparent loss of nerve and very hasty scurrying back to Newcastle.[71]

'The Percies' strategy was a combination of audacious extemporization and sound military judgement'.[72] Hotspur's assessment of the fighting capacities of all the various forces across England and the border was very accurate. The only variable was the king and any army he might muster. This was the random card Percy couldn't predict or double guess. He gambled that Henry would not be able to move fast enough to frustrate his seizure of Shrewsbury and that's the bit he got wrong. Ultimately, it was the only thing that mattered.

On 10 July, the king wrote to the Council from Higham Ferrers in Northampton-shire stating he was taking forces north to *assist* Percy before heading for Wales and a reckoning with Glyndwr. This was only a day after Hotspur had arrived at Chester to unfurl his rebel standard. Peter McNiven makes the excellent point that, regardless of how he might view Northumberland's adventures in Scotland as being merely private enterprise, he couldn't ignore the threat posed by Albany's army. While he didn't want to underwrite Percy ambition, he couldn't afford a major reverse which might undo all the advantages won at Homildon.

Throughout, the influence, insidious rather than official, of George Dunbar who had his own game to play on the border must never be underestimated. While the slippery Scottish magnate might have had little to gain from Percy aggrandisement, he had everything to lose if they got beaten and the Scots reasserted full control of their marches. While one scenario might not bring him any closer to recovering his estates, the other would see him cut off completely. This subtle schemer was probably trying to persuade the king that the influence of the Percies in the north needed to be both balanced and corralled by someone with all the right credentials and that he was naturally the only suitable candidate.[73]

Checkmate

It seems Hotspur did not anticipate the king's march north, ironically coming to his assistance and he'd gambled the rebels would have secured both the north and west by the time Henry got wind of their enterprise and had a chance to react. But the king was already on the road. By 16 July, he'd both marched as far as Lichfield and worked out what was afoot, sending out letters to raise further levies from a dozen counties.[74] He gave orders for the internment of leading Percy adherents in Yorkshire and swerved his army sharp left to head for Shrewsbury.

For both sides this was now the focal point of the campaign. It was the chief crossing place over the upper Severn and Prince Henry's base. From Lichfield, King Henry could have continued along the ancient artery of Watling Street but in fact marched north to Stafford, where the royal army bivouacked during the night of 19 July. Up to this point he mustn't have been quite certain Hotspur was moving on Shrewsbury, though this would seemingly have been obvious at Lichfield. He made up for this on the 20th, pushing his army the full 32 miles (51km) through Newport and Haughmond to reach Shrewsbury's suburbs just ahead of the rebels. Hotspur had been driving his own forces south from Chester via Whitchurch and Wem in a bid to reach the town first. For once Harry Percy, master of haste, was too slow. Walsingham credits Dunbar with more sage advice urging Henry on with classical exhortations from Lucan:

> Avoid delay it always hinders plans
> the foe now fears, his strength not yet amassed.[75]

Harry Percy got remarkably close, and his skirmishers were probably infiltrating the northern fringes of the town as early as evening on the 19th, but Prince Hal, who commanded over a thousand men, refused to be intimidated even though some of the outlying streets were torched. Both his own men and the townsfolk stayed loyal and prepared to defend their homes next day. Before Hotspur could tighten his grip and begin to squeeze, the king's outriders were clattering across the English bridge to the south on the evening of the 20th. Harry Percy had just lost the most important race of his life.

Dusk

> *King*: How bloodily the sun begins to peer
> Above yon bulky hill
> The day looks pale at this distemperature.
> *Prince*: The southern wind
> Doth play the trumpet to its purposes
> And by his hollow whistling in the leaves
> Foretells a tempest and a blustering day.
> *King*: Then with the losers let it sympathize
> For nothing can seem foul to those that win.[76]

Meanwhile, it would be a worried Hotspur who camped that night by the small hamlet of Berwick, surely a stroke of darkest irony? Walsingham and subsequent writers certainly thought so:

> Hotspur now bid his page gird him with the sword he had worn at Homildon, and on being informed that the weapon had been left overnight at the village where they had halted – he changed colour exclaiming 'now I see that my ploughshare is drawing to its last furrow, for a soothsayer once told me in my own country that I should perish at Berwick. Alas, he deceived me by that name which I believed to mean Berwick in the north' . . .[77]

Predictions, even if this incident is apocryphal, mattered in an age of faith and religiosity. Harry Percy (unlikely) hadn't realised he'd been bivouacked at another place called Berwick – so like Macbeth, 'despair thy charm'.

For Worms Brave Percy – The Battle of Shrewsbury, 21 July 1403

A battle is a dramatic action that has its commencement, its middle and its end. The order of battle taken by the two armies, and the first movements to come to action, constitute the prelude. The contra movements of the attacked army form the plot. This causes new dispositions, brings on the crisis, from whence springs the result.

Napoleon Bonaparte

My heart is broken by the terrible loss I have sustained in my old friends and companions and my poor soldiers. Believe me, nothing except a battle lost can be half so melancholy as a battle won.

Duke of Wellington[1]

If you visit any of the First World War Western Front battlefields, Delville Wood on the Somme for example, you're struck firstly by the beauty of the wonderful South African War Memorial there, but also, as with so many others, by the spread of visible traces, mainly shell craters and warnings about unexploded ordnance (and there are plenty still around).[2] Industrial warfare leaves traces, but medieval war isn't like that at all. Generally, there's extraordinarily little if anything to tell you what horrors were enacted on a site. Shrewsbury field today is delightfully well ordered, almost manicured, with excellent interpretation. It was quite different that July day roughly 600 years ago. For battlefield archaeologists, grave-pits represent their holy grail and just as hard to find. Towton (1461) has been the exception when part of a mass interment was uncovered, anecdotally it must be said, and there are the famous remains from the Swedish fight at Visby a century earlier. Shrewsbury Field like so many others has, so far, kept its treasures well hidden.

The Arena

In gratitude for, and in commemoration of, this victory, Henry the Fourth erected on the spot Battlefield Church; and from the circumstance of the battle having been fought on St Mary Magdalen's eve, he, in compliance with the prevalent opinions of the age, and probably also from his considering himself in some degree indebted to her for the victory, caused the church to be dedicated to St. Mary Magdalen.[3]

At the time of the battle the ground over which it was fought belonged to the Hussey family, a gentry name, who gave their name to Albright Hussey. In 1403 the manor house encompassed a small chantry chapel dedicated to St John the Baptist and the incumbent was Roger Ive of Seaton, installed some five years beforehand on 22 October 1398.[4] After the conflict, Hussey gifted his priest a parcel of land on which to raise a memorial chapel.

Three years after that, by royal licence dated 28 October 1406, king Henry effectively stamped his seal on the site and 2 acres of Hussey's land, 'situated in the field called Bateleyfield in which a battle had lately been fought between the king and Henry Percy deceased and other rebels'.[5] Henry IV was happy to take credit for the chapel's foundation and airbrush Roger Ive's original initiative out of the historical picture. And for quite a while he got away with it, but local historian John Brickdale Blakeway was later able to set the record straight.[6] Ive surrendered the land in late 1409, enabling Henry to assume control of and credit for the monument which was neatly re-branded as a royal initiative.

This chapel was, as mentioned, dedicated to St Mary Magdalen – suitable enough as the fight occurred on the Feast of St Praxedes, eve of the Feast of the Virgin. It can be assumed that the 2-acre rectangular enclosure marks the site of likely mass interments, being at the epicentre of the melee. During the mid-nineteenth century, quantities of human bones were, it is said, uncovered while workmen were digging to extend and drain the Corbet vault inside the church.[7] This rather echoes the situation at Elsdon church (see Act 5 above), equally tantalising but of course equally inconclusive. A subsequent charter dating from 1440 refers to the land granted being bounded by a ditch, together with two inlets and outlets, 'one extending along the lands of Richard Hussey, twenty feet and the other containing in breadth fifteen feet'. Brooke identified these as the entry and exit points for a track which ran over Hussey's land from the main Whitchurch road to the east towards Albright Hussey lying further west.[8]

Nor was this chapel the only structure within the curtilage, Ive built and ran a small secular college, staffed in due course by five chaplains, together with a small infirmary for the poor. Henry IV was a benefactor of this hospital and Battlefield College kept going until the reign of Edward VI, after which it fell into disuse. Leland recorded its existence.[9] As for the chapel this became, post-Reformation, the parish church. It's a fine building (now in care of the Churches Conservation Trust) but, over the decades, attendances tailed off as local populations shrank, and the place fell into terminal decline. Victorian antiquarian and battlefield writer

Richard Brooke described it as 'roofless and dilapidated'.[10] However, a strongly worded footnote cautioned against excessive zeal for restoration or improvement of the building:

> When I visited the church in May 1856, I was very sorry to hear that a subscription had been entered into, for the purpose of what was termed 'renovating' this curious and interesting edifice. As far as respects removing the modern pillars, and the plastered ceiling from the chancel, and making the latter appear more in accordance with its ancient state, few persons would object to that measure; but it ought to be borne in mind that the chancel will accommodate, and much more than accommodate, the whole number of church-goers of the very scanty population of Battlefield parish; and that the renovation or rebuilding of any other part is wholly unnecessary, with reference to the spiritual requirements of the parishioners.
>
> It would evince great want of taste and judgment to renovate or restore the ancient nave and tower. The remains are most valuable to the historian and archaeologist. The interval was so very short, comparatively speaking, between the erection of the church in the reign of Henry IV, and the seizure of the edifice and its contiguous college and hospital in the reign of Henry VIII, that we cannot doubt that the remains are now an authentic and interesting example of church architecture of the reign of the former monarch.
>
> The parties who wish for or recommend the renovation of the nave, or the restoration of the whole of Battlefield Church, may possibly find some architect, who, like an old-clothes man, may undertake to 'renovate' the article which he is accustomed to deal in, or, in other words, to make it 'as good as new'; but when the alterations in this church are finished, they may probably furnish an example of a lamentable destruction of a very ancient, curious, and historical relic of times gone by.[11]

Andrew Boardman has looked exhaustively at the evidence and thoroughly interrogated all the sources and there is little to disagree with in most of his findings. He looks at the various field names, Hateleyfield (surely a version of Bateleyfield), Old Field, Husifield, King's Croft, and Bullfield in Harlescott. Several maps from the nineteenth century show Old Heath, Old Farm, and sundry variants on the 'Old' strain, lying south of Battlefield church; these have fuelled some controversy. Speed's map of the county (1596–1610) suggests the fight occurred in a space known as 'Olfeilde' which, as Boardman, believes, could be a variant of Boleffyld or Bull Field.[12] In 1403, the Hussey family also owned Husifield, a large enclosure lying south or south-west of the memorial church.

King's Croft, south-east of the chapel and bordering onto the Whitchurch Road, marks the traditional location for the king's division, though the name is later, and this ground was, at the time, just part of Bull Field, which was then considerably larger in extent. This is borne out by some sources; the *Chronicle of London* where a supplementary note confirms the battle took place in Bull Field as was, latterly Bateleyfield 'where the church now stands'.[13] Andrew Boardman concludes, quite rightly, that Bull Field and Bateleyfield are one and the same.[14] It seems likely Bull Field was an area of open grazing which lay towards the lower portion of a more intensively farmed and planted arable zone that climbed north towards the rebel battle line. The presence of these crops would prove significant.

What certainly weren't there are those 'ponds' that Wyntoun mentions, subsequently echoed by Ramsay. Colonel Burne relies on Brooke's mid-nineteenth century examination of the site and he dismisses these traces as much later than 1403. Burne, walking the ground a century after Brooke, believes the most westerly of these depressions was probably a clay pit, used for brickmaking while the rectory (1861) was under construction. Brooke had thought the middle opening was probably evidence of some amateur archaeology – looking for battlefield relics. The third, he considered, was a typical Shropshire 'marl' (fertiliser) pit. It's also been thought these could have been fishponds associated with the college, but still, very definitely, after the battle.[15] When Wyntoun (who of course, had never been anywhere near) writes of a 'strictum passum' (narrow passage), he's referring to a restriction of the general direction of approach taken by the king's army. Such a feature would occur roughly 2,000yd (1,829m) north of the town leading up from the former bed of the river. It can safely be assumed that the battlefield itself was clear of any such obstructions.

Prelude

Worcester: Your father's sickness is a maim to us.[16] Or, as Hardyng says, Percy senior '. . . came not out of Northumberland but fayled hym foule without witte or rede'.[17] This was considered in Act 7 above and Peter McNiven's view that Hotspur was not anticipating support from his father bringing a northern army, or indeed from Glyndwr, seems reasonable. What he had hoped to achieve with his largely Cheshire army was to neutralise Prince Henry's garrison at Shrewsbury and prise open the marches as a springboard for a further advance. And he'd failed. The king's timely arrival had scuppered that plan and severely restricted his remaining options, which now boiled down to simply fight or flee.

Percy was hemmed in on the wrong side of the Severn. To advance and sidestep the royal army he'd have to find another crossing or face attempting to withdraw his scratch-built forces with the king in close pursuit. This would test a seasoned

THE BATTLE OF SHREWSBURY
21st September 1403

To Whitchurch

To Shrewsbury

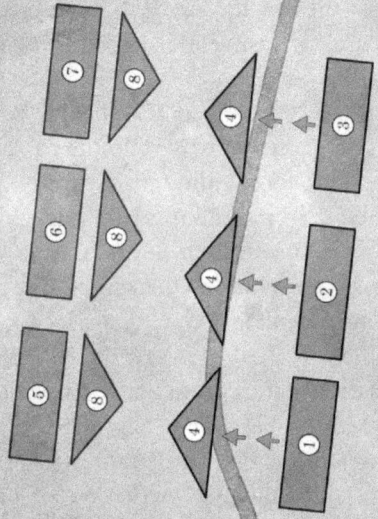

N

YARDS

0   500

BULL FIELD

HATELY FIELD
(field of peas)

HUSSEY FIELD

Albright Hussey

① Prince of Wales
② King Henry IV
③ George Dunbar Earl of March
④ Royalist archers advance
⑤ Earl of Worcester
⑥ Hotspur
⑦ Earl of Douglas
⑧ Rebel archers

army; Hotspur did not command a seasoned army. With hardened northerners under the Percy banner, he might have pulled it off, but this wasn't that kind of army. If he couldn't effect an orderly withdrawal, then he'd have to give battle and for that he needed to find the right ground. Even if he could get clear, what then? The chances were his army would disintegrate anyway and he'd have no more than his original handful to scamper back north and hope to link up with his father's levy in Yorkshire. Tellingly, he would have lost the initiative which, so far, he'd managed quite cleverly. But now he'd need to think fast.

Walsingham allows Hotspur a rousing address to his no doubt shaken men:

> We must . . . give up what we have begun and turn our weapons against those who come against us. You see for certain the royal standard, and we do not have the time to look for a hiding place, even if we wanted to. So be of good courage. Stand your ground as this day will either advance us all, if we win, or free us from high hopes of rule, if we lose. For it is fairer to fall in war for our country than to be put to death after the battle by the sentence of our enemy.[18]

This is an eloquent way of admitting you don't have a back-up plan.

Success in war can be divided between a happy blend of good planning and inspired improvisation. So far, Hotspur's planning had been sound but now it was time to extemporise, and quickly. On the eve of battle Hotspur's forces were bivouacked around the village of Berwick, 2 miles (3.22km) north-west of Shrewsbury, while the king's army camped by Haughmond Abbey, 3½ miles (5.6km) north-east. It can be discounted that Hotspur was waiting for Glyndwr, more likely he was trying to find some means of outflanking Shrewsbury.

In any event, time was against him. Prince Hal was on his heels. So, next morning, the day of battle, his rebel force moved off east towards Harlescott then due north to deploy on their chosen ground. Now, whether this was just thought for the day or whether Percy had spotted the potential on his approach march it is difficult to say but a good general always keeps his eye open. Wellington knew he intended to stand on the Ridge of Mont St Jean, if he had to, before Napoleon ever left Elba. Hotspur was 39, survivor of two big battles and many small ones, not the impetuous youth Shakespeare portrays, and it is therefore likely he'd this terrain in mind before he marched on the 21st.

As ever with medieval battles, numbers are hard to calculate. Hardyng states Hotspur led 9,000 'knights, squires, yeomen and archers'.[19] Walsingham gives him a larger force, 14,000 'of the finest men'.[20] It is highly likely the king could command rather more, probably he had say 14,000 against Hotspur's 10,000 at best. It is known that on 17 July 1403, the king paid 4 barons, 20 knights, 476 esquires, and 2,500 archers whom he'd contracted with at Burton upon Trent the hefty sum of £8,108.00. Clearly then it was in Henry's interest to fight now rather than let the rebels march clear and risk a possible junction with Northumberland's northern levy, thus handing back the initiative which the king had now so neatly captured. He couldn't afford to dole out second chances. Now was best.

The scene in Hotspur's makeshift camp can be conjured up. It is not known how much baggage his army was dragging along but probably not much or as little as possible. Hotspur would want a pared down force, lean and ready for action, an extension of his hobiler pedigree. Sergeants would be bellowing orders before dawn when short summer darkness gave way to rising light and its chorus. Scouts would have reported the presence of royal outposts and approaches. Hotspur, quartered with the Betton family in Berwick, wouldn't have got much sleep. Did the tragic irony of his first fight haunt him? No one can say if there was ever any truth in the Berwick prophecy, but the medieval mind was accustomed to signs and portents. He'd know how desperate his situation was, but all was far from being lost.

At least his Cheshire men weren't strangers to march discipline, their elan was clearly intact and pride in their perceived elite status would have sustained them. Getting the army moving, dousing fires, doling out morning rations, a downing of Dutch courage. Most would realise they'd likely fight that day and possibly not live to see the end of it, death in battle or a traitor's death jigging at rope's end. Armies on the move take up a lot of room. For instance, in 1914 a foot battalion of the BEF marching over the hot pave in Northern France or Belgium occupied roughly a space of 1,000yd (914m) and more. If Hotspur did have 9,000/10,000 men, that's a 9-mile (14.5km) marching column, even discounting the inevitable tail of baggage and non-combatants. They'd need to move fast and light.

Most were probably mounted on ponies, knights and gentry on horseback, spilling out over the fields, probably less splendidly colourful than most accounts would have us believe. It is not known if officers rode in full harness, very possibly on this warm summer's morning they did. Great clouds of dust and piles of steaming dung would mark their passage; any locals would shift fast out of the way. Armies weren't good news whoever's side they might be on. Banners may have been furled, probably were until deployment, this morning's work was about speed not ostentatious show, there was nobody to impress. Nothing about them would shine but their weapons; smiths would have been busy sharpening edges giving that 'dreadful note of preparation'.

Once Hotspur's marching columns had reached his chosen ground, probably by mid to late morning, their officers would shake them out into line, deploying by companies of a hundred under a centenar, sub-divided into weak platoons of twenty, led by vintenars. It is not known how Hotspur ranged his forces. Boardman shows Worcester commanding the right, Hotspur in the centre, with Douglas on the left. But this may not be convincing, Douglas had only a small party of Scottish knights with him (see Act 7) and the English weren't too keen on taking orders from Scots, besides which their respective dialects would have been barely comprehensible. Instead, Hotspur may have split his force into two battles or divisions, Worcester, the most senior noble, on the right and he himself the left. Archers, it can be surmised, formed a line along his entire frontage, though it's always possible bowmen stood either in wedges between bodies of infantry or in wings on each flank, no one can say for certain.

The ground was good, the slope descended gently towards the south, and the rebels were protected by the next best thing to barbed wire – the medieval equivalent, a broad sweep of maturing peas. Walsingham mentions this and suggests Hotspur's men tied the bushes together to form an improvised barrier, crude perhaps but the peas would make themselves useful. It was perhaps now midday or after and, banner trailing banner, in a cloud of dust and the reverberating tramp of men and horses, King Henry's army began to appear along the Shrewsbury road.

Henry would know he had numbers on his side beside the tactical initiative. He had forced Percy to accept battle against the odds, facing an altogether more homogeneous royal army. Proud banners flaunting in that summer's afternoon, dull ochres of field and meadow and track, glowing with a pageant of gold; pennons of many knights and lords flying proudly beneath the King of England's great banner:

> Advance our standards, set upon our foes
> Our ancient world of courage fair St George
> Inspire us with the spleen of fiery dragons![21]

Such displays aimed to overawe, and it worked. Even as the armies shook themselves out, a company of Hotspur's rebels, led by Richard Horkesley, decamped, and pelted downhill to join the king, the cheers and jibes of the royalist knights ringing across the rising plain. A bad moment for Harry Percy, wondering how many might follow, but none did. The Cheshire men hated King Henry and that kept them in their ranks. By now the royal army, deployed in either two or three divisions, was occupying a line between the Whitchurch Road and Albright Hussey, probably just south of where the church now stands (see Map 4).

It seems likely, as most writers agree, that Prince Henry led the left of his father's battle line, the king himself the centre. Andrew Boardman suggests that George Dunbar, as indefatigably wily as ever, took the right. However, Burne asserts there were only two divisions, conforming to Hotspur's own disposition, and this seems more probable. This deployment gave King Henry a frontage of about 1,000yd (914m), which with a density of say a dozen men per yard equates to 12,000 fighting men, not far off the chronicler's figures. Brooke and Burne both suggest the lines may have been slightly shorter, with say some 300–500yd (275–450m) between opposing forces. King Henry's proud flags now fluttered over what became King's Croft, Bateleyfield, and Hussey Field. Henry had appointed Edmund, young Earl of Stafford, as Constable of England, an onerous responsibility and a dangerous one.[22]

Percy might have suffered defections and more on his side might have been flaky but, as Walsingham concedes, he had 'the better position'.[23] He still had a hard core of his own affinity along with those following his redoubtable uncle plus Douglas' tough Scotsmen. Knights such as Sir Richard Venables of Kinderton in Cheshire and Sir Richard Vernon, a Shropshire knight and captain of Beaumaris Castle, with those famous or notorious Cheshire bowmen, stood ready beneath their White Hart banner.

The stage was set.

Parley

> *Blount*: If that the king
> Have any way your good deserts forgot
> Which he confesseth to be manifold
> He bids you name your griefs; and with all speed
> You shall have your desires with interest
> And pardon absolute for yourself and these
> Herein misled by your suggestion.[24]

Medieval generals didn't like battles as a rule, too unpredictable, too hard to control, and the risks too great. Henry IV was no exception. He'd not fought a major battle before and, even if the odds favoured his cause, he'd be wary. Hotspur and Worcester were proven captains, those Cheshire men with their fearsome warbows, the best around. Henry had reacted effectively to the crisis; one he had not sought and doesn't necessarily appear to have anticipated. The *Dieulacres Chronicle* informs us that the king had written 'amicable' letters to Hotspur from Burton on 16 July offering some form of mediation.[25]

His emissaries now were Thomas Prestbury, Abbot of Shrewsbury and Haughmond together with Thomas Langley, his Clerk of the Privy Seal, men calculated to soften a confrontation, not sharpen it.[26] The story, certainly Shakespeare's version, is that Hotspur was too haughty and hot-blooded to engage in talk and sent his uncle Worcester, a skilled, normally silver-tongued diplomat, to do the bargaining. But Worcester plays a double game and mispresents the king's otherwise positive replies as insults and so stokes the fire, prompting his impetuous nephew to launch the attack:

And the story is that although the king made every reasonable concession and humbled himself more than was fitting for a royal person, this same Sir Thomas Percy, when he returned to his nephew, brought back the opposite answer to the one given by the king, thus embittering the young man's mind and driving him into battle even against his will.[27]

Nonetheless, it must be kept in mind that Hotspur wasn't a 'young' man, he was almost 40, a decent age for the time and not necessarily as hot-headed as in the days of his youth. This account doesn't quite ring true.

Hardyng, however, tells it quite differently and it should be remembered that he was after all there. He says he witnessed a dispatch of the Percy manifesto taken to the king by those two esquires, Thomas Knayton and Roger Salvayn. Moreover, he claims Worcester wasn't involved at all.[28] He goes on to state that 'after a long trete [talk] the prince began to fight'.[29] So Hardyng is saying the precise opposite of Walsingham and it was the royalists who initially moved to contact.

Obligingly, Hardyng reveals the content of this manifesto, probably the king was already aware, but it was strong stuff and didn't leave a lot of room for negotiation. The Percies claimed: 1. Henry had taken an oath at Doncaster, solemnly swearing he'd not come to claim the throne but merely to recover that which was rightfully his; 2. He'd also sworn there'd be no unfair taxation – a matter dear to all Englishmen's hearts. Nonetheless, he'd seized the crown; 3. Murdered Richard II 'by the space of fifteen days and so many nights (which is horrible among Christian people to be heard) with hunger, thirst and cold to perish – to be murdered'; 4. Henry had stolen the throne contrary to his earlier oath and dispossessed Edmund Mortimer who was rightfully next in line; 5. Further the Percies accused Henry of stuffing his Parliament with placemen so he could exercise unlawful, tyrannical control; and 6. He'd failed to ransom Mortimer from the Welsh and even prevented the Percies from doing so. When they'd agreed terms and brokered a true, Henry had accused them of treason and conspired to destroy them.[30] There was not a lot to talk about here, Henry was pretty much damned if he conceded any of these. He had a simple choice, be utterly humiliated and forced to abdicate, after which he could measure his life expectancy in days if he was lucky, or fight. He opted for battle, let God decide.

> *Hotspur*: I thank him, that he cuts me from my tale
> For I profess not talking; only this – Let each man do his best: and here draw I
> A sword, whose temper I intend to stain with the best blood that I can meet withal
> In the adventure of this perilous day. Now, Esperance! Percy! and set on Sound all the lofty instruments of war

And by that music let us all embrace;
For, heaven to earth, some of us never shall
A second time do such a courtesy.[31]

De Fonblanque also puts inspiring war cries of 'Esperance Percy' and 'St George, upon them!' into the mouths of the opposing armies as they braced themselves to fight.[32] God would indeed now decide, with some assistance from George Dunbar, 9th Earl of Dunbar and March.

Crisis

'So, Henry Percy's archers began the battle, and there was no place on the ground for their arrows, for they all lodged in bodies, and the men on the King's side fell like the leaves that fall in the cold weather after frost.'[33] This was new, unique. In many battles English bowmen, those terrible 'men of the grey goose feather', had shot down their opponents, Scots, French, and Spaniards, with their clothyard storm. Now, for the first time, they were killing each other. 'But the King's archers did their job as well and sent a dense shower of shafts into the ranks of the enemy. So, on both sides, men fell in great numbers just as the apples fall in autumn, when shaken by the south wind . . .'.[34] Hotspur's army received assistance from that humble crop of peas which impeded the steady advance of the king's bowmen, reminiscent of the difficulties their red-coated descendants would experience trying to feel their way forward though head-high wheat and rye south of the crossroads at Quatre Bras on 16 June 1815 and with similar, deadly consequences.

Walsingham likes his homely similes but he's right about the effect. For the first time two longbow formations were battering each other at about 200yd (183m). Boardman shows the king's missile troops moving forward pretty much in line with the church to begin this archery duel, but this doesn't seem quite right. Probably they moved further forward and that was how they became entangled among the peas. We've no idea of just how awful that exchange of arrows would be. Probably not until the use of rifled guns during the American Civil War when troops blazed away over similar ranges, wreaking terrible havoc with conical Minie bullets, would this level of killing occur and a warbow had at least three times the rate of shooting. Black powder arms swiftly blotted out the field with dense clouds of sulphureous smoke, arrows don't. Bullets, at such high muzzle velocity, strike with numbing force, shafts don't; you feel the agony instantly.

In that first fatal moment, the summer sky is blotted out by arrows, with each army perhaps deploying 7,000 archers shooting at maybe 10 flights per minute – well within their capability, that's 140,000 shafts in the air during that first moment. Both are shooting at massed targets, both sides deploy men who've trained for this since childhood. One side, Hotspur's, fields the acknowledged masters of their chosen weapon edged with collective grudge. Most would have had a ready supply of four dozen arrows, in two sheaves each of twenty-four. Once those were shot, they'd need re-supply from the baggage train. It would take about five or six minutes to shoot off their initial ammunition and it could be speculated that the missile duel barely lasted much longer than that.

Once one side advanced to contact, the archers might disperse and reform on the flanks to keep shooting over the heads of their attacking comrades or down tools, pick up polearms and get stuck in.[35] Bodkins and broad heads, weighing around 4oz (113g), thump home with fearful force, punching men aside as though shot with heavy calibre bullets. Nobody who survived this would ever forget it, it would define their lives as surely as going over the top did for those who came through 1 July 1916. The carnage was similar. Men would be shot through their faces, bodies, limbs, and feet, some pinned by multiple hits.

It's difficult to speak to surgeons who've treated arrow wounds but there is a good deal of speculation as to how these resemble or differ from gunshot injuries:

> Low velocity bullets with little penetration like a 9 x 18mm or 9 x 19mm would penetrate your skin and lose velocity very quickly once most of the energy was transferred on impact, they usually hit a bone and stop, or they go in a few inches and stop.
>
> Compare the same 9mm bullet to a broadhead launched from a compound bow with a 150lb draw, the arrow will do more damage to a unarmoured target and removing it on your own would be VERY dangerous as broadheads are made for slicing, while it's in you may not be bleeding out but if you remove it you could nick an artery or a major vessel group and you'd have no chance of stemming the flow of blood because of the surface area of the wound. I'd rather get shot multiple times by bullets to be honest, they are small and fragment which can cause serious risks but it's better than taking something like an arrow to the chest, I'd compare an arrow hit to being hit by a shotgun slug.[36]

Earlier accounts referred to, describing the Battle of the Standard in 1138, describe King David I of Scotland's feared Norse-Gaels being studded like porcupines as English archers shot. That would have been the earlier shorter form of stave, nothing like the terrible potency of the great warbow. The man next to you could have been struck through the face or body or doing a frantic dance of death as shafts penetrated limbs, smacking home like an axe into wood. His screams will fill your ears, his agonies your eyes, stink of his piss and shit your nostrils as bladder and bowels void themselves. This is effectively industrial warfare, centuries before industry, nearly the killing power of machine guns and it's Englishman against Englishman.

Later, during the Wars of the Roses (1453–87), it would be perceived wisdom that whoever lost this opening bout had to attack, or their casualties would mount so rapidly that survivors would bolt. And they did, Walsingham tells us '. . . many thousands fled from the place of the battle at the same time, as they thought the King had been killed by arrows'.[37] Hotspur's Cheshire archers lived up to their fearsome reputation and clearly achieved 'fire superiority' which caused an unspecified number of the king's men to drop weapons and run for it.

Hotspur attacked. He launched his division against that of the king (it is assumed here that both sides deployed each in two divisions), while Worcester (presumably) engaged Prince Henry on their respective wings. This is uncertain; Walsingham refers to Percy and Douglas, 'the bravest soldiers anyone has ever seen', launching their charge aiming to kill Henry – 'turning their weapons against nobody but the person of the king'.[38] Contact occurred likely at the base of the rise, though the king's division may have given ground to absorb the impact of their enemies' furious onslaught.

The implication here is that the whole weight of the rebels' attack fell on the right flank of the royalist forces, so Hotspur was aiming for a single bold stroke to decide the fight and capitalise on the success of his archers. Did these bowmen hang back to keep shooting or did they join the melee? Chroniclers don't really give us a clue, but my supposition is that most now fought as billmen or with falchion and buckler.[39] At this juncture they were probably of more use to Hotspur as infantry. Just possibly, they split into companies and fulfilled both roles.

Whether Prince Henry was attacked by Worcester or whether the earl threw the weight of his division behind to add greater momentum to his nephew's charge is difficult to assess. Perhaps the rebels though the prince's wing was already in disarray after the archery duel and that applying greater force to that crucial point justified the risk of leaving their left flank effectively in the air. Colonel Burne's theory of Inherent Military Probability would dictate that they'd at least try to mask the royal left wing to prevent envelopment (which is in fact what finally occurred).

King Henry was definitely 'must kill' target of the day: 'Thinking that he was worth ten thousand of his men, they looked for him, mowing down those who stood in their way and searching for him with death-dealing spears and swords'.[40] Luckily, the king had George Dunbar by his side. Henry was a brave knight and fought like a lion, but the Scottish earl knew his loss would mean certain defeat so persuaded Henry to leave the press for long enough to allow his line to stabilise and soak up the furious brunt of the attack. This mightn't have been heroic, but it was sage advice, and you could say Dunbar saved the day by saving the king. Henry's most recent biographer, Chris Given-Wilson, is in no doubt: 'battle hardened Dunbar who proved the greater asset on the day, his influence on the outcome . . . thought by some to have been pivotal'.[41] King Henry evidently thought so, as Dunbar was permitted to brand his herald as 'Shrewsbury Herald'.[42]

Wyntoun, as might be expected, casts Douglas as hero. The Tineman did have a knack of choosing the losing side in all his battles but he was a tough customer who 'wreaked so much slaughter that beside the others he killed with his great mace three men disguised as kings in the hope that each was the real King Henry'.[43] Did the king have proxies on the field, decked out in his livery? There's some suggestion the Earl of Stafford died wearing the royal colours, though it's possible he fell in the opening archery duel and his loss, as commander, prompted the panic. Bower certainly credits Douglas with annihilating several proxies, but this may well be apocryphal.

Henry might well be tempted, even if this was somewhat bad form, unchivalrous even, to call for a few volunteers to double up. A bit like leading the forlorn hope in later centuries, the risk might be compensated with subsequent honours if the volunteer survived. If Bower is to be believed, at least three didn't. Adam of Usk records: 'there also fell two noble knights in the King's armour, each made conspicuous as though a second king . . .'.[44] Even if he heeded Dunbar's sound advice to take himself temporarily out of danger, Henry was credited with disposing of no less than three-dozen rebels in the melee beforehand, a respectable score, even if it's likely to have been exaggerated. Fighting raged hotly around the royal standard. Besides Stafford, Sir Walter Blount also went down, 'the standard thrown to the ground and all those around it killed'.[45] *Gregory's Chronicle* claims Stafford was slain wearing the king's 'Cote armure' (livery) and died defending the flag. Perhaps he'd swapped colours when Dunbar persuaded Henry to take cover, a brave young man who's courage cost him his life.[46]

On the royal left, Prince Henry appears to have suffered a very nasty arrow wound quite early on, '. . . wounded in the face'.[47] A bodkin, probably a ricochet rather than a direct hit, struck him in the cheek.[48] But, as the later Tudor writer Edward Hall tells us, he continued fighting in the place of maximum danger and to encourage his men. Indeed, it was Hal who'd win the day, regrouping stragglers from the earlier panic and swinging his division in against the flank of Hotspur's swollen column. This clearly suggests the whole rebel line had advanced as one giant formation, gambling on a rapid exploitation and risking their exposed flank. This enabled the future victor of Agincourt to both save his father's throne and ensure the Lancastrian dynasty would survive.

Result

Once Hotspur's attack had run out of steam, he'd just have succeeded in punching a deep salient into the king's line. Without momentum, the juggernaut just becomes a mass, vulnerable on the flanks which is just where Prince Hal's counterattack struck home. It was now a battle of attrition, and it was nasty. Men half blind in plate, soon assailed by raging thirst, and swiftly reaching exhaustion would become disorientated. Dust and the steam from thousands of sweating men would further obscure any wider view. Few would be killed by a single blow, but a disabling wound, bringing the sufferer to his knees, would expose him to a further flurry, his skull then shattered, pierced through the visor or groin by daggers, hacked by bills, stamped on, kicked and slashed. Not a swift death, nor an easy one.

Illustrations from the period show the field heaped with the press of the slain, garnished by a slew of severed limbs, blood would run in great rivulets, splattering the living. Once one side broke in rout, casualties would begin to mount. Armoured men trying to flee towards horses tethered at a distance would be easy prey. Those less encumbered or not enfeebled by wounds might survive the race, others would not. The victors, their horses brought forward by grooms, would be swooping, circling, and striking like hawks.

Abbot Whethamstede, who may have been an eyewitness, graphically chronicles the fate of some of Warwick's men, fleeing from the debacle at 2nd St Albans in 1471:

> . . . The southern men, who were fiercer at the beginning, were broken quickly afterwards, and the more quickly because looking back, they saw no one coming up from the main body of the King's army, or preparing to bring them help, whereupon they turned their backs on the northern men and fled. And the northern men seeing this pursued them very swiftly on horseback; and catching a good many of them, ran them through with their lances.[49]

The Towton mass grave excavated during the 1990s, has provided a grim insight into the brutality of fifteenth-century warfare. Some forty-three skeletons were unearthed; most of these had suffered a series of massive head injuries, puncture wounds, and calamitous fractures with evidence of specific and deliberate dagger thrusts to the back of the skull, either a *coup de grâce* or cold-blooded execution. In either event the victim would have been stripped of head protection at the fatal moment.[50]

At some point Hotspur, perhaps sensing the hoped-for moment of triumph, so tantalisingly close, was beginning to slip away, gathered up a commando of thirty men, probably including Douglas for a final surge towards the king, or at least whoever looked most likely. This tactic wasn't new; Duke William at Hastings had sent in a chosen cadre of knights to do for King Harold, they succeeded. James IV of Scotland at Flodden in 1513 tried the same tactic and died in the attempt. As did Hotspur. We're not sure if the knights on either side fought mounted or dismounted, both had risks but probably they formed up on foot for the charge. It was Harry Percy's last gambit and, at some point he went down, either to an archer's well-placed shaft or an unknown assailant.

Any man who killed Harry Hotspur would be sure to brag about it so possibly it was an archer who accounted for the rebel leader. It does seem Prince Henry, having reformed his own bowmen on that wing, ordered his men to shoot into the tightly packed enemy column. Again, Inherent Military Probability would dictate he'd do so, too good an opportunity to miss, too obvious and inviting a target. Did Hotspur raise his visor at an inopportune time to get a better view? It can be surmised that detached archers, specialists in killing, today known as snipers, stalked the field seeking out unwary targets among enemy officers. 'Butcher' Clifford at Dintingdale and Lord Dacre next day at Towton were both neatly and fatally sniped when they removed bevors to take water.[51] These stellar marksmen were not relying on a lucky random shot, they'd be tracking their victim waiting for him to do something daft.

Shadows were lengthening that summer's day as afternoon blended into evening. Nobody can be sure exactly when Harry Percy bit the dust, but it is known there was an eclipse of the moon at about 2030. Such a phenomenon, then unexplained, would have chilled superstitious men to the bone, the strange half-light blood red. This eclipse heralded the final act in that day's tragedy. Once it was shouted out that Harry Hotspur was down, his men would lose heart very quickly, the fact of his demise turned stalemate automatically into defeat. For all his status Worcester wasn't his nephew, lacked that stellar quality, the talisman of charisma which had brought the rebels to within an inch of victory.

'A Day Rather to be Celebrated with Tears than Triumphs'[52]

Suddenly another shout is heard! 'Hotspur is dead! Long live the King! Hotspur is dead!' Louder and louder rises the cry till it swells into a chorus of triumph that carries dismay into the rebel ranks. 'Hotspur is dead!' His followers look around in vain for the waving plume and the uplifted sword they know so well. Never again shall they hear the ringing tones that have so often led them to victory. Low lies the hero, trampled under the feet of friends and foes, an arrow through his brain. Young Harry Percy's spur was cold.[53]

Panic is a pandemic, it spreads like wildfire and has no vaccine, unless a few brave officers can rally their men. None did. It usually starts at the rear, those in the front line are too blinded by red mist and hemmed in. Once that trickle begins, it rapidly swells into a stream, a river, a torrent, and finally a flood. Men who've been fighting like lions only a moment ago, the fire in their veins turns instantly to water, and they run like rabbits. Worcester, Venables, and Vernon were all captured, they wouldn't be expecting any clemency, nor did they receive any. For Thomas Percy, Earl of Worcester, a sorry end to so illustrious a career.

Archie Douglas was most unlucky. Despite the sterling service his famous war axe had done, he was taken by Sir James Harrington, having been wounded yet again in the groin and this time losing a testicle.[54] He did at least survive, though once again becoming a prisoner. Dusk was on the fugitives' side and besides, the king's men were as exhausted and just thankful to be alive. Many rebels still were hunted down like cornered rats, traitors don't merit mercy. Some, like a squire to the Duchess of Norfolk, weighed down by harness, wounds, and tiredness managed to crawl into hidey-holes, in his case a hedge, and escape detection.

Walsingham gives us a note of casualties: 'On the King's side fell ten knights, many esquires, several servants and about three thousand were seriously wounded. On the rebel side most of the knights and esquires of Cheshire fell, in number about two hundred, not counting servants and foot soldiers, whose numbers I do not know'.[55] Adam of Usk suggests as many as 16,000 dead but this seems unlikely.[56] If Walsingham refers to 3,000 wounded from the king's army, then taking a standard ratio of dead to wounded of 3 to 1 this gives about 1,000 killed. It can safely be assumed that rebel losses were much higher, somewhere between 2,000 and 3,000.

And what of those many wounded? Despite the presence of brilliant practitioners and innovators such as Bradmore, available medical services were both rudimentary and sparse. Wounds, sensibly, were cauterised with hot pitch. Anaesthesia, with solutions mixed from herbs, was by no means unknown however, and surgical techniques perhaps more sophisticated than might be assumed. The king would have surgeons in his train and most lords might have their own. Even if your chances of survival from any head, chest, or intestinal wound were limited, it's worth reflecting on the sophisticated reconstructive surgery carried out on the Towton Archer.[57]

On 17 June 1815, in the wake of Prussian defeat at Ligny, Napoleon and his staff picked their way through the smouldering, blackened shells of villages that had lined the stream. Corpses were stacked like cordwood, lying as they'd fallen, the emperor's attendants had to shift piled bodies to create a passage, burnt-out alleyways were choked shoulder high with walls of dead. Similar sights would have greeted the victors of Shrewsbury next morning, when the red mist had cooled, and the chill of reaction set in. Most who'd fought would never have seen a battlefield the day after before, most would pray they'd never experience the like again. Men would lie in the grotesque contortions of violent death, sack-like and waxen in their indifference.

Spattered brains, ruptured and trailing intestines, wet, discarded offal marinating in a stew of human waste. During those short hours of darkness, the human jackals who crept out after sunset like rats to strip and pillage would have been at work. Many wounded would have quietly slipped away or those silent foxes hunting valuables silenced them with a practised stroke. Among the piles, many still moving, writhing in their agonies, animating the tumbled heaps with unnatural movement, their weakening groans a final dirge. I've spoken to men who served in the Falklands Campaign of 1982, and they told me that they'd extremely limited recollection of the killing which took place during their final battles but what they did remember and could never forget was walking the same ground the morning after, freed from red mist and seeing just what it was they'd done.

Provosts would have been allotted the ghastly job of digging mass graves. There were no great send-offs for those rebel dead by Shrewsbury, these were nobody's heroes, a despised enemy reduced to chattels to be got rid of. Those of us who live in rural areas will recall the foot and mouth epidemic of 2001, when funeral pyres for mountains of slaughtered livestock lit up the night skies and troops charged with the grisly task were seen on quiet country lanes as though we were at war. Nobody really wanted to ask. It was unnatural, deserted fields and empty byres, shameful somehow. The suffering of the animals didn't really count, they were livestock – commodities. So too the dead of Shrewsbury, even though they had been Englishmen, they weren't really like 'us', losers never are, they weren't liked, and they wouldn't be missed.

Not for them the heroic, Homeric torch-lit send-off. Mass graves, shallow and scraped in a hurry, tired and brutalized men fearful of contagion, dumping reeking faeces-covered corpses into the pits. These graveyard squads would be busy, cloths wrapped over their faces against the smell, smoke possibly to ward off contagion. Stripped of everything except their anonymity, bodies trundled on carts from ground to pit. This job was best done quickly and as near to hand as might be managed. No weeping widows, no cortèges, no dignity. This was disposal not interment. The wages of treason.

So ended 'the sorry battaille of Shrewsbury between English men and Englishmen'. Hotspur's body was taken by Thomas Neville, 5th Baron Furnivall, to Whitchurch for burial. However, when rumours circulated that Percy was still alive, the king had the corpse exhumed and displayed in the marketplace at Shrewsbury. After this, the king dispatched Percy's head to York, where it was impaled on one of the city's gates; his four-quarters were sent to London, Newcastle upon Tyne, Bristol, and Chester before they were finally delivered to his widow who had him buried in York Minster.[58]

> After him came a man spurring hard
> A gentleman almost forspent with speed
> that stopp'd by me to breathe his bloodied horse
> He asked the way to Chester; and of him
> I did demand, what news from Shrewsbury
> He told me, that rebellion had ill luck
> And that young Harry Percy's spur was cold.[59]

The man was dead, but his legend was only beginning.

Fair Rites of Tenderness – Legacy

For worms, brave Percy: fare thee well great heart!
Ill-weaved ambition, how much art thou shrunk
When that this body did contain a spirit
A kingdom for it was too small a bound
But now two paces of the vilest earth/Is room enough . . .
William Shakespeare,
The First Part of King Henry IV, Act V, sc. iv

When the old Earl of Northumberland, loudly disavowing his dead son's treachery, rode with due humility into York, he passed Hotspur's severed head spiked above Micklegate Bar.[1] Henry Percy survived by the skin of his teeth, half drowning in humiliation. Stripped of his office of Constable of England, cripplingly fined, and cast out, but he, for the moment, kept his head and his lands. Despite this suffering, he didn't learn and within two years was conspiring afresh. He would have known that this time there'd be no second or even third chances, neither he nor the king had likely viewed his submission as anything other than a temporary truce.[2] Henry Percy had lost his eldest son and a much-loved brother, and as his biographer observes, he'd have done best to count himself lucky to still be alive and able to enjoy the bulk of his estates, but Percies tended not to think that way. Admitting defeat wasn't really an option.[3]

The Last Gasps

This time round he allied with Richard le Scrope, Archbishop of York and Thomas Mowbray, Earl of Nottingham. De Fonblanque tries to exonerate the old earl by envisioning him as a tool of his fellow conspirators but this is mere hagiography, he certainly knew what he was doing.[4] This current attempt was a predicable fiasco and Percy, accompanied by Lord Bardolph with a few hundred spears, escaped into Scotland. Scrope and Nottingham lost their heads, Northumberland all his vast acres; he'd played neatly into the king's hands. The ageing rebel toured Europe seeking support and found none. In summer 1407, empty-handed, he was back in Scotland still trying to scrape together an army.

Northumberland's current preferred candidate for the throne of England was Edmund Mortimer, 5th Earl of March.[5] Percy's star was waning, desperation ousted discretion and his foray into England that winter was effectively stillborn. Bad weather gave men a good excuse to stop at home. Leaving dismal, dreach, and unenthusiastic Northumberland behind, the would-be kingmakers stumbled into Yorkshire where they hoped their luck might change. It didn't. Having got down as far as Thirsk, Percy and Bardolph proclaimed their manifesto. Nobody cheered.

On 19 February 1408, a freezing Monday in a relentlessly cold winter, the old fox stood at bay on Bramham Moor, an ordinary belt of common land, a couple of miles south-west of Tadcaster. It is not known what size army the earl commanded but it was likely quite small, more in hundreds than thousands, a far and humiliating cry from Hotspur's host at Shrewsbury. Percy's force had moved through Boroughbridge and Wetherby, then on to Tadcaster where he was presumably hoping to raise further contingents from among his tenants there. As it was, his 'troops' were said to be a motley crew drawn from a raft of occupations, seized from bench or plough with few knights and men-at-arms. Thomas Rokeby, High Sheriff of Yorkshire with a body of local militia, probably around the same or similar numbers, was in hot pursuit. He set up a blocking position at Grimbald Bridge by Knaresborough, obliging Percy to try and edge past through Tadcaster where his recruiting was as successful as his strategy. The rebel earl turned to fight on Bramham Moor; he didn't have much choice.[6]

It was last ditch, and he probably knew this was a ditch too far. The battle was forced on him as he deployed his meagre 'army of liberation' to fight for their lives. Rokeby got his men onto the field at around 1400 and wasted no time on preambles. Details of the fight are sparse, but it's likely Rokeby's archers won that vital first round though it was he who advanced to contact. The action broiled over an area covering both sides of the Toulston Road, spilling over Camp Hill, Headley Hall, and Oglethorpe Hills.

De Fonblanque gives the earl and his lieutenant Bardolph suitably heroic deaths:

> Northumberland and Bardolph fought with all their native courage, stimulated by the energy of despair . . . The unequal contest is furious but short; the battle axe wielded by Bardolph's giant arm deals death around with every sweep, until transfixed by a lance through his throat he is overpowered, while him companion, bleeding from many a wound, falls dead.[7]

Some Percy apologists suggest Rokeby had lured Northumberland into an ambush, but this seems unlikely, Percy stage-managed his own destruction perfectly well.

Lord Bardolph in fact went down quite early on and the Earl's affinity crumbled into rout. Percy showed no great tactical insight but seems to have died in a desperate rearguard action, probably in small hollow nestling between Oglethorpe Hills and Old Wood, 250yd (239m) north off Toulston Lane. He was 66 and had taken his family's fortunes to the very zenith and crashed them down into the slush that now soaked up his life blood. Princes in the north no more. His venerable noggin 'with its fine head of white hair' alongside that of Bardolph was carried, stuck on a lance, down to King Henry, then at Stony Stratford.[8] This severed head was soon decorating London Bridge while his quartered carcass was variously garnishing locations at Newcastle, Berwick, York, and Lincoln.

Percy v Neville, the Road to Anarchy

Hotspur's death followed by that of his slippery parent might have been good news for the Nevilles and a relief to the Crown, but their joint loss had significant consequences. Nevilles did very well indeed out of their staunch Lancastrian adherence and the Percy lion was, at least for now, eclipsed. Nonetheless, Hotspur's son carefully and meticulously clawed back fragments of his great patrimony, grovelling, and abasing as much as he needed to start the long road back to rebuilding an affinity. It took him thirty years and the main block remained those Nevilles. Eventually, their simmering rivalry would ignite into a low-intensity regional war, the sparks of which lit up a wider conflict in a divided realm and, you could say, led to another thirty years of sporadic civil war and magnatial in-fighting, we call the Wars of the Roses. And just possibly, none of it ever need have happened anyway if it wasn't for those two great houses in the north of England, Percies and Nevilles. This too was part of Harry Hotspur's legacy.

When, in the north, Percy adherents tried to ambush a Neville wedding party, the affair on the surface may appear as little more than a local, bloodless brawl. Nonetheless, it could be said to represent the first significant, armed clash between these two pre-eminent northern affinities which were also active in the wider movement to reform and ultimately remove the Lancastrian administration.[9] That policy, begun by John of Gaunt, of buttressing the power of the Nevilles as a counterweight to the Percies was continued by Henry VI and the rise of the former was, not infrequently, at the expense of the latter.[10] Neville prestige was particularly high in County Durham, where the influence of their rivals was noticeably weaker.

Richard, Earl of Salisbury inherited the bulk of the Neville holdings in Yorkshire, centred on the valuable estates of Middleham and Sheriff Hutton. The worth of this legacy, Salisbury being the son of the Earl of Westmorland's second wife, sparked a deep division with the senior branch, which retained the title and lands in the north-west. Undisturbed by this family rift, Salisbury went on to steadily build up the scale of his holdings. His own eldest son, another Richard, added the dazzling Beauchamp inheritance and the earldom of Warwick to his titles and was to mature into a key figure of the political landscape, bringing the power of his name to its ultimate zenith before crashing to ruin: 'Warwick the Kingmaker'.

The three ridings of Yorkshire were parcelled out, in terms of land ownership, between four of the greatest magnates of the realm, including the Crown as Duchy of Lancaster, the Percies, Nevilles, and the Duke of York, Salisbury's brother-in-law. The Percy holdings east of the Pennines were interspersed with those of Salisbury and York, though the latter showed little interest in his northern estates.[11] Having taken the years from 1416–40 for the 2nd Earl of Northumberland to recover the bulk of his father's lost inheritance, Salisbury, who had been elevated to his earldom in 1429, had had ample time to consolidate his hold on manors in Cleveland, Westmorland, Cumberland, and the important lordship of Raby.[12]

Most aggressive of the Percy brood was the 2nd earl's younger son, Lord Egremont, who had threatened the life of the Sheriff of Cumberland, Thomas de la Mare, an adherent of Salisbury.[13] Egremont, who had gained his lordship in 1449, at the age of 25, typified all the adverse traits of his name: '. . . quarrelsome, violent and contemptuous of all authority, he possessed all the worst characteristics of a Percy for which his grandfather [Hotspur] is still a byword'.[14] Salisbury's sister, Eleanor, was married to Northumberland, but the ties of blood counted for little in a game with such high stakes. Both families possessed mature and ambitious patriarchs, each with a brood of young, restless, and potentially lawless sons, and no shortage of available manpower.[15]

When Thomas Neville married Maud Stanhope this proved a provocation too far for the volatile Egremont. The bride had been married before, to Robert, Lord Willoughby of Eresby, who had died the previous summer. She was also, and significantly, the niece and co-heiress of Ralph, Lord Cromwell, a choleric character himself but one who had acquired the leases on two choice manors at Wressle and Burwell in Lincolnshire, previously in the hands of the Percies.

In February 1440 Cromwell had purchased the reversionary interest. Northumberland, whose line had spent lavishly on Wressle, had litigated in vain. When Cromwell married his niece to a Neville, he was adding insult to injury.[16] Tension had been mounting throughout the early summer of 1452. In June, the king had summoned both Egremont and John Neville, by the end of that month, Neville was laying plans for an ambush of his own. On 2 July, Henry dissolved Parliament and journeyed north to confront his quarrelsome vassals. He proposed that Percy and his affinity should be ready to serve in Gascony which would have got them nicely out of the way. However, the proposal came to nothing.

The king established a commission of Oyer and Terminer, the membership of which included both the rival earls, Viscount Beaumont, and some fourteen others.[17] A fortnight later, the commission was re-issued but to little effect. Salisbury, who unlike Northumberland, sat in the Council, undoubtedly used his influence to pack the membership with allies, including such Neville stalwarts as Sir James Pickering, Sir Henry Fitzhugh, and Sir Henry le Scrope of Bolton.[18] Despite the commission's excellent credentials, it proved ineffective amidst a rising tide of disorder and, by the end of July, a new and perhaps less overtly partisan body was set up under the guidance of Sir William Lucy, a knight of Northamptonshire and Council member, his leadership supported by leading counsel. Immediately Sir William set to work, summoning Ralph Neville, Sir John Conyers, Sir James Pickering, Sir Ralph Randolf, Sir Thomas Mountford, Richard Aske, Thomas Sewer, and John Alcombe. On 10 August nine Percy adherents were summoned, together with both Sir Ralph and Sir Richard Percy.[19]

Undeterred by the failure at Heworth, Richard Percy and a band of thuggish adherents now embarked on a spree of vandalism, culminating in the kidnapping of Lawrence Catterall, the bailiff of Staincliff Wapentake, who was roughly dragged from his devotions in Gargrave church on 9 September. He was subsequently incarcerated, at first in Isel Castle and, latterly, at Cockermouth, obviously the luckless man had, in some unrecorded way, offended the Percies.[20] The unrest continued; on 25 September, a brace of Percy retainers, a John Catterall and Sir John Salvin, pillaged the house of William Hebdon, vicar of Aughton. This may have been in reprisal for John Neville's plundering of the Earl of Northumberland's property at Catton.[21]

On 8 October King Henry wrote plaintively to both earls, asking them to exercise some degree of control over their headstrong siblings. At this time, the king's mental health was already causing concern, he had no history of instability and his queen and the court faction were not inclined to advertise the fact. The exact nature of the king's malady has never been definitively diagnosed, though catatonic schizophrenia has been suggested.

Whatever the cause, the plain fact was that Henry's deteriorating mental condition contributed to his administration's weakening grip on law and order. By 17 October Egremont had assembled perhaps fifty armed retainers, who mustered at Topcliffe. Rather less than half of these were from the Percy heartland of Northumberland or the City of Newcastle.[22] Heedless of feeble royal admonitions, both sides were squaring up for a scrap and a confrontation of sorts probably occurred at Sandhutton on 20 October.

Here, Salisbury and Warwick, joined by Sir John and Sir Thomas Neville, were bolstered by such trusty friends as Sir Henry Fitzhugh and Sir Henry le Scrope. Not to be outdone, the Percy affinity were led by the earl and Lord Poynings, Lord Egremont, and Sir Richard Percy. The standoff seems to have amounted to little more than bravado on both sides but the magnates themselves had now clearly shown their hands in the fracas. Battle lines had been drawn, even if very few blows had yet been struck.[23]

As the tempo of strife rose the king's grasp on reality declined and it had, by now, become impossible to hide the fact of his condition. Matters were further stirred by the birth, on 13 October of a son, Edward of Lancaster. With this York's hopes of securing the succession from a childless monarch vanished like the mist. Increasingly vociferous, the duke, as the senior magnate, was clamouring to be appointed as regent during the term of the king's illness, a demand the queen and Somerset were equally determined to resist. On 25 October, the Council convened at York with both Salisbury and Warwick in attendance. Both Northumberland and Lord Poynings were pointedly absent.[24] The duke of York had married Salisbury's sister, Cicely, the celebrated 'Rose of Raby'. As a man he was '. . . a somewhat austere, remote, and unsympathetic figure, with little capacity of inclination to seek out and win support from his fellow noblemen or from the wider public'.[25]

York had no love for Somerset, whom he perceived, almost certainly correctly, as the main block to his inclusion in the king's inner circle. No sooner was York in office than his former rival was consigned to a sojourn in the Tower.[26] Meanwhile, Lord Cromwell, notoriously litigious, had been at odds in the courts with Henry Holland, Duke of Exeter. The matter had become so heated between these two choleric peers that, in July 1453, both had been temporarily incarcerated. With the Neville marriage Cromwell found an ally in Salisbury, Exeter, inevitably, sought common cause with the Percies.[27] On 27 March 1454, the duke of York was formally installed as protector and, less than a week later his brother-in-law was appointed as Chancellor.

Secure in his high office, Salisbury summoned Egremont and Richard Percy to attend upon his convenience on pain of forfeiture and outlawry.[28] Whereas the Percies might disdain the king's feeble complaints, Salisbury, in the mantle of Chancellor, could not be ignored. York's appointment marked a period of more decisive governance, though the Nevilles were clearly, as ever, motivated by self-interest. Sensing the mood, Sir Thomas Neville of Brancepeth (not Salisbury's son but a younger brother of the earl of Westmorland, and no friend to his cousins) took the opportunity to 'take up' the property of Sir John Salvin at Egton in Eskdale. This was accomplished with a body of two-dozen armed retainers who lifted some £80 worth of 'gear'.[29]

In May 1454, York, as Protector, sent a strongly worded summons to the earl of Northumberland, ordering him to appear before the Council on 12 June. Lord Poynings and Ralph Percy were summoned to appear ten days beforehand. Already, on 3 April, Exeter had been removed from his lucrative and prestigious post of Lord Admiral.[30] Not unsurprisingly, the Percies were not minded to follow the path of humility.

On 6 May, they showed what respect they had for the new Chancellor by vandalising his house in York and roughing up one of his tenants, John Skipworth. Many of these now involved in this fresh rash of disturbances had been 'out' on Heworth Moor the previous summer. By the middle of May Egremont was mustering his affinity at Spofforth and there, on the 14th, he was joined by Exeter, bridling at his humiliation. Riotous behaviour broke out in the streets of York, alarming the burgesses, especially after the mob had brutally assaulted the Mayor and the Recorder. A wave of anarchy now swept through the North Riding, while Exeter, not to be outdone, busily stirred up trouble in Lancashire and Cheshire.[31]

Needless to say, an invigorated Council, supported by York, as Protector, was not inclined to remain inert while these troubles flared. Sir Thomas Stanley, the Duchy of Lancaster's Receiver for the counties of Lancashire and Cheshire, ably assisted by Sir Thomas Harrington, saw Exeter off in short order. The Protector himself entered the City of York on 19 May – the rioters fled the streets.[32]

Exeter, whose thuggish traits matched those of Egremont, was, nonetheless, one of King Henry's closest blood relations, tracing his line through John of Gaunt. It is conceivable he perceived, in this localised brawl, the chance to light a fuse that might unseat York and see him appointed in his stead.[33] On 21 May, with Egremont and his affinity, he reappeared in York and set about further intimidation of the much abused mayor and burgesses. Disorder flared up once again through the shire. Egremont was sufficiently inflamed to solicit aid from James II of Scotland. The Scots had recently violated the previous year's truce and the herald dispatched to Edinburgh to register the Council's protest was kidnapped at Spofforth. This smacked of rebellion and the rebels, as they could now be termed, planned to lure the Protector into an ambush beneath the walls of York.[34]

York summoned both the ringleaders to appear on 25 June and used the interval to consolidate his position and build up local forces. By 15 June, he was reinforced by Warwick and Lord Greystoke, a week later Lord Clifford, the earl of Shrewsbury, and Sir Henry Fitzhugh added their retinues. Several summonses had been issued and, several individuals suffered forfeiture or even outlawry, Exeter, Egremont, and Sir Richard Percy all failed to appear.[35]

For all their violent posturing the rebels had completely failed to achieve any serious objective. Exeter crept back to London. By 8 July he was in captivity, and by the 24th he had been safely incarcerated in Pontefract Castle. York did not feel sufficiently secure in the north with the Percies still at large to return to the capital.[36] Matters continued in this tense vein until the autumn when a further confrontation took place; this time at Stamford Bridge, heavy with ancient blood, some miles east of York and held by the Nevilles. Whether any actual fighting occurred is doubtful, but the Percy faction were confounded by treachery, when one of their own bailiffs, Peter Lound with some two-hundred followers, deserted.

The Nevilles, led by Thomas and John pounced on their discomfited enemies and captured both Egremont and Sir Richard Percy.

If the Nevilles felt they had cause for satisfaction, their triumph was short-lived for, in December 1454, Henry VI recovered his wits and was deemed able to resume the reins of government, the office of Protector was thus redundant. On 7 February Somerset was freed from the Tower and reinstated to all his many offices. A month later Salisbury bowed to the inevitable and resigned as Chancellor. A mere seven days after his departure Exeter was set at liberty. Somerset and the queen would be in the mood for retribution rather than compromise, a further and greater trial of strength now appeared inevitable.

What had changed since that earlier showdown at Blackheath was that York was not now entirely isolated – true the Courtenays, disgruntled at the duke's handling of their feud with Bonville, had switched their allegiance to the court faction. Now, however, York had the powerful support of the Neville earls, Salisbury and Warwick, with their large affinities. Somerset had blundered in allowing the alienation of the Nevilles who, with York, now believed the duke with Wiltshire, Exeter, Beaumont, and Northumberland, was at the head of a faction now intent upon their destruction. The situation was considerably more volatile than it had been in 1450; the scene was thus set for armed confrontation.

On 22 May 1455, the first armies clashed in the streets of St Albans, Northumberland was among the dead, as were Somerset and Lord Clifford; first blood had been drawn. A third Earl of Northumberland died at Towton, Sir Ralph Percy went down at Hedgeley Moor in 1464 and, in an ultimate humiliation, John Neville, Lord Montagu, was created earl by Edward IV. As ever the Percies staged a comeback, and the 4th earl proved a more circumspect character that played all sides effectively, though he eventually died very ingloriously trying to suppress a tax riot.[37] It could be said this was all part of Hotspur's legacy and his loutish grandson was a chip off the old block, his family despite his own unfortunate demise still pursued the same degree of swaggering bullying.

Henry Percy – My Life with the Bard

Our view of Hotspur is hugely influenced, perhaps definitively so, by Shakespeare when he wrote *The First Part and the Second Part of King Henry IV*. These form part of his cycle of history plays which have remained popular since first being performed in 1597–8.[38]

What the critics said: 'In 1784, Thomas Davies, in a collection of essays on Shakespeare's plays, observed that "in the opinion of Thomas Warburton, and I believe all the best critics, the *First Part of Henry IV* is, of all the author's plays the most excellent."'[39] The title page from the earliest surviving edition (1598) is illuminating: 'The History of Henry the Fourth; with the Battle of Shrewsbury between the King and Lord Henry Percy, surnamed Henry Hotspur of the North'.[40]

There are four major and inextricably linked principal characters: the king himself, uneasy on his usurped throne and at odds with both his powerful, indeed over mighty kingmakers, most loudly Hotspur, his own son Hal, seen as feckless and immature, and Falstaff, the classic comic foil. This Hotspur is truly another Hector, obsessed and driven by his pursuit of a chivalric ideal, a fine contrast to the prince who, in today's terms, is an idle waster. Yet, the essence of the drama is Hal's path to noble kingship and his flowering in the next play as Henry V, combining chivalric honour with ruthless realpolitik.

Naturally, Shakespeare uses an abundance of dramatic licence; this isn't history it's storytelling. When Hal and Percy meet in their Homeric final duel (the one that never happened), Hotspur goes down lamenting, 'O' Harry, thou hast robbed me of my youth'.[41] No, he hasn't; Percy was over twenty years older and by no means a youth; by the longevity stakes of the era, he was well into middle age. Percy is seen not so much as a pure rebel, after all Henry himself was merely a successful version, but as a kingmaker driven by an attack of conscience. He sees his family's previous support as a badge of shame, and he has set out to right a hideous wrong and salvage the family honour. While the *real* Hotspur was probably more focused on the family silver, Shakespeare gives him the chance to assume a greater degree of nobility by championing Mortimer's claim on the basis Henry had proved a worse tyrant than his predecessor.

We must always bear in mind that Shakespeare's history cycle is heavily influenced by the output of Tudor chroniclers. The overall burden of carefully constructed Tudor propaganda is that Henry's usurpation of the throne in 1399 offended God's sense of order and all the troubles that followed came as the Almighty's sanction against the English. Order and the correct balance wasn't restored until Henry VII defeated and killed Richard III at Bosworth in 1485. The first Tudor removes the last Plantagenet for the universal weal of the kingdom. Henry Tudor was, like Henry IV, a successful usurper whose claim to the throne was far more tenuous, if indeed it existed at all. Shakespeare's portrayal of Hotspur is a complex matter.

Falstaff, everybody's foil and by no means a fool, scorns honour – no more than a word he says, no more than 'Air' . . . 'who hath it, he who died o' Wednesday'.[42] His cynicism is countered by Hotspur's obsession and blind adherence. Percy sees honour as something tangible, a physical manifestation of all that is noble; honour is all, it banishes fear, he will fight any odds if honour flows from it.[43] At Shrewsbury he is almost cornered possibly without the parcel of allies he was expecting but he scorns despair with an Arthurian flourish. Like El Cid exhorting his followers to fight steep odds, the harder the fight, the greater the honour and renown to be won; death in a good fight can never bring dishonour.

What is hard to define is exactly how the medieval mind (as opposed to the Tudor version) would perceive the constituent parts of honour:

> First we must be more specific: what concerns us most of all is traditional male honour. Originally, to be honourable meant quite different things for men and for women. Whereas men took pride in sexual exploits, say, female honour was based on its opposite, chastity. Women were also expected to be passive and silent. The passivity demanded from them meant that they had only limited possibilities for maintaining their honour themselves.

Old Europe was a patriarchal society. An important part of men's honour was precisely to keep up the honour of women (women who did fight went beyond what was expected). Men performed this task by attacking and taking revenge on other men whose actions had compromised their wife's, daughter's, or mother's honour. But a man also reacted with violence when another man tried to diminish his honour directly, by insulting him, say. Thus, for men, honour and its defence were practically the same. Male honour depended on physical courage, bravery, and a propensity for violence. Being attacked or being insulted equally counted as stains upon a man's honour, which could only be washed away by counterattack. This idea probably originated among castes of warriors, but already in the Middle Ages artisans, merchants and peasants shared it moreover, any conflict between two or more men had repercussions for their honour.[44]

Honour is somewhat derided in our contemporary society, all too often associated with 'honour' killings in minority ethnic and religious groups and used to disguise the base and cowardly murder of a female relative who is perceived to have transgressed in some way. As explored earlier, it meant something hugely different to Hotspur, and Shakespeare picks up on this to characterise his hero – he becomes the epitome of chivalric notions of honour, still very current nearly two centuries later. Nonetheless, this remains an artist's view, Shakespeare's Hotspur is a dramatic creation conjured up by a selective view of historical sources. His audiences aren't paying for a lecture – they demand to be entertained.

Then there's Hotspur and women, or Shakespeare's version. He shows Percy as a rather distant husband, perhaps afraid his chivalric priorities will be deflected by womanly charms. He's almost an aesthete in his obsession, a warrior monk, a Hospitaller or Templar:

> this is no world
> to play with mammets [false gods or fake kings] and to tilt with lips.[45]

The Bard has ensured Hotspur's fame, without the plays it's hard to imagine this memory of Harry Percy would have endured so long or so loudly, overlooked like his thuggish grandson Egremont whose own death, heroic enough, at Northampton in 1460, barely raises a footnote.

Shakespeare's version endures and shows every sign of sustained vitality. His plays have been performed for over four centuries and attitudes to the portrayal of history and historical characters have migrated with the times. First performed toward the very end of Elizabeth's golden reign, they were banned under the dour strictures of the Commonwealth, then joyfully revived after 1660 and into the eighteenth century by, among others, the seemingly indefatigable Samuel Phelps:

> In his 18 years as manager of Sadler's Well's theatre, Phelps mounted nearly all of Shakespeare's plays as well as reviving several forgotten plays by Shakespeare's contemporaries. He first played Falstaff in *Henry IV, Part One* in 1846. His portrayal was very well received, and he went on to revive the role hundreds of times in his career. One particularly elaborate production in 1864 was staged to celebrate the tercentenary of Shakespeare's birth. Phelps had left Sadler's Wells by this time and had been enlisted by the managers of Drury Lane to help revive the fortunes of the grand old theatre. *Henry IV, Part One* with Phelps as Falstaff helped enormously. The scenery was particularly impressive. A pictorial replica of the representation of the battle of Shrewsbury was published in the *Illustrated London News*, accompanied by warm praise:
>
> 'The Shrewsbury battlefield was divided by a long ridge, and the numerous combatants, arrayed in bright armour, were concealed under its shelter, until, rising from their ambush, they filled the stage with their glittering figures, all in vivid action and stirring conflict. The brilliant effect . . . roused the audience to repeated plaudits. The new scenery . . . has been painted by Mr. Beverley, and the whole constitutes the worthiest dramatic effort of the time'.[46]

Grand Revivals

After the end of the Second World War and once austerity began to lift, there was another grand revival:

> It was not until 1951, however, that a Shakespeare company at Stratford had the resources to turn the history cycle into an impressive event. After the Second World War two successive artistic directors, Jackson and Anthony Quayle had turned the Shakespeare Memorial Theatre into a prestigious venue. Stratford's major contribution to the 1951 Festival of Britain was a season of four history plays – *The Tragedy of*

King Richard II, The First Part of King Henry IV, The Second Part of Henry IV, and *The Life of King Henry V* – staged on a single permanent set with actors carrying through their roles from one play to the next. As T.C. Worsley pointed out, 'only an organization such as Stratford has now become would be capable of presenting these four plays in this way'. Anthony Quayle had assembled a large, highly skilled cast. He played Falstaff himself, Michael Redgrave played both Richard II and Hotspur, Harry Andrews was Henry IV, and Richard Burton – at the time a relatively unknown young Welsh actor, was cast as Hal.

The project was heavily influenced by post-war theories about the connectedness of Shakespeare's history plays. Each play fed into the next, presenting the interwoven stories of Richard II's deposition and Prince Hal's gradual transformation into Henry V. Anthony Quayle wrote of the project: 'In approaching our tasks the producers – Michael Redgrave, John Kidd and myself, together with our designer Tanya Moiseiwitsch – never doubted but that the plays were written as one great tetralogy . . . We well knew that each play was strong enough to stand on its own feet, and that economic necessity had for many years forced them to do so; but the more we studied the more we felt that this practice of presenting the plays singly had only resulted in their distortion, and that their full power and meaning only became apparent when treated as a whole'.[47]

Shakespeare and therefore his characters were being re-defined in a shifting world of sharpening political perspectives:

This approach had the effect of radically altering general perceptions of Shakespeare's history plays. The project elevated Shakespeare's status as a political writer because it argued the existence of an elaborately planned historical series, and it elevated the status of Prince Hal because he became the central hero of a rediscovered national epic. The casting was integral to the over-all conception of the tetralogy and created an important shift of emphasis in *Henry IV, Part One*. Although Redgrave as Hotspur and Quayle as Falstaff were the acknowledged stars, both were prepared to rein in their performances to allow Richard Burton's Hal to dominate the story. Redgrave's Hotspur was a rough, impetuous Northumbrian, attractive in many respects, but less thoughtful, modest, and ultimately less interesting than Hal. Quayle's Falstaff was also designed to be less attractive than was usual. He seemed less genial, less in tune with Hal, more grotesque and more self-conscious in his role as the prince's jester than before.[48]

For the political left Hotspur seems hardly an ideal role model, an aristocratic gangster, bully, and militarist; he fits all their 'must-hate' stereotypes yet he's one of the few (if any) Shakespearean characters to be played by two on-screen Bonds – Sean Connery, as mentioned in 1960, then Timothy Dalton fifteen years later (Dalton was succeeded by the equally glamorous Hugh Quarshie). Norman Rodway played him in Orson Welles 1965 version, *Chimes at Midnight*, and most recently Tom Glynn-Carney in Netflix's idiosyncratic version *The King* in 2019. This is basically a deeply flawed and self-indulgent film, presumably intended for a 'Woke' audience and Hotspur reverts to stereotype, a brutish, aggressive, and foolish thug. He and Hal roll around a lot in a badly choreographed scrap.

Hotspur – The Verdict

What's the final say on Harry Hotspur then? Is he just a violent boor, charismatic knight errant, hero or fool, noble or treacherous, clever or plain daft? The answer is all of these, depending on circumstances or perspective. That's part of the problem we have, as with all historic characters, we've got to try and view them through the prism of their times not ours. Hotspur was born into a great magnatial family, one which was set to rise yet further, having come a long way in a few generations. With the earl as his father there seemed no limit on what ambition might achieve.

Being typical of his class, he is raised in a knightly elitist school which reveres tradition and martial glory, this is his very life blood, chivalry is his holy grail, an ideal of manly virtue which guides like a lodestar. That reality falls far short of the aspiration shouldn't blind us to its appeal or indeed to the sincerity with which it's held. His contemporaries would have seen nothing anomalous here; for the most part they felt the same. He was a luminary in the stellar league of European chivalry, never was his courage in question and that mattered as much if not more than most else. His defeat at Otterburn was a noble reverse, his role redeemed by sterling valour on the field. This was what he aspired to and he was successful.

At the same time, he was born into an era of dark ferocity when the simmering cauldron of the border wars bubbled into a fresh round of troubles. Not much courtesy here, both sides raided, robbed, raped, and murdered pretty much as their standard default position. Extreme and relentless violence was the only game in fashion. The mere fact his enemies gave him the epithet they did indicates he was able to excel in this school of extremely hard knocks. Viewed through the perspectives of the day, this was a form of achievement and a significant one.

Was he capable of cruelty – yes, he clearly shows that after Homildon, was he a swaggerer and a bully, imperious, priggish, and haughty? Yes, to all of those but then so were most noblemen of his day. Medieval magnates were a gentlemanly mafia, better manners, same morality; a caste apart who saw themselves elevated to an Olympian degree above mere commoners and most mere commoners accepted this social order. It seemed immutable, unchanging and for a long time it was, ordained and sanctioned by the God everybody believed in. Not a cosy God of church suppers and coffee mornings but a divine dictatorship based on fear. Piety was as much a part of life as breathing, God was everywhere and omnipotent. All the Hotspurs knew that however wide their acres, however tangible their power, however resonant their deeds, they came under God who had the power, at a stroke, to cast them down into the dust. You could kill a rival in battle and decorate woodwork with his body parts, but you might still endow a chapel to sing Masses for his soul, and in so doing help preserve your own.

Harry Hotspur wasn't a medieval rebel in the sense some biographers assert, the act of rebellion doesn't necessarily make you a stereotypical rebel. Hotspur was at the extreme edge of typical of his caste and time. He didn't strive ever to change the prevailing order just to move it around, so it better suited his family's ambitions. This too was within normal boundaries. A gentleman's role was to further his name, to increase family lands, and enhance prestige. This could be achieved by dynastic alliances, judicious acquisitions (in which the Percies traditionally excelled), as rewards for good service or as spoils of war, or indeed as any combination.

It is worth focusing on the fact Hotspur, as has been stressed, was born into an era of increased cross-border aggression when the Scots, cowed for a generation after Neville's Cross, began to fight back and cleverly. George Dunbar understood that fighting pitched battles against the English was too risky – even though, unusually for a Scottish commander, he defeated Percy at Otterburn. He believed in the same strategy as his French contemporary Bertrand du Guesclin adopted, guerrilla-style asymmetric war, nibbling at the flanks till they finally caved in, exploiting the enemy's weaknesses not playing to his strengths. It's perhaps one of the real ironies of Hotspur's life that it was really March who guided him to victory and Homildon and Douglas who abandoned a strategy of caution for the recklessness of the charge.

Warrior in Bronze

This was the dangerous world of Harry Percy, one he did not create but was born into, born to be a player and he was, at the end of the day, a top player in a league of wolves – for your enemies to grant you a respectful sobriquet was praise indeed. The last word goes to Robert Brooks, writing on Hotspur's new statue in Alnwick:

At fourteen feet [4.3m] high and brandishing a sword, he's certainly eye-catching as these exclusive pictures show. And in just under a month, the magnificent new statue of legendary Northumbrian knight, Sir Henry 'Hotspur' Percy, will be hoisted into place at the Duke's Memorial Garden on Pottergate in Alnwick, just yards from the castle which was his home more than six centuries ago.

The site was chosen from a wide number of possible locations throughout Alnwick, because it offered a large area, free from traffic, where people could gather to view it. Other options, such as next to the Bondgate Tower or the Market Place, were ruled out because of complex listed building regulations and potential conflict with vehicles. Geoff added: 'We realise that the statue will be visited by a lot of people, including groups of children, and this is a safe place to gather. We hope it will become a feature for the town.'[49]

Perhaps the figure in armour is more symbolic than intended. We think of Hotspur, history and stage portrays him as a warlord, a man identified by his war gear rather than his deeper personality. We don't trouble to look beneath the steel carapace. What might lie inside is far harder to interpret, obscured by time and fiction. We also tend to see biography in Manichean terms, the subject is a good guy in which case he can do no wrong or a bad guy and vice-versa. The case of Richard III is a fine example of this – to his disciples the last Plantagenet is a shining beacon, horribly maligned by those annoying, and highly successful, Tudors.

*   *   *

'History is written by the victors; legends are woven by the people; writers fantasise. Only death is certain.'[50] I suspect Hotspur would have agreed.

Appendix 1

The Ballad of Chevy Chase

The epic verses that so moved Elizabethan hero Sir Philip Sidney have been accepted as some of the earliest in the border ballad tradition. The version which Sidney heard was that of *The Hunting of the Cheviot*, at least according to Bishop Percy writing in 1765 and it might be it was the famous soldier's enthusiasm for this that prompted the composition of *Chevy Chase*. The exact relationship between *The Hunting of the Cheviot*, *Chevy Chase* and the equally well-known *Battle of Otterburn* is uncertain. Scott gives us *The Battle of Otterburn* in his *Minstrelsy* and this comes from the Herd manuscript, published in Herd's *Scottish Songs* from 1776. Later writers such as John Marsden take the view that its provenance is at least a couple of centuries older.[1] Here then is *Chevy Chase*:

> God prosper long our noble king,
> Our lives and safeties all!
> A woeful hunting once there did
> In Chevy Chase befall.
>
> To drive the deer with hound and horn
> Earl Percy took his way;
> The child may rue that is unborn
> The hunting of that day!
>
> The stout Earl of Northumberland
> A vow to God did make,
> His pleasure in the Scottish woods
> Three summer's days to take.
>
> The chiefest harts in Chevy Chase
> To kill and bear away.
> These tidings to Earl Douglas came,
> In Scotland where he lay:
>
> Who sent Earl Percy present word
> He would prevent his sport.

The English Earl, not fearing that,
Did to the woods resort,

With fifteen hundred bowmen bold,
All chosen men of might,
Who knew full well in time of need
To aim their shafts aright.

The gallant greyhounds swiftly ran
To chase the fallow deer:
On Monday they began to hunt
Ere daylight did appear;

And long before high noon they had
An hundred fat bucks slain:
Then having dined, the drivers went
To rouse the deer again.

The bowmen mustered on the hills,
Well able to endure;
Their backsides all with special care
That day were guarded sure.

The hounds ran swiftly through the woods
The nimble deer to take,
That with their cries the hills and dales
An echo shrill did make.

Lord Percy to the quarry went
To view the slaughter'd deer;
Quoth he, 'Earl Douglas promised once
This day to meet me here;

'But if I thought he would not come
No longer would I stay'
With that a brave young gentleman
Thus to the Earl did say:

'Lo, yonder doth Earl Douglas come
His men in armour bright –
Full twenty hundred Scottish spears

All marching in our sight.

'All men of pleasant Tividale
Fast by the river Tweed.'
'O cease your sports!' Earl Percy said,
'And take your bows with speed,

'And now with me, my countrymen,
Your courage forth advance!
For there was never champion yet
In Scotland nor in France

'That ever did on horseback come,
But if my hap it were,
I durst encounter man for man,
With him to break a spear.'

Earl Douglas on his milk-white steed,
Most like a baron bold,
Rode foremost of his company,
Whose armour shone like gold:

'Show me,' said he, 'whose men you be
That hunt so boldly here
That, without my consent do chase
And kill my fallow deer?'

The first man that did answer make
Was noble Percy, he Who said,
'We list not to declare
Nor show whose men we be.

'Yet we will spend our dearest blood
Thy chiefest harts to slay.'
Then Douglas swore a solemn oath
And thus in rage did say:

'Ere thus I will out-braved be
One of us two shall die!
I know thee well, An earl thou art
Lord Percy! so am I.

'But trust me, Percy, pity it were,
And great offence, to kill
Any of these our guiltless men
For they have done no ill:

'Let thou and I the battle try,
And set our men aside.'
'Accurst be he,' Earl Percy said,
'By whom it is denied.'

Then stepped a gallant squire forth, —
Witherington was his name, —
Who said, 'I would not have it told
To Henry our king, for shame,

'That e'er my captain fought on foot,
And I stand looking on:
You be two Earls,' quoth Witherington,
'And I a Squire alone.

'I'll do the best that do I may,
While I have power to stand!
While I have power to wield my sword,
I'll fight with heart and hand!'

Our English archers bent their bows,
Their hearts were good and true;
At the first flight of arrows sent
Full fourscore Scots they slew.

To drive the deer with hound and horn,
Douglas bade on the bent;
Two captains moved with mickle might,
Their spears to shivers went.

They closed full fast on every side,
No slackness there was found,
But many a gallant gentleman
Lay gasping on the ground.

O Christ! it was great grief to see
How each man chose his spear,
And how the blood out of their breasts
Did gush like water clear!

At last these two stout Earls did meet
Like captains of great might;
Like lions wud they laid on load
And made a cruel fight.

They fought, until they both did sweat,
With swords of tempered steel,
Until the blood, like drops of rain,
They trickling down did feel.

'O yield thee, Percy!' Douglas said,
'In faith, I will thee bring
Where thou shalt high advanced be
By James our Scottish king;

'Thy ransom I will freely give,
And this report of thee,
Thou art the most courageous knight
That ever I did see.

No, Douglas'; quoth Earl Percy then,
'Thy proffer I do scorn;
I will not yield to any Scot
That ever yet was born!'

With that there came an arrow keen
Out of an English bow,
Which struck Earl Douglas to the heart,
A deep and deadly blow;

Who never spake more words than these
'Fight on, my merry men all!
For why? my life is at an end,
Lord Percy sees my fall.'

Then leaving life, Earl Percy took

The dead man by the hand;
And said, 'Earl Douglas! For thy life
Would I had lost my land!

'O Christ! my very heart doth bleed
With sorrow for thy sake;
For sure a more redoubted knight
Mischance could never take.'

A knight among the Scots there was
Who saw Earl Douglas die;
Who straight in wrath did vow revenge
Upon the Lord Percy:

Sir Hugh Montgomery was he called,
Who, with a spear full bright,
Well mounted on a gallant steed,
Ran fiercely through the fight;

And past the English archers all,
Without all dread or fear,
And through Earl Percy's body then
He thrust his hateful spear.

With such a vehement force and might
His body he did gore,
The staff ran through the other side
A large cloth yard and more.

So thus did both those nobles die,
Whose courage none could stain.
An English archer then perceived
The noble Earl was slain;

He had a good bow in his hand
Made of a trusty tree;
An arrow of a cloth yard long
To the hard head haled he,

Against Sir Hugh Montgomery
His shaft full right he set;

The grey goose-wing that was thereon,
In his heart's blood was wet.

This fight did last from break of day
Till setting of the sun;
For when they rung the evening bell
The battle scarce was done.

With stout Earl Percy there was slain
Sir John of Egerton,
Sir Robert Harcliffe and Sir William,
Sir James that bold baron;

And with Sir George and Sir James,
Both knights of good account,
Good Sir Ralph Raby there was slain,
Whose prowess did surmount.

For Witherington needs must I wail
As one in doleful dumps,
For when his legs were smitten off,
He fought upon his stumps.

And with Earl Douglas there was slain
Sir Hugh Montgomery,
And Sir Charles Morrel that from the field
One foot would never fly;

Sir Roger Hever of Harcliffe too, —
His sister's son was he, —
Sir David Lambwell, well esteemed,
But saved he could not be;

And the Lord Maxwell in like case
Did with Earl Douglas die;
Of twenty hundred Scottish spears
Scarce fifty-five did fly;

Of fifteen hundred Englishmen
Went home but fifty-three;
The rest were slain in Chevy Chase

Under the greenwood tree.

Next day did many widows come
Their husbands to bewail;
They washed their wounds in brinish tears,
But all would not prevail.

Their bodies bathed in purple gore
They bore with them away;
They kissed their dead a thousand times
When they were clad in clay.

This news was brought to Edinburgh,
Where Scotland's king did reign,
That brave Earl Douglas suddenly
Was with an arrow slain.

'O heavy news!' King James did say,
'Scotland may witness be
I have not any captain more
Of such account as he!'

Like tidings to King Henry came
Within as short a space,
That Percy of Northumberland
Was slain in Chevy Chase.

'Now God be with him!' said our king,
'Sith 'twill no better be,
I trust I have within my realm
Five hundred as good as he!

'Yet shall not Scots nor Scotland say
But I will vengeance take,
And be revenged on them all
For brave Earl Percy's sake.'

This vow the king did well perform
After on Humble Down;
In one day fifty knights were slain,
With lords of great renown,

And of the rest of small account,
Did many hundreds die:
Thus ended the hunting in Chevy Chase
Made by the Earl Percy.

God save our king, and bless this land
With plenty, joy and peace,
And grant henceforth that foule debate
'Twixt noblemen may cease!

Appendix 2

The Art of War in Hotspur's Day

Real war was always a major and expensive undertaking. To provide a reliable supply of trained fighting men, as a replacement for the outmoded feudal host, Edward III had developed the contract system. The monarch, as commander in chief, entered into formal engagements, indentured contracts in writing, with experienced captains, who were then bound to provide an agreed number of men at established rates for a given period.[1]

Protracted and wide-ranging campaigns in France made the reputations of famous captains such as Robert Knollys, John Chandos, and numerous Percies, including Hotspur's uncle the Earl of Worcester. Service on the Border Marches was never likely to have the same degree of lustre. Frequently, it was the magnates who acted as main contractors, sub-contracting knights, men-at-arms, and archers in turn.[2] The provision of indentures and annuities was, as it appears, also employed by lords to bind their retainers. Humphrey Stafford, 1st Duke of Buckingham, killed in the Wars of the Roses battle at Northampton in 1460, had ten knights and twenty-seven esquires in his service. One of the former, Sir Edward Grey, was granted a life annuity of £40 in 1440; those further down the social scale might receive annual emoluments of £10 to £20.[3] Much of the evidence dates from the later fifteenth century, though it's almost certain things were remarkably similar a few decades earlier.

In addition to his professional retainers a lord could call out his tenantry, many of whom might also have military experience, especially in much-buffeted Northumberland. To these he might, if numbers were needed, round up a following of master-less men happy to have the protection of a great man's livery. A surviving indenture, dating from 1452, and entered into by the Earl of Salisbury and his tenant Walter Strickland, knight of Westmorland, lists the complement which Sir Walter was to muster: Billmen – 'horsed and harnessed' 74; mounted bowmen to the number of 69; dismounted billmen 76, with 71 foot archers, an impressive total of 290.[4] Archers, in most companies, were still the predominant arm, outnumbering bills by anything from 3 to 1 to 10 to 1.

When Sir John Paston was preparing to sail for Calais, he begged that his brother recruit four archers: '. . . likely men and fair conditioned and good archers and they shall have four marks by year and my livery'.[5] In short, these were to be permanent retainers, paid an annual wage. A particularly skilled archer belonging to a lord's household might command equal remuneration to a knight.

At any time, the king still had power to issue what were termed 'Commissions of Array' which empowered his officers to call up local militias who, in theory at least, were to be the best armed and accoutred men from each village in the county. This system, though time honoured, was much open to abuse. The antics of Falstaff provide a comic parody.[6] Contemporary letters from the Stonor correspondence, relating to the Oxfordshire half hundred of Ewelme, comprising some seventeen villages in that county, show that the catchment yielded eighty-five recruits, seventeen of whom were archers. The village of Ewelme itself provided six:

> Richard Slyhurst, a harness and able to do the King service with his bow, Thomas Staunton [the constable] John Hume, whole harness and both able to do the King service with a bill. John Tanner, a harness and able to do the King service with a bill, John Pallying, a harness and not able to wear it, Roger Smith, no harness, an able man and a good archer.

Those without any armour are described as: 'able with a staff'.[7]

Surviving muster rolls from the period also provide an insight into local levies. One held at Bridport in Dorset on 4 September 1457, before the king's officers, reveals that a man was expected to possess a sallet, jack, sword, buckler, and dagger. Of those on parade that day around two-thirds carried bows and had arrows; other weapons on show included poleaxes, glaives, bills, spears and axes, staves, and harness.[8] Dominic Mancini has left a vivid, eyewitness account of the appearance of the troops Richard of Gloucester with the Duke of Buckingham brought into London in 1483 to provide muscular deterrence for any citizen who might be tempted to think of resisting the usurpation:

> . . . There is hardly any without a helmet, and none without bows and arrows; their bows and arrows are thicker and longer than those used by other nations, just as their bodies are stronger than other peoples, for they seem to have hands and arms of iron. The range of their bows is no less than that of our arbalests; there hangs by the side of each a sword no less long than ours, but heavy and thick as well. The sword is always accompanied by an iron shield . . . they do not wear any metal armour on their breast or any other part of their body, except for the better sort who have breastplates and suits of armour. Indeed, the common soldiery have more comfortable tunics that reach down below the loins and are stuffed with tow or some other soft material. They say the softer the tunics the better do they withstand the blows of arrows and swords, and

besides that in summer they are lighter and in winter more serviceable than iron.[9]

These were those roaring northerners much loathed by their southern contemporaries and some would undoubtedly be grandsons of men who'd followed Hotspur's banner.

Civil wars do not promote chivalric conduct, vendettas tend to mar fair play and the decline in knightly values was much bemoaned by contemporary chroniclers, though vestiges persisted. In his work *Le Jouvencel* the chronicler Jean le Beuil, writing in about 1466, gives an insight into the mind of the fifteenth-century gentleman:

> What a joyous thing is war, for many fine deeds are seen in its course, and many good lessons learnt from it . . . You love your comrade so much in war. When you see that your quarrel is just and your blood is fighting well, tears rise in your eyes. A great sweet feeling of loyalty and pity fills your heart on seeing your friend so valiantly expose his body to execute and accomplish the command of our Creator. And then you prepare to go and live or die with him, and for love does not abandon him. And out of that there arise such a delectation; that he who has not tasted it is not fit to say what a delight is. Do you think that a man who does that fears death? Not at all, for he feels strengthened, he is so elated, that he does not know where he is; truly, he is afraid of nothing.[10]

Hotspur didn't fight those sorts of more gentlemanly wars, insofar as reality ever matched literary aspiration. His fighting was mainly guerrilla style against fast-moving raiders and in a war where atrocity was normal currency. The list of slaughters which accompanied battles, or which mired the wrack of defeat does not bear this chivalric ideal out. Thirst for revenge, fear, greed, and sheer expediency were all powerful realities. Hotspur was the traitor at Shrewsbury and chivalry stopped short of rebellion.

In terms of how high medieval generals thought in terms of strategies, these tended to be based purely upon the offensive conversely, tactics often assumed the defensive. Command was most frequently exercised by the magnates themselves; Divisional commanders would often be family or high-ranking members of the commander in chief's family or affinity. Hotspur fought with his brother Ralph at Otterburn, possibly with his father at Homildon, and his uncle at Shrewsbury, all the officers in each of his battles would be known to him, knighthood and chivalry were the basis for a true band of brothers even though they frequently behaved rather more murderously.

Campaigns in this era were typically of short duration, avoiding the need to keep forces victualled and in the field through the harshness of winter. Commanders might seek a decisive encounter. Rarely was an offer of battle refused. This doesn't imply medieval generals sought battle as a given, most preferred to avoid a head-on clash instead opting for manoeuvre, frightfulness, and sieges. Border scraps such as those wherein young Harry Percy earned his spurs and his name tended to be swift, sudden, and unforgiving, set-piece sieges such as Edward III's leaguer of Berwick in 1333 were relatively rare.

To stake all on the outcome of a single battle involved high risk.[11] Once forces were committed, a commander had little prospect of decisively influencing events. The soundest tactics can be undone by the fog of war – as Hotspur found out at Otterburn. Those border hobilers, sometimes called 'prickers', were deployed for scouting and vedette work. A lack of intelligence as to the enemy numbers and location could lead to disaster, again as Percy discovered. Knights and men-at-arms typically dismounted to fight on foot. Horses were sent to the rear, to be mounted only when the enemy was in rout. Pursuit of a beaten foe was rigorous and merciless, the slaughter indiscriminate. A wealthy captive in the French wars could be the making of a yeoman's fortune but a lord whose lands stood to be attainted by the victors had no commercial value. Personal animosities were a constant factor, exacerbated on the borders by the pernicious prevalence of the 'feid' or vendetta.[12]

Armies were still marshalled into three divisions or 'battles', the van, or vaward, main battle, and rear, or rearward. Deployment was in linear formation, knights and men-at-arms dismounted and ready, archers moving to the fore to shoot, all beneath the banner of their captain or lord. In the late fourteenth and early fifteenth centuries a commander had limited forces at his disposal. A single, significant defeat in the field would likely ruin his cause and not infrequently dramatically shorten his life.

Communications were dependent upon flags. Supply and victualling remained constant headaches and the spectre of treachery as omnipresent as Banquo's ghost. Hotspur fought against George Dunbar, the Scottish Earl of March at Otterburn, had him as a vital ally at Homildon, and faced him again as an enemy at Shrewsbury. After his death, his father tried to place the blame for the Shrewsbury campaign onto him. Heroes didn't necessarily have many friends and, as was said of the unfortunate captain Nolan after the Charge of the Light Brigade at Balaclava in 1854, 'dead men carry a heavy burden'.

Although armies deployed in line with opposing divisions aligned, this neat arrangement could go awry, depending upon weather and terrain, as in the twilight of Otterburn. A commander with a good eye for ground might try to deploy an ambush party for a flank attack. The Scottish flanking move at Otterburn in 1388 ultimately proved decisive, as did Prince Henry's attack at Shrewsbury fifteen years later.

Late medieval captains were, for the most part, literate and familiar with the tenets of their trade. Many, if not most, would have read the classical authors, such as the late Roman theorist Vegetius, whose *Epitoma Rei Militaris* was revised in the fifteenth century by Christine de Pisan. She also wrote the *Livre des fais d'armes et de chevalerie*, subsequently translated and popularised by Caxton as *The Book of the Fayttes of Armes and Chyvalrye*. It should not be assumed that Hotspur or his contemporaries were illiterate brawlers; they were not. These were professional fighting men for whom war was their trade and one at which they strove to excel.

In this era, the continental system of 'lances' was not popular in England. Companies were led by captains ('centenars') and formed up according to their chosen arms.[13] Platoons, perhaps four to a company, were officered by NCOs or 'vintenars'.[14] Banners were important, as morale boosters, signalling devices, and rallying points. The use of liveries did, at least, promote some degree of uniformity. In practice this consisted of a loose tunic or tabard which the soldier wore over his jack or harness in the lord's colours. The Percies, for instance, fielded a livery of russet, yellow, and orange with the badge of the Percy Lion rampant sewn onto the shoulder.

Going to the wars was, for the gentleman, a costly business. The late fourteenth and early fifteenth centuries heralded a final flowering of the armourer's art, fine plate armours that could resist even the deadly arrow storm. Italian harness of this era was skilfully and beautifully constructed to maximise deflection. Defences for the vulnerable areas at the shoulder, elbow and knees were strengthened.[15] A harness of this period might weigh about 60lb (30kg) and would not greatly inhibit the mobility of a robust man, trained since boyhood to move and fight in armour.[16] Medieval knights, even when fighting on foot, frequently bore a less onerous burden than the average 'Tommy' of the First World War, loaded with rifle and pack, ammunition bandoliers, wire, and tools and all on his back. In the 1450s the Earl of Warwick ('The Kingmaker') as his party piece would vault fully armoured onto the back of his horse. This was most impressive, particularly as the earl was in his forties.

Italian and German styles came together in Flanders, a flourishing centre of manufacture where Italian armourers produced a hybrid style that features the flexible, fluted plates of the Gothic combined with the more rounded pauldrons (shoulder defences) and tassets (thigh guards) of their native style. Such armours were sold in quantities in England as evidenced by their regular appearance in funerary monuments. For head protection the bascinet had not yet been replaced by the stylish sallet.[17] Although knights could move freely, even in full plate, thirst and heat exhaustion were constant threats even in winter campaigning.

Dressing for war was best achieved at leisure, before the enemy was in the field, as a contemporary author, writing in *c.* 1450, explains:

> To arme a man. Ffirste ye must set on Sabatones [armoured over shoes] and tye hem up on the shoo with small points [laces] that woll not breke. And then griffus [greaves, plate defences for the calves] and then cuisses [thigh defences] and ye breche [leggings] of mayle. And the Tonlets. On the Breast and ye Vambras [upper arm defences] and ye rerebras [lower arm] and then gloovis [plate gauntlets]. And then hand his daggere up on his right side. And then his shorte sworde on his lyfte side in a round rynge all naked to pull it out lightli [the sword is carried without a scabbard, hung in a ring for quick release]. And then put his cote upon his back. And then his basinet [bascinet – a form of helmet in use prior to the sallet] pyind up on two greet staples before the breste with a dowbill bokill [double buckle] behynde up on the back for to make the basinet sitte juste. And then his long swerd [sword] in his hande. And then his pensil in his hande peynted of St. George or of oure ladye to bless him with as he goeth towarde the felde and in the felde.[18]

While knights and men-at-arms would wear full harness, archers tended to favour padded jacks or brigandines, as the account from Dominic Mancini, quoted earlier, suggests. This fabric garment was finished with plates of steel or bone riveted between the inner and outer layers or, as in the cheaper version, simply padded and stuffed with rags and tallow. The ubiquitous jack was far cheaper, lighter and, for many purposes, more practical. Some were fitted with sleeves of mail to afford protection to the arms. Though archers traditionally didn't wear leg harness, billmen and men-at-arms would wear whatever they could afford or were able to loot, a seasoned campaigner augmenting his kit from the spoil of dead and captives. As an alternative to the expensive bascinet, foot soldiers might rely on the basic 'kettle' hat.

Horsemen's lances, grown heavier than the original Norman spear, were carried couched under the arm and used primarily for thrusting. The weight was such that the weapon had to be held with the point angled across the saddle, a difficult business that could only be accomplished with plentiful training. When used on foot the shaft was generally cut down in length to make for easier handling.

Around this time the knight's sword was reaching the apex of its development. Blades were designed for both cut and thrust. Long and elegantly tapering, with a full grip that could be hefted in one or two hands, in section resembling a flattened diamond; simple quillons, curved or straight, a wheel, a pear or kite-shaped pommel. This was the hand and a half or 'bastard' sword, the very 'King of Swords'. Such precision instruments were reserved for the gentry, extremely expensive to buy. Commoners carried a simpler, lighter, and considerably cheaper sidearm, a short single-edged blade with the quillons curving around up to the hilt to provide a form of crude knuckle guard.

Gentlemen and footsloggers both bore daggers. The long-bladed rondel with tapering triangular blade, hardwood grip, disc guard, and pommel was a popular style. Ballock knives, whose wooden handle featured two rounded protuberances of suggestive form, rather resembled the later Scottish dudgeon dagger. As handy as a tool as a weapon, daggers were carried by all ranks and might be used to stab an opponent or plant vegetables as the situation required. In battle the thin-bladed knife could be used to deliver a *coup de grâce* to an armoured enemy, either thrust directly through the eye slit of the steel visor or into the more vulnerable areas of armpit or genitals.

Only later, during the sixteenth century, did the term 'longbow' come into usage. A plainer expression, war or 'livery bow' was more commonplace during the fourteenth and fifteenth centuries. Retained or liveried archers normally carried their own bows but, in the long continuance of the French wars, the Office of Ordnance began issuing standardised kit on campaign to replace those lost or damaged. Thus, quantities of bows were manufactured to a standard or government pattern, like the infantry musket of following centuries. Yew was the preferred timber, though ash, elm, and wych-elm were also favoured. The weapon was usually between 5ft 7in (1.675m) and 6ft 2in (1.850m) in length, the cross section corresponding to a rounded 'D' with a draw weight of between 80 and 120lb, (40 and 60kg). A modern target bow has an average draw of around 45lb (22.5kg).

Arrows were crafted from a variety of woods. Roger Ascham, tutor to Elizabeth I and a noted sixteenth-century authority, advocated aspen as the most suitable, though ash, alder, elder, birch, willow, and hornbeam were also utilised. The shafts were generally around 2ft 6in (75cm) in length, fletching formed from grey goose feathers. Arrowheads came in a variety of forms, flat, hammer headed, barbed, or wickedly sharp needle-pointed piles or bodkins, designed to punch through plate and mail. Livery quality arrows were issued to retainers, 'standard' grade was just that, and 'sheaf' arrows came in bundles of two dozen.[19]

At each extremity, the bow was tipped with cow-horn, grooved to take a linen string and, when not in use, the stave was carried unstrung in a cloth cover. To draw, an archer gripped the bow with his left hand, about the middle, where the circumference of the wood was about 4½in (22.5cm) then he forced the centre of the bow away from him to complete the draw, using the full weight of his body to assist, rather than relying on the strength in his arms alone. Such strength, stamina, and expertise demanded constant drill. Practice at the butts was compelled by statute. The bow could kill at 200yd; every archer wore a leather or horn 'bracer', strapped to his wrist to protect against the vicious snap of the bowstring.

Effectively used, bows had proved to be a battle-winning weapon; at Homildon in 1402 a Scottish army would be completely routed by archers alone (see Act 7 above). Few who suffered the deadly hail of an arrow storm could have forgotten the experience. If gentlemen, secure in fine plate, enjoyed greater protection than their predecessors then the rank and file were less fortunate. Time and romance have, over the intervening years, cast a shroud of pageantry over the harsh realities of medieval combat. The truth is somewhat less attractive.

A commander with an eye for ground would always seek the position of best advantage, though elements in the topography, adverse weather, mist, and darkness could combine to upset the best-laid plans and, as at Otterburn, each side might find themselves equally confounded. Once begun close-quarter combat became an intensely personal affair; a hacking, stamping melee of bills and other polearms, sword, and axe. Men, half blind in plate, soon assailed by raging thirst and swiftly reaching exhaustion would become disorientated.

Dust and the steam from thousands of sweating men would further obscure any wider view. Few would be killed by a single blow, but a disabling wound, bringing the sufferer to his knees, would expose him to a further flurry, his skull then shattered, pierced through the visor or groin by daggers, hacked by bills, stamped on, kicked, and slashed. Not a swift death, nor an easy one. Illustrations from the period show the field heaped with corpses, severed limbs, blood would run in great rivulets, splattering the living.

Once one side broke in rout, casualties would begin to mount. Armoured men trying to flee towards horses tethered at a distance would be easy prey. Those less encumbered or not enfeebled by wounds might survive the race, others would not. The victors, their horses brought forward by grooms, would be swooping, and circling like eagles. Abbot Whethamstede, who may have been an eyewitness, graphically chronicles the fate of some of Warwick's men, fleeing from the debacle at 2nd St Albans in 1461:

> . . . The southern men, who were fiercer at the beginning, were broken quickly afterwards, and the more quickly because looking back, they saw no one coming up from the main body of the King's army, or preparing to bring them help, whereupon they turned their backs on the northern men and fled. And the northern men seeing this pursued them very swiftly on horseback; and catching a good many of them, ran them through with their lances.[20]

The Towton mass grave excavated during the 1990s, has provided a grim insight into the brutality of fourteenth- and fifteenth-century warfare.[21] Some forty-three skeletons were unearthed; most of these had suffered a series of horrific head injuries, puncture wounds, and calamitous fractures with evidence of specific and deliberate dagger thrusts to the back of the skull, either a *coup de grâce* or cold-blooded execution. In either event the victim would have been stripped of head protection at the fatal moment.[22]

By contemporary standards, the available medical services were both rudimentary and sparse. The perceived presence of evil humours was the source of copious bleedings, quacks cast horoscopes and peddled bizarre potions. Wounds, sensibly, were cauterised with hot pitch. Anaesthesia, with solutions mixed from herbs, was by no means unknown however, and surgical techniques perhaps more sophisticated than might be assumed. Gerhard von Wesel, travelling in England in 1471, has left an eyewitness account of the army of King Edward IV as the survivors of Barnet trudged wearily back into London: '. . . Many of their followers were wounded, mostly in the face or the lower part of the body; a very pitiable sight'.[23] These, it must be remembered, were the victors.

Appendix 3

Otterburn – What the Chroniclers Said

While gossipy Froissart may be our most comprehensive primary source, there are numerous others, though these chroniclers often cause more confusion than they add clarity. The *Westminster Chronicle* tells us that on 12 August the Scots invaded England. Henry Knighton informs that the Scots entered England on the western side near Carlisle, plundering the countryside and capturing 300 men, including Sir Peter Tyrell (Sheriff of Carlisle) and other knights. He then says they escaped back over the border with no major losses. Walter Bower lets us know the Earl of Douglas had promised he'd join forces with the western attack near Carlisle. Instead, he gathered 7,000 fighting men and attacked in the east.[1]

The *Cronykil of Scotland* records that in 1388 (no month specified) the Earl of Fife raided England. At the same time, William Douglas sailed to Ireland with 500 men. The Irish of Dundalk gave him money to leave. He then returned and went south into England where he joined the Earl of Fife's army in 'Ryddysdale' (Redesdale). What can be said is that with a strong commando of say 3,000 spears, Douglas and March blazed a trail through Northumberland to waste County Durham, the *Westminster Chronicle* ramps up their numbers to an unlikely 30,000, destroying everything in their path en route to Newcastle, convincing the Earl of Northumberland that their forces were far stronger than they were.

1388 wasn't a vintage year for Richard II, embroiled with the Lords Appellant and the 'Merciless Parliament'; he probably didn't have much time to focus on his northern border. Besides, he had the Percies, his faithful hounds, to keep the back door shut. On 12 April Hotspur was confirmed as East March Warden and Captain of Berwick. This was made even sweeter by the eclipse of Sir Ralph Neville while his kinsman John, Lord of Raby succumbed to a lingering terminal illness which finally did for him that October. A Neville loss was ever a Percy joy.

When the Lords Appellant decided to have another crack at the French in June, this empowered the Scots to plan a clever, three-pronged riposte of their own. William Douglas of Nithsdale with Sir Robert Stewart of Durisdeer would launch a diversionary blitz in Ireland where they won a fight at Dundalk, torched Carlingford, and beat up Man before getting home unchallenged. The Earl of Fife, accompanied by Archibald the Grim, would attack through the WestMarch while the Earls of March, Moray, and Douglas would lead their own deep raid down the eastern side, another diversion but a powerful one. It was a sound strategy and it yielded dividends. In the west, Fife ravaged the Eden Valley, burnt Appleby, and menaced Carlisle, though, as ever, the city itself remained strong. In this careful and wisely limited overall strategy we can detect George Dunbar's savvy guidance.

This eastern force mustered towards the end of July (there are difficulties with dates) at Jedburgh with a forward base at Southdean kirk near Bonchester Bridge.[2] Froissart gives us an interesting anecdote; apparently an English spy had infiltrated the orders group in the church and overheard the bones of their plan. So far so good, dressed as a Scottish knight, he prepared to ride off but found the locals had, as ever, beaten him to it and nicked his horse. He then made the cardinal error of trying to slip nonchalantly away on foot but gentlemen ride, they don't yomp. He was soon in irons and giving up his secrets.

Froissart next tells us how the plan unfolded:

> The Scots went to County Durham, peaceably to start with, but then started to kill, burn and make war. News of this came to Newcastle and Durham and that the Scots could be detected by the smoke of the fires they set. The Earl of Northumberland sent his sons, Henry and Ralph to Newcastle while he stayed in Alnwick in case the Scots passed that way. From Durham and Newcastle was 12 leagues and all towns were burnt unless behind closed walls. The Scots crossed the Tyne again, to Newcastle. *Scrimmishing* took place and in one episode of hand to hand combat Douglas managed to take Percy's pennon.
>
> He told Percy he would fly it from his castle at Dalkeith, for all to see. Percy's response was that Douglas would not make it back across the border with the pennon, to which Douglas answered that he'd fly it outside his lodgings that night and Percy could see if he could get it back.[3]

The *Westminster Chronicle* just says the Scots attacked the English with losses on both sides while Douglas sent an abusive message to Henry Percy. *Scotichronicon* is even more succinct; Douglas arrived in Newcastle where the county's militia were waiting for him bolstered by additional ad hoc forces from as far away as York.[4]

Chroniclers generally seem to agree that there was some random skirmishing around Newcastle but none of them refer to the business of a captured pennon. Engaging as this is from Froissart, it doesn't mean it happened and even if it did that it was significant. Neither Douglas nor Percy were daft young lads, both experienced border fighters and actual single combat between champions was rare. This tale, however stirring and seductive, as the main cause of the battle which ensued should be viewed with scepticism. That Percy realised he'd been humbugged and that the Scots were far fewer than advertised must have become clear outside Newcastle's walls and the urge to teach them a lesson both imperative and tactically sound.

Froissart goes on to relate that:

> . . . next morning Douglas left Newcastle and arrived at Ponteland where he captured the castle of Edmund of Aphel before continuing to Otterburn some 8 leagues [44km] from Newcastle. They [the Scots] fortified their camp by siting it near the marshes. They placed their wagons at the entrance to the marshes and had all their livestock within the marshy land. The following day they attacked Otterburn castle, but it stood in marshland and they grew tired of their attack. The Scottish Earls had a council and most wanted to return via Carlisle, *but Douglas wanted to wait and see* if Percy would come and try to retrieve his pennon [author's italics].
>
> He [Douglas] still believed Otterburn castle was pregnable (i.e., could be stormed). Percy was desperate to pursue Douglas and reclaim his pennon, but the council who met in Newcastle said it was better to lose a pennon than 2 or 3 hundred knights and squires. However, once word arrived in Newcastle about what Douglas and his men had done Percy and his troops set off in Pursuit. He was told about Ponteland and Otterburn and that Douglas had only around 3,000 men with him. The Bishop of Durham had set off for Newcastle with an army in support, but Percy did not wait for him.[5]

Scotichronicon just tells us Percy went in search of the Earl of Fife's army but finding it too large decided to attack the army of Douglas instead.

John Hardyng, who was a Percy adherent and a zealous one, informs us that the Scots left Newcastle via Morpeth, moving northwards to Otterburn, where Percy engaged them with a small army. That's it and not very enlightening. Meanwhile the *Cronykil of Scotland* claims Percy saw that the Earl of Fife's force was strong and turned instead towards Earl Douglas who was in his country. Percy followed Douglas with 10,000 men and rode until he came to Otterburn in Redesdale.[6]

Harry Percy had perhaps 6,000–7,000 men, easily twice as many as March and Douglas. The traditional site of the battle is marked by a battle stone (not in its original position, however) and, as shown on the Ordnance Survey map, lies a mile or so (1.6km) north of the present township, with the waters of Rede on the left and rising ground to the right. Hotspur, coming from the south, light thickening, deployed for an immediate attack, detaching, it is said, a portion of his army under Umfraville to sweep northward around the Scots flank, an unlikely tactic given the gathering dusk and one that's been discounted above. The present A696 follows the route of the eighteenth-century turnpike. In Hotspur's day the road, as has been mentioned, lay along the dead-straight arrow from Cambo and past Harwood then down to Elsdon.

The *Westminster Chronicle* reveals both sides' plans: the Scots' intention was that their main strength would work around behind the English, cutting off their retreat. The English plan was similar, with Percy leading a frontal attack and Sir Matthew Redmayne the rear. However, Percy was too hasty and rushed off at Vespers (about 1800 hours) without organising his men into battle formation. He killed Douglas in his own tent, but the Scots, alerted by the noise and still in their armour, fought back. Henry and Ralph Percy were captured, 550 English died. The English were confused in the dark, especially by voices that sounded the same as their own and killed some of their own men in error.[7]

Bower in *Scotichronicon* says Douglas had pitched camp at Otterburn and was dressed for the feast of St Oswald (5 August) and without his armour on when a scout alerted him to Percy's rapid advance. The Scots rushed to put on their armour, but Douglas didn't fix his correctly which led to him being fatally wounded in the face and neck in the ensuing battle by an unnamed soldier. He was not found until the next day. Percy's men were crowded together, so he decided to split his army in two, with him and his brother leading one contingent and Redmayne and Ogle the other. The Scots took flight pursued by Redmayne and Ogle. Percy's contingent was rejoicing at the sight of the retreating Scots, but unknown to them Douglas had gathered his best men who advanced on horseback, hidden by thickets and thorn breaks. Shortly before sunset, they dismounted and attacked the English, who outnumbered them 3 to 1. The English line was broken by a Scot, John Swinton, enabling the Scottish troops to break through.[8]

It's more likely Hotspur directed an initial assault on the Scottish camp while he held his main brigade in readiness for a counterattack from a second Scottish camp higher up which held most of the knights and men-at-arms. This tactic proved successful, the servants and baggage masters holding the enclosed lower camp, even when partially reinforced, couldn't hold and were swept clear away with the English on that flank pursuing; so far so good. Meanwhile, Douglas, shielded by dead ground, prepared to strike at Hotspur's flank, a manoeuvre the Scots had trained for, having just such a scenario in mind. The melee was long and hard, hand-to-hand through the gloaming.

Froissart paints a dramatic scene:

> After laying siege to the castle at Otterburn, Douglas' men were tired. They ate and lay down to sleep. Percy's men arrived at their

lodgings but found servants when they had expected lords. There was fighting which allowed Douglas and his men time to put their armour on. It was a clear moonlit August night. Douglas and his men had already reconnoitred the area and knew of a 'little mountain' which would hide them from view. They set off for it silently. The English were busy fighting so were taken by surprise when Douglas and his men came from behind the mountain. Battle commenced. Both sides fought nobly, and the English had the best of it at first. When Douglas felt his men were weakening, he grabbed an axe and hurled himself into the fray. Eventually he was struck by three spears simultaneously, one to his shoulder, one to his breast (which also sliced his belly) and the third to his thigh.[9]

It's implied that even light summer darkness deprived the English of any chance of using their warbows effectively, and as the fight wore on the long day's march began to take its toll. In part Hotspur is still fighting as a quasi-guerrilla fighter, relying on dash and elan rather than more sedate, methodical reliance on the arrow storm. When Douglas' attack smashed home the Northumbrians faltered, though the Scottish Earl, leading the charge with berserker fury, was brought down with a catalogue of wounds and died, initially unnoticed in the half-light. As his army disintegrated the wounded Hotspur was taken prisoner, together with his brother Ralph. John Hardyng boasts Percy both killed Douglas and sent Redmayne, Grey, and Umfraville to cut off the Scottish retreat. However, the Scots regrouped and captured Percy who was taken to Dunbar and ransomed. Umfraville, Grey, and Ogle held the field and were unaware of Percy's whereabouts. He also tells us the battle was on St Oswald's Day (5 August).

The *Cronykil of Scotland* is more measured: Douglas received warning that Percy was nearby. He and his knights hastily tried to get their armour on. Some failed to do so properly. Percy divided his forces into two battles, and he had the larger brigade. Percy hoped to engage Douglas while the others under Redmayne and Ogle would ride round to the right to attack the camp. Douglas came around the Englishmen's flank screened by bushes. The English were watching the Scots flee from Redmayne and Ogle's attack but when Percy and his men saw more Scottish banners, they set off to fight in disarray. The battle began at sundown and continued all through the night. It resulted in a Scottish victory. Percy and his brother were captured, while about 1,000–1,500 men and horses were killed. Douglas too was killed but no one knew how this had happened.[10]

Both Hotspur and his brother Ralph fought well, the younger Percy found himself surrounded and under attack from all sides, he took more than a few hits to the extent his armoured greaves were full of blood, spilling from the joints. John Maxwell, knighted later on the field for his coup, captured the gravely wounded

Ralph and in best chivalric tradition, made sure his wounds were immediately tended.

James, Earl of Douglas was less fortunate. It seems unlikely he had forgotten his helmet; armoured headgear was pretty much de rigueur as head wounds were the most frequent cause of death. You would be well aware if you had not put a helmet on as even the best crafted hugely restricted both vision and hearing and became credibly hot. Froissart tells us Douglas seized a battle-axe to hew his way through the English line and barged forward. Three bills struck him at once (billmen would habitually take on an armoured foe with at least two working together). One point struck at the earl's shoulder, the second on the chest, though his harness deflected the blow downwards but the third caught him on the thigh. He went down and suffered further wounds including a fatal cut to the head.

Some from his affinity had tried to form a ring around him but his own impetuosity and the confused melee meant they couldn't save him. Sir James Lindsay, a cousin of his, with Sir John and Sir Walter Sinclair, along with his chaplain, found the dying earl. The priest, clearly of a more militant persuasion, was preaching the gospel of the axe at this point lending material as well as spiritual sustenance (this earned him an archdeaconry). Douglas knew he was done for but ordered his men to take up his banner and continue the fight. On that heroic note he expired, a most beautiful death.

Froissart does express some uncertainty over the exact manner of Douglas' death:

> Neither the Scots nor the English realised who he was. Henry Percy was captured. Ralph Percy [as has been seen] was seriously hurt and captured. The English outnumbered the Scots but were tired having ridden from Newcastle that day. The Scot, James Lindsay, believing Redmayne was fleeing the battle, set off after him. They fought and Redmayne took Lindsay prisoner. The pursuit by the English of fleeing Scots lasted five miles. When the Bishop, still in Newcastle, heard about the Scots, he set off to support Percy with his contingent, but Hotspur had been too impatient to wait for him, especially when he believed Douglas only had a small force; he [the bishop] set off for Otterburn with his soldiers but was halted by a rider who said the Scots were in pursuit.[11]

The *Westminster Chronicle* lets us know Redmayne was rather more successful, chasing the Scots to the border, killing 500 men, and capturing Sir James Lindsay. Meanwhile, the Scots who had captured Percy were baying for his blood, but his life was saved by the Earl of Dunbar. Knighton confirms the English captured Sir James Lindsay, brother of the Queen of Scotland. The dead numbered 1,000 with an additional 100 near Carlisle out of the 30,000 who fought against the

English and who were put to flight and driven into the 'water'. This presumably means the Solway, but it is unclear.

Bower says after the Scots broke their line, the English began to retreat and throughout the night were pursued. Many were killed or captured. Among the captured were Henry and Ralph Percy. The captives were said to outnumber the captors. One Scottish paladin, Sir John Swinton (destined to die in Northumberland, fourteen years later at Homildon), performed prodigies of valour, almost single-handedly breaking Hotspur's line.[12] Despite the loss of one of their leading captains, the Scots won the field, perhaps 500 died on either side and while the English survivors withdrew, it wasn't a total rout by any means. Though another force under the Bishop of Durham came up next day, battle was not resumed and the Scots, bearing the corpse of their earl, retired unmolested. The *Cronykil of Scotland* confirms Douglas' naked body wasn't discovered till next morning and with a large wound on his neck and more cuts to the face.[13]

The bishop's forces panicked and scattered; Froissart picks up on their dire performance:

> The Bishop decided to return to Newcastle as he was worried that pursuing Scots might gain entry to the town and resume his pursuit in the morning. Many others thought he could have defeated the Scots. He went back the next day with 10,000 men but turned away again because his men were so distracted by the noise of the Scottish horns that they decided not to fight. Ralph Percy and others were sent back to Newcastle to recover from their wounds against their word to surrender or pay their ransoms in due course. He states 1,040 English taken prisoner, 1,840 killed and more than a 1,000 wounded. The Scots lost 100 lives with 200 taken captive. The Scots retreated to Melrose where Earl Douglas was buried. They then began to ransom their prisoners; the date of the battle was 19 August.[14]

Generally, from an English perspective, the news was not well received, the *Westminster Chronicle* notes that when King Richard II heard of the battle, he was furious and met with his Council in Northampton on 22 August. It simply wasn't done for a Scottish army to defeat an English force, the Crown had rather got used to easy victories won at small cost, Dupplin Moor, Halidon Hill, Neville's Cross, and so many wins in France. However, it was decided that it was too close to winter to pursue the Scots so they would wait until next campaigning season and prepare. Meanwhile, the *Cronykil of Scotland* records that when the Earl of Fife heard about the battle he was angered at the loss of life. He returned to Scotland with his own forces via the Solway. The victorious Scots took the body of Douglas home with their wounded and prisoners.[15]

Landscape

Historic England has looked at the evolution of the battlefield landscape and points out an established agricultural and arable use for the valley floor, with evidence of medieval rigg and furrow. Despite this, pastoralism was probably more the norm at the time of the battle and indeed Glendale's fat cattle were frequently the target of Scottish raiders (plus probably a few English). Today both Akeld and Humbleton are small but may, in the fifteenth century, have been much larger, certainly both had chapels.[1] There may also have been more woodland. Since prehistory, the upper slopes of both Humbleton and Harehope Hills have been used as rough pasture; today's timber plantations are much younger. Eighteenth- or early nineteenth-century drainage has substantially firmed up the wet alluvial plain.

Historic England defines the battlefield area:

> Wherever possible, the boundary has been drawn so that it is easily appreciated on the ground. On the eastern side of the battlefield the boundary begins at the junction of the A697 with the road from Gallowlaw. The battlefield boundary proceeds south along the road from Low Humbleton to Humbleton and beyond, following the unmade road that skirts the edge of the Northumberland National Park as far as a series of enclosures on the right-hand side. From here the boundary line follows a path to the summit of Humbleton Hill and then down the other side until it meets the public footpath that runs between Humbleton and Harehope Hills.
>
> The boundary line continues in a westerly direction, runs along the escarpment to the south of Harehope Hill summit and then heads due north until it reaches the public footpath on Harehope Hill's northern slope. Such a boundary circumscribes the position of the Scots on Humbleton Hill and the English archers on Harehope Hill. Following a field divide past the reservoir the battlefield boundary skirts the eastern edge of Akeld, crosses the A697 and from spot height 56 heads north to the dismantled railway running nearly east-west. The boundary line then follows the railway to a copse north of Bowchester where it

turns southwards to return to the road junction in Low Humbleton, so completing the battlefield area. This northern half of the boundary accommodates the body of the English army.[2]

Obviously, this definition includes both hilltops which are very unlikely to have actually featured in the battle.

Glossary

abbatis   An obstacle forming part of a field fortification where branches of trees are laid in rows, ready sharpened with the ends pointing towards the general direction of the enemy.

advowson   The lord's right to appoint an incumbent to a living.

affinity   A magnate's following, comprising not just his own vassals or tenants but his friends and allies.

annuity   A grant of a pension for life, payable in annual instalments, usually granted by the Crown or magnates.

appenage   The lands of one of royal blood, with co-existent legal rights and privileges.

attainder   Statutory deprivation of one found guilty of treason, forfeiture of all estates, rights, and privileges in the context of the Wars of the Roses, the inevitable consequence of failure or defeat. The Act of Attainder was passed by Parliament and did not require a conviction of treason from the courts.

banneret   A knight who was entitled to carry his own banner, conferred status over more junior knights, likely to be given a command in battle.

bill   A pole arm, a deadly fusion of agricultural implement and spear, with a curved axe type blade, a spike for thrusting and a hook on the reverse, a formidable weapon in trained hands.

bombard   A heavy siege gun of the fifteenth century, irregular in calibre but throwing a massive ball, perhaps up to 60lb in weight.

bond   An agreement or contract, confirmed by the pledge of cash as a recognisance – a surety for the act to be performed or for the refraining from an act, obviously forfeited should the contracting party default on the terms of the bond.

captain   The officer responsible for a particular place or location but whose authority was limited to his charge.

Chamber	The fiscal aspect or operation of the Royal Household; the management of the Royal accounts as distinguished from the Exchequer, then as now the finances of the state.
Chancery	The executive and administrative function of the Crown.
chevauchée	A large-scale foray aimed at laying waste the territory of an enemy, to belittle the foe and perhaps force him to accept battle.
Commission of Oyer and Terminer	From the French, literally to 'hear and determine', the commissioners were Crown appointees charged to examine and investigate acts of treason, felonies (serious offence), and misdemeanours (lesser offence) committed in a particular county or locality.
constable	The official in charge of a magnate's tenantry who might exercise his office within the lord's residence or with his soldiery in the field.
crenellation	The form of battlements on a castle's parapet, 'licence to crenellate' being required before a castle could be constructed.
demesne	A lord or magnate's personal holdings, those occupied and managed by him as opposed to being parcelled out to a tenant or tenants.
destrier	A warhorse, much prized and of considerable value.
enceinte	The circuit of the walls of a defended castle or town.
feudalism	The system of government and land holding introduced into England by William I; the feudal pyramid, whereby land was parcelled out to the tenants in chief, together with rights attaching thereto, in return for a complex raft of obligations, inherent among which was military service for defined periods and duration. The system prevailed all the way down the social scale from sub-tenants to the unfree agrarian poor or villains. 'Bastard Feudalism' is a complex concept, championed by Stubbs in the nineteenth century but revised by MacFarlane subsequently – it embodies the notion of service being undertaken for cash payment rather than as part of a wider obligation.
fiefdom	A parcel of land, usually substantial, containing a number of manors with rights attached.
fosse	A defensive ditch.
gorget	A section of plate armour designed to protect the neck area.
halberd	A form of polearm with a broad axe blade.

hand and a half sword	The knightly sword of the fifteenth century, often known as a 'bastard sword', the long, tapering, double-edged blade used either for the thrust or the cut.
harness	Full plate armour.
hobiler(ar)	Lightly mounted cavalry or mounted infantry, associated with the light horse of the Anglo–Scottish border.
indenture	A form of legally binding agreement, the engrossment of which was, upon completion, cut into two halves along an indentation, an 'employee' or retainer could be contracted into service by means of an indenture.
jack	A form of protective doublet, stuffed with rags and generally sleeveless, worn by the commons, a more sophisticated form was the brigandine which had metal plates sewn between the facing and lining so that only the rivet heads, in decorative patterns, showed through the fabric covering.
kettle hat	A form of iron headgear worn by men-at-arms, with a wide protective brim, similar in appearance to British helmets, 'tin hats', of both world wars.
lance	A tactical unit built around a knight's following and could therefore vary in size.
leaguer	A siege or blockade.
livery	The distinctive coat ('livery coat') worn by the lord's retainers, bearing his badge, thus the expression 'livery and maintenance' – the retainer is clothed and fed by his employer in return, in effect, for wearing his private uniform (and assuming his private quarrels). The Battle of Empingham or 'Losecote Field' refers to the haste with which the panicked rebels cast off the incriminating livery coats of the erstwhile paymasters Warwick and Clarence.
mainprise	A form of surety or bond.
manor	A form of landholding, a knightly estate usually comprising the residence of the gentleman, a village or villages, woods, fields, mill(s), wine presses, church etc.
march	A frontier territory, administered by a warden, 'marcher' lords were those who held lands along the Anglo–Scottish or Welsh borders.
mesnie (meinie) knight	One of a lord's household knights, i.e., of his domain or demesne.

palatinate	Lands held by a count palatine, who enjoyed exclusive jurisdiction and extensive, quasi-regal privileges. The Bishops of Durham had the secular office of Counts Palatine for Durham and North Durham (Norhamshire in north Northumberland).
poleaxe	A polearm, favoured by the gentry for close-quarter combat, an axe blade, spear head, and a hammer for battering an armoured opponent.
rondel dagger	A fifteenth-century, long-bladed knife, carried by all classes, could be used as a weapon or implement.
sallet	A fifteenth-century helmet with a swept neck guard and often fitted with a fixed or moveable visor, worn above the bevor.
tenant in chief	Magnates who held their lands directly from the Crown, rather than from a superior lord, these were known as sub-tenants.
vassal	One who holds his land from his feudal superior on terms which involve an obligation of service as a condition of the tenancy.

Notes

Abbreviations of Commonly Cited Publications

CDS   J. Bain (ed.), *Calendar of Documents relating to Scotland*, Vol. IV, 1357–1509, Edinburgh, 1881–8

De Fonblanque E.B. De Fonblanque, *Annals of the House of Percy: From the Conquest to the opening of the nineteenth century*, London, R. Clay & Sons, 1887, Vol. 1

Froissart   Jean Froissart, *Chronicles of England, France etc.*, trans. Lord Berners, ed. G.C. Macaulay, London, Macmillan & Co., 1924

Hardyng   J. Hardyng, *The Chronicle of John Hardyng*, ed. F.C. and J. Rivington, England, 1812

Ridpath   G. Ridpath, *The Border History of England and Scotland*, Edinburgh, Mercat Press, 1979

Scotichronicon Walter Bower, *Scotichronicon*, ed. D.E.R. Watt, Edinburgh, John Donald, 2012, Vol. 7

Usk   *Chronicles of Adam of Usk 1377–1421*, trans. C. Given-Wilson, Oxford, Oxford Medieval Texts, 1997

Walsingham   Thomas Walsingham, *Historia Anglicana*, ed. H.T. Riley, Rolls Series, Cambridge Library, 2015

Introduction and Acknowledgements

1. https://www.britannica.com/art/tragedy-literature, accessed 17 March 2021.

Prologue

1. https://www.army.mil/article/50082/warrior_ethos#:~:text=The%20 Army%20Warrior%20Ethos%20states,by%20which%20every%20 Soldier%20lives, accessed 15 February 2021.

Act 1

1. Licence to crenellate was medieval planning consent for a castle.
2. W. Dickson (ed.), 'The Chronicles of Alnwick Abbey', *Archaeologia Aeliana* (1944), Vol. 2, p. 42. The kalends was the first day of the month in the Roman calendar.

3. http://www.northumbriana.org.uk/langsoc/, accessed 28 December 2020.

4. See A.J. Macdonald, *Border Bloodshed* (Edinburgh, Tuckwell Press, 2000), Chapter 1.

5. Barded = horse trappings.

6. The Black Death – bubonic plague – struck England in 1349 but took some while to spread to the north and longer still to Scotland. It isn't possible to calculate the percentage death rate on the borders, which was likely less than further south but nonetheless terrible.

7. De Fonblanque, p. xxi.

8. R. Lomas, *A Power in the Land: The Percys* (East Linton, Tuckwell Press, 1999), p. 3.

9. De Fonblanque, p. 3.

10. Ibid., p. 3.

11. Percy may well have crossed with d'Avranches, De Fonblanque, p. 11.

12. Lomas, *A Power in the Land*, p. 9 and De Fonblanque, pp. 21–2.

13. Lomas, *A Power in the Land*, p. 10.

14. A motte and bailey was a timber and earth fortification with a defended outer bailey and conical mound.

15. Lomas, *A Power in the Land*, pp. 10–11.

16. De Fonblanque, p. 17.

17. Ibid.

18. M. Lynch, *Scotland: A New History* (London, Pimlico, 1992), p. 53.

19. J. Kinross, *Walking and Exploring the Battlefields of Britain* (London, David & Charles, 1988), p. 48.

20. Lomas, *A Power in the Land*, p. 28.

21. Ibid., p. 29.

22. Ibid., p. 30.

23. Ibid., p. 37.

24. Ibid.

25. The Umfravilles were Lords of Redesdale with their main castles at Harbottle and Prudhoe.

26. It wasn't until much later that a full system of three separate marches on both sides came into being, allowing a magnatial family like the Percies such wide-ranging powers as only having two marches conferred clearly had its dangers.

27. Lomas, *A Power in the Land*, p. 44.

28. A banneret commanded a tail of men at arms from between ten and twenty in number.

29. G.W.S. Barrow, *Robert Bruce* (Los Angeles, University of California Press, 1965), pp. 206–8.

30. Ibid., p. 245.

31. Lomas, *A Power in the Land*, p. 47.

32. Ibid., p. 49.
33. *Scotichronicon*, Book XIII, p. 217.
34. Lomas, *A Power in the Land*, p. 56.
35. Ibid., p. 57.
36. Ibid., p. 61.

Act 2

1. Sir N. Pevsner and I. Richmond, *Northumberland*, 'The Buildings of England' Series (London, Penguin, 1992), p. 557.
2. https://www.britannica.com/topic/chivalry, accessed 17 November 2020.
3. Homer, *Iliad*, 2.12.310–28.
4. M. Keen (ed.), *Nobles, knights, and men at arms in the Middle Ages* (London, Hambledon Press, 1996), p. 39.
5. Beginning in 1198, the Northern or Baltic Crusades were attempts by Christian knights to colonize and convert the Baltic lands, generally by force of arms, a handy and worthy training and proving ground for European chivalry.
6. Keen (ed.), *Nobles, knights, and men at arms*, p. 112.
7. Ibid., p. 2.
8. Lomas, *A Power in the Land*, p. 59.
9. J.J. Pay (trans.), *De Arte Honeste Amandi* (New York, 1941), I, c, 1, p. 28.
10. De Fonblanque, p. 112.
11. Quoted by La Curne de Ste-Palaye, *Memoires de l'ancienne chivalries* (Paris, 1759), I, p. 276, n. 28.
12. William Shakespeare, *The First Part of King Henry IV*, Act V, sc. iv.
13. Account of the Deed of Arms at St Inglevert in the *Chronographia Regum Francorum*, ed. H. Moranville (Paris, 1897), Vol. iii, pp. 97–100.
14. Froissart, pp. 434–46.
15. The file was released in 1979.
16. https://www.poetryfoundation.org/poems/43926/the-canterbury-tales-general-prologue, accessed 23 November 2020.

Act 3

1. De Fonblanque, p. 100.
2. The Most Noble Order of the Garter was instituted by Edward III in 1348.
3. De Fonblanque, p. 101.
4. Gaunt and Percy were both descendants, one through the male and the other via the female line, of King Henry III. Lancaster's wife Blanche was also Percy's first cousin. Henry Percy then married Margaret Neville whose brother, as Earl of Westmorland, subsequently became his nemesis in 1403. The marriage

alliance did nothing to dispel the Percy/Neville rivalry, see De Fonblanque, p. 102.

5. Ibid., p. 106, in a note confirms that Thomas had been awarded the degree of Batchelor of Arts, conferred by the Pope himself.
6. Walsingham, p. 101.
7. Jean III de Grailly, Captal de Buch (1330–76), Froissart's great exemplar of chivalry. The first Battle of Soubise, the more famous second fight took place during the Huguenot wars.
8. See map in Macdonald, *Border Bloodshed*, p. 12.
9. TNA, SC6/951/5 and see Macdonald, *Border Bloodshed*, p. 17.
10. Macdonald, *Border Bloodshed*, p. 22.
11. William Shakespeare, *Romeo and Juliet*, Act 1, Prologue.
12. Rot. Scot, 1, 985 and T. Rymer (ed.), *Foedera, Conventiones, Litterae* . . . (1704–35), Vol. iii, 971.
13. See J.M.W. Bean, 'The Percies and their Estates in Scotland', *Archaeologia Aeliana*, 4th Series, xxxv (1957), pp. 91–9, they in fact clung on to Jedforest till 1404 and the fallout from Shrewsbury.
14. Hector Boece, *The Buik of Croniclis of Scotland*, trans. W. Stewart, ed. W.B. Turnbull, Vol. iii (Cambridge Library Collection, 2012), p. 396 and note De Fonblanque, p. 110.
15. J. Campbell, 'England, Scotland and the Hundred Years War', in *Europe in the Later Middle Ages*, ed. J.R. Hale at al. (Illinois, North-western University Press, 1965), pp. 184–216 and Macdonald, *Border Bloodhsed*, p. 45 et seq.
16. Froissart, p. 213.
17. Andrew Wyntoun, *The Origynale Cronykill of Scotland*, ed. David Laing (Edinburgh, Edmonstone and Douglas, 1872–9), III, 13.
18. Macdonald, *Border Bloodshed*, p. 49.
19. TNA, 401, *Exchequer Rolls, Army*, 45, Edward III.
20. De Fonblanque, p. 111.
21. John Wycliff (d.1384), was a religious reformer, philosopher, and academic.
22. De Fonblanque, p. 120.
23. G. Ridpath, *The Border History of England and Scotland* (Edinburgh, Mercat Press, 1776), p. 241.
24. Sadly, the rest was thoroughly purged in the mid-nineteenth century to make room for the railway station. Still, the elegant span of the Royal Border Bridge, which soars like a living sculpture over the river, offers significant compensation.
25. Walsingham, p. 77.
26. Ridpath, *Border History of England and Scotland*, pp. 241–2.
27. Walsingham, p. 77.
28. Ridpath, *Border History of England and Scotland*, p. 242.
29. Walsingham, p. 78.

30. Ibid.

31. Ibid., p. 239.

32. Mortimer was a Norman name, probably from Mortemer in the Seine Maritime, active in the service of William I as early as 1054. After the Conquest they became powerful marcher Lords on the troublesome Welsh border and highly active in the Second Barons' War. Roger Mortimer, 1st Earl of March led an unsuccessful rising, the Despenser War, against Edward II but then became Queen Isabella's lover and accomplice in a successful coup. He may or may not have arranged the gruesome murder of the deposed king in Berkeley Castle and ruled, effectively as military dictator, for three years before young Edward III carried out a countercoup at Nottingham in 1330 and removed his head. 'Anglo-Scottish relations in the reigns of Robert II & Robert III', thesis, University of Glasgow, 1971 Glasgow, 1971 http://theses.gla.ac.uk/72755/1/10647029.pdf, accessed 20 April 2021.

33. Rymer (ed.), *Foedera, Conventiones, Litterae . . .*, Vol. vii, p. 353. See also, E. Hamer, 'Anglo–Scottish relations in the reigns of Robert II & Robert III', thesis, University of Glasgow, 1971 http://theses.gla.ac.uk/72755/1/10647029.pdf, p. 158, accessed 20 April 2021.

34. Ridpath, *Border History of England and Scotland*, p. 242: a mark = 13*s*. 4*d*. or about £0.67p, roughly £4.5 million in today's money.

35. Ridpath, *Border History of England and Scotland*, p. 243.

36. *Scotichronicon*, p. 249.

37. Ridpath, *Border History of England and Scotland*, p. 243.

38. *Scotichronicon*, p. 248 and Wyntoun, *Origynale Cronykill of Scotland*, V, p. 283.

39. Ridpath, *Border History of England and Scotland*, p. 243.

40. De Fonblanque, pp. 134–5.

41. In theory each district was measured by the span of a day's 'march', though more probably on horseback.

42. These incidents occurred mainly in the sixteenth century, Sir Walter Kerr of Cessford and Sir John Carmichael were two examples and Queen Mary's Bothwell came close.

43. Ridpath, *Border History of England and Scotland*, p. 244.

44. *Scotichronicon*, p. 250.

45. Ibid., p. 251.

46. Ridpath, *Border History of England and Scotland*, p. 245.

47. Clement VII – Robert of Geneva ('the Butcher of Cesana), elected by French cardinals, who opposed Urban VI, the 'anti-pope'.

48. A.W. Boardman, *Hotspur* (Stroud, Sutton Publishing, 2003), p. 43.

49. Ridpath, *Border History of England and Scotland*, p. 245.

50. Baron de Clifford, the title was created in 1299 and the family, Anglo-Normans active in border affairs, the 1st Baron fell at Bannockburn.

51. *CDS*, 340, p. 77.
52. A livre was a form of currency, first established by Charlemagne and equal in value to a pound of silver (0.45kg), divided into 20 sous.
53. *Scotichronicon*, p. 253.
54. Ibid., p. 254.
55. Ridpath, *Border History of England and Scotland*, p. 246.
56. *CDS*, 347, p. 78.
57. Walsingham, p. 239.
58. Ibid.
59. Ibid.
60. Ibid., p. 244.
61. The barony was created for Sir Richard le Scrope in 1371 and became dormant on the death of the 11th baron in 1630.
62. Boardman, *Hotspur*, pp. 46–7.
63. Sir N. Harris Nicolas, *The Controversy between Sir Richard Scrope and Sir Robert Grosvenor, in the Court of Chivalry*, 2 vols (London, 1832), Vol. II.
64. Walsingham, p. 248.
65. Ibid.
66. De Fonblanque, p. 126.
67. Ibid.
68. Jack Straw was identified as one of the three prime movers in the Peasant's Rebellion.
69. Walsingham, p. 251.
70. An indenture was a document where the terms were repeated and then it was cut erratically across the divide so that the two halves would indent or fit together to prove authenticity.
71. *CDS*, 377, p. 83.
72. G.F. Beltz (*Lancaster Herald*), *Memorials of the Order of the Garter* (London, William Pickering, 1811), pp. 315–16.

Act 4

1. *The Works of Joseph Addison: Complete in Three Volumes: Embracing the Whole of the 'Spectator,' &c* (London, Harper & Brothers, 1837), p. 117.
2. https://www.northumberlandnationalpark.org.uk/; https://www.revitalising redesdale.org.uk/; http://www.battlefieldstrust.com/.
3. Froissart, p. 371.
4. Charles Wesencraft published his monograph in 1989.
5. See, Boardman, *Hotspur*, pp. 51–81 and P. Armstrong, *Otterburn 1388* (Osprey 'Campaign' Series, Oxford, 2006).
6. Thomas Percy, *Reliques of Ancient English Poetry*, ed. J.V. Pritchard, Book One: I 'Chevy Chase' (London, J. Dodsley, 1775).

7. Ridpath, *Border History of England and Scotland*, p. 247.
8. R. White, *History of the Battle of Otterburn fought in 1388 etc.* (Newcastle upon Tyne, Emerson Charnley, 1857), p. 30.
9. This is Burne's means of justifying assumptions if faced with lack of evidence; what would a competent commanding general do here? It is not a popular theory among academics but then very few of these have commanded men in battle, unlike Colonel Burne.
10. White, *History of the Battle of Otterburn*, p. 31.
11. Ibid.
12. Ibid., p. 39.
13. Ibid.
14. Sir J.H. Ramsay, *Lancaster and York*, 2 vols (Oxford, Clarendon Press, 1892).
15. C.J. Bates, *History of Northumberland* (London, Elliott Stock, 1895), p. 182.
16. W. Sitwell, *The Border* (Newcastle upon Tyne, Andrew Reid, 1927), p. 214.
17. Ibid., p. 216.
18. A.H. Burne, *More Battlefields of England* (London, Methuen, 1952), pp. 127–40.
19. Ibid., p. 136.
20. Macdonald, *Border Bloodshed*, p. 108.
21. Boardman, *Hotspur*, p. 63.
22. Froissart, p. 371.
23. 'King Robert's Testament' was the equivalent of Lawrence's *Seven Pillars of Wisdom* of its day.
24. Boardman, *Hotspur*, p. 68.
25. Ibid., p. 69.
26. Pevsner and Richmond, *Northumberland*, p. 537.
27. Dr E.C. Robertson, 'On the Skeletons exhumed at Elsdon and their probable connection with the Battle of Otterburn', *History of Berwickshire Naturalists' Club 1879–1881* (Berwick-upon-Tweed, Martin's Printing Works, 1882), pp. 506–9.

Act 5

1. De Fonblanque, p. 151 and *Issue Rolls*, 12 Ricard II, 15 July 1389, *CDS*, 395, p. 87.
2. *CDS*, 395, p. 87.
3. *Scotichronicon*, p. 262.
4. *CDS*, 425, p. 94.
5. Walsingham, p. 262.
6. Ibid., p. 30.
7. Walsingham, p. 266.
8. *CDS*, 436, p. 95.

9. Walsingham, p. 267.
10. Ibid., p. 269.
11. *CDS*, 419, p. 93.
12. De Fonblanque, p. 161.
13. Ibid., p. 162.
14. Ibid., p. 160.
15. Ibid., p. 161.
16. *CDS*, 474, p. 101.
17. Ibid., 481 and 482, p. 102.
18. The Holy Roman Emperor, or German-Roman Emperor, was seen by the Papacy as the natural successor to the Roman Empire in the West, dating from Charlemagne's days and therefore *primus inter pares* of the crowned heads of Europe.
19. Walsingham, p. 298.
20. Ibid., p. 301 and n., Richard gave those Cheshire men who'd fought for him at Radcot Bridge a bounty of 4,000 marks.
21. Ibid., p. 301.
22. Ibid., p. 302.
23. Ibid., p. 301.
24. Ibid., p. 302.
25. Ibid., p. 303.
26. Ibid., p. 304.
27. Ibid.
28. Ibid., p. 305.
29. Ibid., p. 306.
30. William Shakespeare, *Macbeth*, Act III, sc. iv.
31. Walsingham, p. 307.
32. De Fonblanque, p. 174.
33. Rymer (ed.), *Foedera, Conventiones, Litterae . . .*, Vol. viii, p. 85.
34. Walsingham, p. 308.
35. Ibid., p. 309.
36. De Fonblanque, p. 177.
37. Ibid., p. 186, n.
38. Boardman, *Hotspur*, p. 96.
39. TNA, E404 (Warrants under the Privy Seal), no. 46.
40. *Chronicles of the Revolution, 1397–1400*, trans. C. Given-Wilson (Manchester, Manchester University Press, 1993), pp. 35–6.
41. Hardyng, pp. 349–54.
42. *Chronicle of Evesham Abbey*, trans. D.C. Cox (Evesham, Vale of Evesham Historical Society, 1964), p. 129.
43. Walsingham, p. 309.

44. Sir Thomas Erpingham (1355–1428) loyally served three generations of Lancastrian kings.
45. De Fonblanque, p. 182.
46. Ibid., p. 184.
47. Walsingham, p. 309.
48. Ibid., p. 311.
49. Hardyng, pp. 349–54.
50. This was originally linked to the rituals of knighthood, bathing being a symbol of purity, the order wasn't fully established until George I's time, in 1725.
51. E.D. Kennedy, 'Dieulacres Chronicle 1337–1403', London, Gray's Inn, Ms. 9, ff. 129–47.
52. These two officers, Earl Marshal and Lord High Constable, shared responsibility for royal security alongside caring for the monarch's stabling and horses.
53. Shakespeare, *1 Hen. IV*, Act I, sc. i.
54. Died *c*. 1415.
55. Walsingham, p. 319.
56. Ibid. and Usk, pp. 100–1.
57. Usk, p. 95.
58. F.C. Hingeston-Randolf, *Royal and Historical Letters of Henry IV King of England and France and Lord of Ireland: 1863–1864* (Cambridge, Cambridge University Press, 2013), pp. 69–70.
59. Boardman, *Hotspur*, p. 122.
60. The text here is reproduced by kind permission of Alnwick Castle and translated by Chris Hunwick, but the originals are in the British Library, though also listed in De Fonblanque's appendices.
61. Ibid.
62. Ibid.
63. Ibid.
64. Ibid.
65. Usk, p. 107.

Act 6

1. Macdonald, *Border Bloodshed*, p. 137.
2. He followed the aptly named Archibald the Grim, a bastard son of the famous James the 'Black' Douglas, Bruce's ferocious and able lieutenant. Archibald did well in the Scottish service and David II, in 1369, appointed him Lord of Galloway. With the death of the legitimate 2nd Earl at Otterburn in August 1388, Archibald scooped up the other Douglas lands and titles becoming 3rd Earl, the most powerful man in Scotland.

3. This was quite a plum, site of King John's Palace and utilised by kings from Henry II to Richard II, thus it was in Henry IV's gift, the royal heart of Sherwood Forest.
4. Ridpath, *Border History of England and Scotland*, p. 256.
5. The Lord of the Isles was head of an ancient Norse-Gael confederacy under the hegemony of the chiefs of Clan Donald, while nominally vassals of the Scottish Crown, they were largely autonomous until 1493.
6. Macdonald, *Border Bloodshed*, p. 139.
7. Ibid., p. 141.
8. Robert III had mental health issues and appears to have been both depressive and incapable, so he relied on his very able and ambitious younger brother.
9. Macdonald, *Border Bloodshed*, p. 147.
10. Douglas was tried for the duke's murder more for the sake of form than any prospect of a conviction.
11. Thomas H. Cockburn-Hood, *The House of Cockburn of that Ilk and Cadets Thereof* (Edinburgh, 1888), pp. 43–4.
12. Sir J.B. Paul, *The Scots Peerage* (Edinburgh, 1905), pp. 137–8, where it is stated that the Sir Patrick Hepburn of Hailes who died at this battle was 'younger of Hailes', the son, not the father who survived him.
13. De Fonblanque, p. 206.
14. Boardman, *Hotspur*, p. 128.
15. J.L. Kirby (ed.), *Calendar of Signet Letters of Henry IV and Henry V 1399–1422* (London, HMSO, 1978), letter 77; see also De Fonblanque, p. 206, n.
16. Bower suggests this figure and it's generally agreed upon, Hardyng, as seen, gives the much higher and wholly improbable total of 40,000.
17. The 'bludy hert' was a powerful talisman, signifying Black Douglas' final doomed charge to retrieve a casket containing Bruce's heart in Spain en route to the Holy Land.
18. Macdonald, *Border Bloodshed*, p. 154.
19. *CDS*, 620, p. 403.
20. Ridpath, *Border History of England and Scotland*, p. 371. Newcastle Militia – probably marched north up the coastal route either before or as the Scots invaded (it is known that Douglas penetrated as far south as the Tyne).
21. Walsingham, p. 251.
22. http://www.battlefieldstrust.com/media/488.pdf, accessed 11 February 2021.
23. Armstrong, *Otterburn*, p. 83.
24. Hardyng, p. 359.
25. Ibid.
26. *Scotichronicon*, pp. 45–7.
27. Numbers: according to Bower, as mentioned, the Scots numbered 10,000; the only other authority to make an estimate stated that the Scots 'assembled

atop the hill of "Hamilton", near the town of "Vallor" [Wooler], to the number of about twelve or thirteen thousand fighting men'. The same source, the *History of the Life and Reign of Richard II*, numbered the English at 12,000 lances and 7,000 archers, see G.B. Stow (ed.), *Historia Vitae et Regni Ricardi Secundi* (Pennsylvania, University of Pennsylvania Press, 1977), p. 174.

28. If the Scots did possess a missile arm, these would likely be using the short bow rather than the more powerful English warbow, insufficient 'firepower'.
29. Walsingham, p. 251.
30. A.G. Bradley, *The Romance of Northumberland* (London, Methuen, 1908), p. 58.
31. *Scotichronicon*, pp. 45–7.
32. *CDS*, letter from Henry IV, 20 September, no. 620, p. 403.
33. Kirby (ed.), *Calendar of Signet Letters of Henry IV and Henry V*, letter 81; see also Ridpath, *Border History of England and Scotland*, p. 371.
34. *Chronicles of the Revolution*, p. 121.
35. *Chronographia Regum Francorum*, Vol. iii, p. 203; Macdonald, *Border Bloodshed*, points out that Heilly had been a comrade of the Earl of Crawford in his naval actions.
36. Hardyng, p. 359.
37. Macdonald, *Border Bloodshed*, p. 154.
38. Ibid.
39. Wyntoun, *Origynale Cronykill of Scotland*, p. 401.
40. Shakespeare, *1 Hen. IV*, Act I, sc. i.

Act 7

1. Ridpath, *Border History of England and Scotland*, p. 257.
2. Walsingham, p. 327.
3. https://www.escholar.manchester.ac.uk/api/datastream?publicationPid=uk-ac-man-scw:1m1843&datastreamId=POST-PEER-REVIEW-PUBLISHERS-DOCUMENT.PDF, accessed 16 March 2021.
4. J. Bean, 'Henry Percy 1st Earl of Northumberland', *ODNB*, 43, pp. 664–70.
5. S. Walker, 'Sir Henry Percy (Hotspur)', *ODNB*, 43, pp. 702–4.
6. A. Brown, 'Thomas Percy Earl of Worcester', *ODNB*, 43, pp. 737–9.
7. *Scotichronicon*, pp. 259–60 and Bower gives the putative King Richard's date of death as 13 December 1419.
8. *Scotichronicon*, Book VIII, pp. 289.
9. P. McNiven, 'The Scottish Policy of the Percies and the Strategy of the Rebellion of 1403', p. 500, https://www.escholar.manchester.ac.uk/api/datastream?publicationPid=uk-ac-man-scw:1m1843&datastreamId=POST-PEER-REVIEW-PUBLISHERS-DOCUMENT.PDF.

10. *Chronicles of the Revolution*, pp. 191–2.
11. J.H. Wylie, *History of England under Henry IV*, 4 vols (London, Longmans Green & Co., 1884–98), Vol. i, p. 246.
12. R. Davies, 'Sir Edmund Mortimer', *ODNB*, 39, pp. 375–6 and Hardyng, p. 359.
13. J.M.W. Bean, 'Henry IV and the Percies', *History*, xliv (1959), pp. 212–27.
14. McNiven, 'The Scottish Policy of the Percies and the Strategy of the Rebellion of 1403', p. 503.
15. Hardyng, p. 353.
16. *Chronicles of the Revolution*, p. 214.
17. Ibid., p. 204.
18. Ibid., p. 214.
19. McNiven, 'The Scottish Policy of the Percies and the Strategy of the Rebellion of 1403', p. 504.
20. Ibid., p. 505.
21. R. Horrox (ed.), *Parliament Rolls of Medieval England* (Woodbridge, Boydell Press, 2012), viii, 162–3.
22. McNiven, 'The Scottish Policy of the Percies and the Strategy of the Rebellion of 1403', p. 505.
23. Nothing now remains, https://www.thecastlesofscotland.co.uk/the-best-castles/other-articles/cocklaw-castle/, accessed 16 March 2021.
24. Walsingham, p. 326.
25. Wyntoun, *Origynale Cronykill of Scotland*, VI, p. 405.
26. https://www.facebook.com/ProjectHawick/posts/the-siege-of-cocklaw-hawick-the-rebellion-of-1403by-the-roadside-at-ormiston-two/1885960164806544/, accessed 16 March 2021.
27. *Scotichronicon*, p. 1153, n., guns, though becoming dominant in siege warfare, were not much used as yet on the border due the enormous difficulties entailed in transportation.
28. *Scotichronicon*, pp. 1156–7 and Wyntoun, *Origynale Cronykill of Scotland*, XXII, p. 405.
29. McNiven, 'The Scottish Policy of the Percies and the Strategy of the Rebellion of 1403', p. 511.
30. Ibid.
31. Hardyng, pp. 351–2.
32. McNiven, 'The Scottish Policy of the Percies and the Strategy of the Rebellion of 1403', p. 512.
33. Ibid., p. 513.
34. Ibid.
35. *An English Chronicle of the reigns of Richard II, Henry IV, Henry V and Henry VI*, ed. Revd J.S. Davies (Oxford, Camden Society, 1856), p. 27.

36. Ibid.
37. McNiven, 'The Scottish Policy of the Percies and the Strategy of the Rebellion of 1403', p. 514.
38. TNA, Chester 25/10, no. 2.
39. McNiven, 'The Scottish Policy of the Percies and the Strategy of the Rebellion of 1403', p. 514.
40. Ibid., p. 515.
41. Hardyng, p. 352.
42. De Fonblanque, p. 213.
43. Edward Hall, *Chronicle containing the History of England during the reign of King Henry IV and succeeding monarchs to the end of the reign of King Henry VIII* (London, 1809), pp. 28–9.
44. E.D. Kennedy, 'Dieulacres Chronicle 1337–1403', in *Encyclopedia of the Medieval Chronicle*, ed. G. Dunphy and C. Bratu, https://referenceworks.brillonline.com/browse/encyclopedia-of-the-medieval-chronicle, accessed 20 December 2020, pp. 177–80.
45. Ibid.
46. Walsingham, p. 327.
47. J.L. Gillespie, 'Richard II's Cheshire Archers', p. 1, https://www.hslc.org.uk/wp-content/uploads/2017/05/125-2-Gillespie.pdf, accessed 16 March 2021.
48. Ibid.
49. Ibid., p. 2.
50. Ibid.
51. Kennedy, 'Dieulacres Chronicle 1337–1403', in *Encyclopedia of the Medieval Chronicle*, p. 172.
52. Walsingham, p. 228.
53. *CDS*, iv, 136.
54. TNA, Chester 3/22, no. 5.
55. Hardyng, p. 361.
56. McNiven, 'The Scottish Policy of the Percies and the Strategy of the Rebellion of 1403', p. 519.
57. J.E. Lloyd, *Owen Glendower* (Oxford, Clarendon Press, 1931), p. 71 and McNiven, 'The Scottish Policy of the Percies and the Strategy of the Rebellion of 1403', p. 519.
58. McNiven, 'The Scottish Policy of the Percies and the Strategy of the Rebellion of 1403', p. 520.
59. Lloyd, *Owen Glendower*, p. 70 and McNiven, 'The Scottish Policy of the Percies and the Strategy of the Rebellion of 1403', p. 520.
60. McNiven, 'The Scottish Policy of the Percies and the Strategy of the Rebellion of 1403', p. 521.
61. Ibid.

62. Walsingham, p. 361.
63. Ibid.
64. His appointment in south-west Wales naturally raises the question of whether he had also connived with Glyndwr, McNiven, 'The Scottish Policy of the Percies and the Strategy of the Rebellion of 1403', p. 521.
65. Hardyng, pp. 321–62.
66. Walsingham, p. 361.
67. McNiven, 'The Scottish Policy of the Percies and the Strategy of the Rebellion of 1403', p. 517.
68. Walsingham, p. 361.
69. Ibid.
70. McNiven, 'The Scottish Policy of the Percies and the Strategy of the Rebellion of 1403', p. 525.
71. Ibid., pp. 529–30.
72. Ibid.
73. Ibid.
74. *Calendar of Patent Rolls, 1401–1405*, p. 297 and A.H. Burne, *The Battlefields of England* (London, Methuen, 1950), p. 64.
75. Walsingham, p. 327.
76. Shakespeare, *1 Hen. IV*, Act V, sc. i.
77. Walsingham, p. 396, Wyntoun, *Origynale Cronykill of Scotland*, XXII, p. 406 and De Fonblanque, p. 222.

Act 8

1. Letter from the field of Waterloo, 18 June 1815.
2. http://www.greatwar.co.uk/somme/memorial-delville-wood.htm, accessed 5 March 2021.
3. R. Brooke, *Visits to Fields of Battle in England, of the Fifteenth Century* (London, John Russell Smith, 1857), p. 9.
4. R.W. Eyeton, *Antiquities of Shropshire* (London, John Russell Smith, 1860), V. 10, p. 86.
5. William Dugdale, *Monasticon Anglicanum: A History of the Abbies and other Monasteries, Hospitals, Friaries, and Cathedral and Collegiate Churches, with their Dependencies, in England and Wales* (London, 1817–30), Vol. 3, pp. 1426–7.
6. J.B. Blakeway, 'Battlefield', *Transactions of the Shropshire Archaeological and Natural History Society* (1889), 2, 1, pp. 321–45.
7. Corbets were successors in title to the Husseys.
8. Brooke, *Visits to Fields of Battle in England*, p. 17.
9. T. Smith (ed.), *The Itinerary of John Leland the Antiquarian* (Oxford, James Fletcher, 1768), p. 83.

10. Brooke, *Visits to Fields of Battle in England*, pp. 11–12.
11. Ibid., p. 12, n.
12. Boardman, *Hotspur*, p. 178.
13. H. Nicholas (ed.), *Acts and Proceedings of the Privy Council* (1834) Vol. 1, liii.
14. Boardman, *Hotspur*, p. 178.
15. Burne, *Battlefields of England*, p. 73.
16. Shakespeare, *1 Hen. IV*, Act IV, sc. i.
17. Hardyng, pp. 371–2.
18. Walsingham, p. 327.
19. Hardyng, p. 352.
20. Walsingham, p. 327.
21. William Shakespeare, *The Tragedy of King Richard III*, Act V, sc. ii.
22. Edmund, 5th Earl of Stafford (1378–1403) had served as Lieutenant for the borders of South Wales, see Walsingham, p. 328, n.
23. Ibid.
24. Shakespeare, *1 Hen. IV*, Act IV, sc. iii.
25. Kennedy, 'Dieulacres Chronicle 1337–1403', in *Encyclopedia of the Medieval Chronicle*, p. 72.
26. *Chronicles of the Revolution*, p. 223, n.
27. Walsingham, p. 328.
28. Hardyng, p. 352.
29. Ibid., p. 361.
30. Hardyng, pp. 352–3.
31. Shakespeare, *1 Hen. IV*, Act V, sc. ii.
32. De Fonblanque, p. 224.
33. Walsingham, p. 328 n., editor thinks borrowed from the *Aeneid*.
34. Ibid., p. 238.
35. J. Barratt, *War for the Throne, the Battle of Shrewsbury 1403* (Barnsley, Pen & Sword, 2010), pp. 52–3.
36. https://www.quora.com/How-would-getting-shot-with-an-arrow-feel-and-result-in-comparison-to-a-gunshot, accessed 4 March 2021.
37. Walsingham, p. 328.
38. Ibid.
39. A falchion was a short, broad-bladed cleaver like weapon, mainly a slashing tool. A buckler was a small round shield, used to parry, block, and beat.
40. Walsingham, p. 328.
41. C. Given-Wilson, *Henry IV* (London, Yale University Press, 2016), p. 224.
42. A. Macdonald, 'George Dunbar, Ninth Earl of Dunbar', *ODNB*, 17, pp. 207–10.
43. *Scotichronicon*, Book VIII. 59.
44. Usk, p. 123.

45. The brother of Sir John and a seasoned campaigner who'd served both the Black Prince and Gaunt, see Walsingham, p. 328 and n.
46. J. Gairdner (ed.), *The Historical Collections of a London Citizen* (London, Camden Record Society, Old Series, 1876), Vol. 17, p. 103.
47. Walsingham, p. 328.
48. Prince Hal was saved by his surgeon John Bradmore (d.1412). Originally a metal, worker, he was serving time for counterfeiting at the time of the battle but his skills and the urgent need of them earned him an immediate reprieve. He attended his patient at Kenilworth Castle and the wounded prince still had some 5 or 6in of bodkin pointed arrow lodged in his cheek, perilously close to the brain stem. Bradmore was the last resort, others having failed. Firstly, he injected honey, a proven antiseptic, into the wound then used a surgical tool he'd devised for the purpose, not unlike a modern wine cork, to lock onto the bodkin and draw it out. The wound was cleaned out with wine or spirit. Bradmore was well rewarded for this service and later wrote a text, *The Philomena*, where he describes the operation, ground-breaking in its day. See F. Getz, *Medicine in the English Middle Ages* (Princeton, Princeton University Press, 1998), p. 8.
49. H.T. Riley (ed.), *Registrum Abbatis Johannis Whethamstede* (1872), Vol. 1, pp. 388–92.
50. A.W. Boardman, *The Medieval Soldier in the Wars of* the Roses (Stroud, Sutton Publishing, 1998), pp. 181–3.
51. The bevor was the plate section covering the lower face and neck.
52. J. Speed, *Historie of Great Britaine* (London, George Humble, 1623), p. 629.
53. De Fonblanque, p. 226.
54. Walsingham, p. 238.
56. Ibid.
56. Usk, pp. 168–71.
57. See V. Fiorato, A. Boylston and C. Knusel, *Blood Red Roses: The Archaeology of a Mass Grave from the Battle of Towton AD 1461* (Oxford, Oxbow Books, 2007).
58. https://historicengland.org.uk/listing/the-list/list-entry/1000033, accessed 4 March 2021.
59. William Shakespeare, *The Second Part of King Henry IV*, Act I, sc. i.

Epilogue

1. Micklegate Bar was frequently decorated with the heads of traitors; in 1461 it accommodated the Duke of York, Earl of Salisbury, Duke of Rutland, and Sir Thomas Neville; the 2nd Earl of Northumberland was one who helped place them there.
2. De Fonblanque, p. 229.
3. Ibid., p. 232.

4. Ibid., p. 233.
5. Edmund Mortimer (1391–1425).
6. Given-Wilson, *Henry IV*, p. 304.
7. De Fonblanque, p. 238.
8. Given-Wilson, *Henry IV*, p. 304.
9. R.A. Griffiths, 'Local Rivalries and National Politics; The Percies, the Nevilles and the Duke of Exeter 1452–1455', *Speculum*, Vol. XLIII (1968), p. 589.
10. H. Weiss, 'A Power in the North? The Percies in the Fifteenth Century', *The Historical Journal*, 19, 2 (1976), pp. 501–9.
11. Griffiths, 'Local Rivalries and National Politics', p. 589.
12. Ibid., p. 590.
13. Ibid., p. 592.
14. Ibid., p. 591.
15. Ibid., p. 592.
16. Ibid., p. 594.
17. Ibid.
18. Ibid., p. 595.
19. Ibid.
20. Ibid., p. 602.
21. Ibid., p. 603.
22. Ibid., p. 604.
23. Ibid., p. 605.
24. Ibid.
25. C. Ross, *Edward IV* (London, Eyre Methuen, 1974), p. 28.
26. Ibid., p. 29.
27. Griffiths, 'Local Rivalries and National Politics', p. 608.
28. Ibid., p. 609.
29. Ibid., p. 610.
30. Ibid.
31. Ibid., p. 611.
32. Ibid., p. 612.
33. Ibid., p. 613.
34. Ibid., p. 616.
35. Ibid., p. 620.
36. Ibid., p. 621.
37. Henry Percy the adroit 4th Earl (b.1449), met an ignominious end on 28 April 1489 when he was killed during a tax riot at York.
38. These comprise: *The First Part of King Henry IV, The Second Part of King Henry IV; The Life of King Henry V; The First Part of King Henry VI, The Second Part of King Henry VI, The Third Part of King Henry VI; The Tragedy of King Richard III.*

39. Shakespeare, *1 Hen. IV*, ed D.S. Kaston, 'The Arden Shakespeare' (London, Thomson Learning, 2002), p. 1.
40. Ibid., p. 4.
41. Shakespeare, *1 Hen. IV*, Act V, sc. iv.
42. Ibid., Act V, sc. i.
43. Ibid., Act I, sc. iii.
44. https://theconversation.com/honour-and-violence-in-europe-through-the-ages-32323, accessed 1 December 2020.
45. Shakespeare, *1 Hen. IV*, Act II, sc. iii.
46. https://internetshakespeare.uvic.ca/doc/1H4_StageHistory/complete/, accessed 1 December 2020.
47. Ibid.
48. Ibid.
49. *Northumberland Gazette*, 22 July 2010.
50. D. Kiš, *Encyclopaedia of the Dead* (Illinois, North-western University Press, 1998), p. 131.

Appendix 1

1. J. Marsden, *The Illustrated Border Ballads* (London, Macmillan, 1990), pp. 21–7.

Appendix 2

1. Indentured contracts were so-called as the counterpart document was carefully cut apart using a jagged line so the two halves when presented would fit perfectly together.
2. T. Wise, *The Wars of the Roses* (Oxford, Osprey, 1983), p. 22.
3. Ibid., p. 23.
4. Sir Charles Oman, *The Art of War in the Middle Ages*, 2 vols (London, Greenhill, 1924), Vol. 2, p. 408.
5. Wise, *The Wars of the Roses*, p. 27.
6. Shakespeare, *1 Hen. IV*, Act IV, sc. i – Falstaff: 'If I be not ashamed of my soldiers I am a soused gurnet I have misused the King's press damnably.'
7. Wise, *The Wars of the Roses*, p. 27. The Stonor correspondence is that of an Oxfordshire family in the Middle Ages, see C.L. Kingsford (ed.), *The Stonor Letters and Papers 1290–1483* (C.S. 3rd Series 29, 30m, London, 1919).
8. Wise, *The Wars of the Roses*, p. 27.
9. Ibid.
10. Boardman, *The Medieval Soldier*, p. 173.

11. When a lord sent his horse to the rear and took his place among the foot, this was perceived as influencing morale as the gentleman was placing himself in equal peril.
12. The pernicious code of vendetta exacerbated tensions with an endless cycle of internecine bloodletting, good for generations.
13. A centenar from the French 'cent' = 100.
14. A vintenar from the French 'vingt' = 20.
15. C. Blair, *European Armour* (London, Batsford, 1958), p. 77.
16. A.V.B. Norman and D. Pottinger, *English Weapons and Warfare 449–1660* (London, Arms & Armour Press, 1966), p. 114.
17. The bascinet was often called a 'pig face' on account of the shaped projecting visor.
18. R.E. Oakeshott, *A Knight and his Weapons* (London, Dufour Editions, 1997), p. 51.
19. C. Bartlett, *The English Longbowman 1330–1515* (Oxford, Osprey, 1995), pp. 23–30.
20. Riley (ed.), *Registrum Abbatis Johannis Whethamstede*, Vol. 1, pp. 388–92.
21. See Fiorato, Boylston and Knusel, *Blood Red Roses*.
22. Boardman, *The Medieval Soldier*, pp. 181–3.
23. Bartlett, *The English Longbowman*, p. 51.

Appendix 3

1. *Scotichronicon*, Book XIV, p. 255.
2. Southdean, or 'Souden', kirk survives on the banks of Jed Water. Built in the eleventh century, an early foundation of David I, the plan and internal dimensions are plainly visible.
3. Froissart, p. 372.
4. *Scotichronicon*, Book XIV, p. 255.
5. Froissart, p. 371.
6. *Scotichronicon*, Book CXCIV, p. 328.
7. *Westminster Chronicle 1381–1394* (Oxford, Clarendon Press, 1982), p. 346.
8. *Scotichronicon*, Book XIV, p. 256.
9. Froissart, p. 374.
10. Wyntoun, *Origynale Cronykill of Scotland*, p. 332.
11. Froissart, p. 377.
12. *Scotichronicon*, Book XIV, p. 256.
13. Wyntoun, *Origynale Cronykill of Scotland*, CXCIV, p. 332.
14. Froissart, p. 379.
15. Wyntoun, *Origynale Cronykill of Scotland*, CXCIV, p. 332.

Appendix 4

1. De Fonblanque notes that an entry in the Syon House papers records that when Dr Thomas Percy, the family's chaplain and chronicler, visited Humbleton (*c.* 1605) the street was still known as Percy's Row, p. 206, n. See also https://historicengland.org.uk/content/docs/listing/battlefields/homildon-hill/, accessed 11 February 2021.
2. Ibid.

Bibliography

Primary Sources

An English Chronicle of the reigns of Richard II, Henry IV, Henry V and Henry VI, ed. J.S. Davies, Oxford, Camden Society, 1856

Bain, J. (ed.), *Calendar of Documents Relating to Scotland*, Vol. IV, 1357–1509, Edinburgh, 1881–8

Barbour, J., *The Bruce*, Edinburgh, Canongate, 2007

Barr, J., *Border Papers*, 2 vols, ed. Revd J. Stevenson and A.J. Crosbie, Edinburgh, 1894

Blind Harry, *The Wallace*, ed. A. McKim, Michigan, Medieval Institute Publications, 2003, Book ii

Boece, Hector, *The Buik of Croniclis of Scotland*, transl. W. Stewart, ed. W.B. Turnbull, Vol. iii, Cambridge Library Collection, 2012

Bower, Walter, *Scotichronicon*, Vol. 7, ed. D.E.R. Watt, Edinburgh, John Donald 2012

Calendar of Charter Rolls, Vol. V, London, 1916

Calendar of Close Rolls, London, 1892–

Calendar of Patent Rolls, London, 1891–

Chronicle of Evesham Abbey, trans. D.C. Cox, Evesham, Vale of Evesham Historical Society, 1964

Chronicles of the Revolution, 1397–1400, trans. C. Given-Wilson, Manchester, Manchester University Press, 1993

Chronographia Regum Francorum, ed. H. Moranville, Paris, 1897

Clarke, M.V. and V.H. Galbraith, '*Dieulacres Chronicle*, 'The Deposition of Richard II', Bul. Jn. Ryl. Lib. 15 (1930)

Dugdale, William, *Monasticon Anglicanum: A History of the Abbies and other Monasteries, Hospitals, Friaries, and Cathedral and Collegiate Churches, with their Dependencies, in England and Wales*, London, 1817–30, Vol. 6

Froissart, Jean, *Chronicles of England, France etc.*, trans. Lord Berners, ed. G.C. Macaulay, London, Macmillan & Co., 1924

Gairdner, J. (ed.), *The Historical Collections of a London Citizen*, London, Camden Record Society, Old Series, 1876, Vol. 17

Given-Wilson, C. (trans.), *Chronicle of Adam of Usk 1377–1421*, Oxford, Oxford Medieval Texts, 1997

Hardyng, J., *The Chronicle of John Hardyng*, ed. F.C. and J. Rivington, England, 1812

Historical Papers and Letters from the Northern Registers, ed. J. Raine, Rolls Series, 1873

Horrox, R. (ed.), *Parliament Rolls of Medieval England*, Woodbridge, Boydell Press, 2012

Kennedy, E.D., 'Dieulacres Chronicle 1337–1403', London, Gray's Inn, Ms. 9

Kennedy, E.D., 'Dieulacres Chronicle 1337–1403', in *Encyclopedia of the Medieval Chronicle*, ed. G. Dunphy and C. Bratu, https://referenceworks.brillonline.com/browse/encyclopedia-of-the-medieval-chronicle, accessed 20 December 2020

Kingsford, C.L. (ed.), *The Stonor Letters and Papers 1290–1483*, Camden Series, 3rd Series 29, 30, London, 1919

Kirby, J.L. (ed.), *Calendar of Signet Letters of Henry IV and Henry V 1399–1422*, London, HMSO, 1978

Knighton, Henry, *Leycestrensis Chronicon*, ed. J.R. Lumby, Rolls Series, Cambridge Library, 2012 Series

La Curne de Ste-Palaye, *Memoires de l'ancienne chivalries*, Paris, 1759

Nicholas, H. (ed.), *Acts and Proceedings of the Privy Council*, 1834

Pay, J.J. (trans.), *De Arte Honeste Amandi*, New York, 1941

Percy, Thomas, *Reliques of Ancient English Poetry*, ed. J.V. Pritchard, Book One: I 'Chevy Chase', London, J. Dodsley, 1775

Riley, H.T. (ed.), *Registrum Abbatis Johannis Whethamstede*, 1872, Vol. 1

Rymer, T. (ed.), *Foedera, Conventiones, Litterae . . .*, 1704–35

Speed, J., *Historie of Great Britaine*, London, George Humble, 1623

Stow, G.B. (ed.), *Historia Vitae et Regni Ricardi Secundi*, Pennsylvania, University of Pennsylvania Press, 1977

The True Chronicles of Jean le Bel, trans. N. Bryant, Woodbridge, The Boydell Press 2011

Walsingham, Thomas, *Historia Anglicana*, ed. H.T. Riley, Rolls Series, Cambridge Library, 2015

Westminster Chronicle 1381–1394, Oxford, Clarendon Press, 1982

The Works of Joseph Addison: Complete in Three Volumes: Embracing the Whole of the 'Spectator,' &c, London, Harper & Brothers, 1837

Wyntoun, Andrew, *The Origynale Cronykill of Scotland*, ed. David Laing, Edmonstone and Douglas, Edinburgh, 1872–9

Secondary Sources

Allen, K., *The Wars of the Roses*, London, Jonathan Cape, 1973

Allmand, C., *Henry V*, London, Methuen, 1992

Allsop, B. and U. Clark, *Historic Architecture of Northumberland & Newcastle upon Tyne*, Northumberland, Oriel Press, 1977

Anderson-Graham, P., *Highways & Byways in Northumberland*, London, MacMillan, 1920

Archer, R.E.C., *Government and People in the Fifteenth Century*, Stroud, Sutton Publishing, 1995

Armstrong, P., *Otterburn 1388*, Osprey 'Campaign' Series, Oxford, 2006

Armstrong, R.B., *History of Liddesdale, Eskdale, Ewesdale, Wauchopedale & the Debatable Land*, Edinburgh, David Douglas, 1883

Banks, F.R., *Scottish Border Country*, London, Batsford, 1951

Barbour, R., *The Knight and Chivalry*, London, Sphere Books, 1974

Barratt, J., *War for the Throne, the Battle of Shrewsbury 1403*, Barnsley, Pen & Sword, 2010

Barrow, G.W.S., *Robert Bruce*, Los Angeles, University of California Press, 1965

Bartlett, C., *The English Longbowman 1330–1515*, Oxford, Osprey, 1995

Bates, C.J., *History of Northumberland*, London, Elliot Stock, 1895

Bean, J.M.W., 'The Percies and their Estates in Scotland', *Archaeologia Aeliana*, 4th Series, xxxv (1957)

——, *The Estates of the Percy Family*, Oxford, Historical Series, 1958

——, 'Henry IV and the Percies', *History*, xliv (1959).

Beltz, G.F. (*Lancaster Herald*), *Memorials of the Order of the Garter*, London, William Pickering, 1811

Bennett, M., *Community, Class & Careerism: Cheshire and Lancashire Society in the Age of Sir Gawain and the Green Knight*, Cambridge, Cambridge University Press, 1983

Bingham, C., *The Stewart Kings of Scotland 1371–1603*, London, Weidenfeld & Nicolson, 1974

Blackmore, H.L., *The Armouries of the Tower of London – Ordnance*, London, HMSO, 1976

Blair, C., *European Armour*, London, Batsford, 1958

Blakeway, J.B., 'Battlefield', *Transactions of the Shropshire Archaeological and Natural History Society* (1889)

Boardman, A.W., *The Medieval Soldier in the Wars of the Roses*, Stroud, Sutton Publishing, 1998

——, *Hotspur*, Stroud, Sutton Publishing, 2003

Bogg, E., *The Border Country*, Newcastle upon Tyne, Mawson, Swan & Morgan, 1898

Borland, Revd R.R., *Border Raids & Reivers*, Dalbeattie, Thomas Fraser, 1910

Bourne, H., *The History of Newcastle upon Tyne; or the ancient and present state of that town*, Newcastle upon Tyne, 1736

Brand, J., *History of Newcastle upon Tyne*, 2 vols, London, H. White & Son, 1789

Brenan, G., *The House of Percy*, 2 vols, London, Freemantle & Co., 1898

Brockett, J., *A Glossary of North Country Words*, Newcastle upon Tyne, T. & J. Dinsdale, 1849

Brooke, R., *Visits to Fields of Battle in England, of the Fifteenth Century*, London, John Russell Smith, 1857

Brown, A.L., 'The English Campaign in Scotland 1400', in *British Government and Administration*, ed. H. Hearder and H.R. Loyn, Oxford, Oxford University Press, 1974, pp. 40–54

Brown, M., *The Black Douglases*, Edinburgh, John Donald, 1999

Burne, A.H., *The Battlefields of England*, London, Methuen, 1950

——, *More Battlefields of England*, London, Methuen, 1952

Caldwell, D.H., *The Scottish Armoury*, Edinburgh, John Donald, 1979

Campbell, J., 'England, Scotland and the Hundred Years War', in *Europe in the Later Middle Ages*, ed. J.R. Hale et al., Illinois, North-western University Press, 1965

Cathcart King, D.J., *Castellarium Anglicanum*, 2 vols, New York, Kraus International, 1983, Vol. 2

Chadwick, H.M., *Early Scotland*, Edinburgh, 1949; new edn London, Octagon Press, 1974

Charleton, R.J., *A History of Newcastle upon Tyne*, London, Walter Scott Publishing, 1894

Charlton, B., *Upper North Tynedale*, Northumberland, Northumberland National Park Authority, 1987

Chesterton, G.K., *A Short History of England*, London, Biblio-Bazaar, 2008

Child, F.J., *The English and Scottish Popular Ballads*, 8 vols, Boston, Houghton, Mifflin & Co., 1965, Vol. 1

Cockburn-Hood, Thomas H., *The House of Cockburn of that Ilk and Cadets Thereof*, Edinburgh, 1888

Crow, J., 'Harbottle Castle, Excavations and Survey 1997–1999', in *Archaeology in Northumberland National Park*, ed. P. Frodsham, Northumberland, Northumberland National Park Authority, 2004, pp. 246–62

Dent, J. and R. McDonald, *Warfare & Fortifications in the Borders*, Newton St Boswells, Scottish Borders Council, 2000

Dickson, W. (ed.), 'The Chronicles of Alnwick Abbey', *Archaeologia Aeliana* (1944), Vol. 2

Dixon, D.D., *Whittingham Vale*, Newcastle upon Tyne, Robert Redpath, 1895

——, *Upper North Coquetdale*, Newcastle upon Tyne, Robert Redpath, 1903

Dixon, M.C., 'The Knightly Families of Northumberland: a crisis in the early fourteenth century', Master's thesis, Durham University, 2000

Dixon, P.W., 'Fortified Houses on the Anglo-Scottish Border: A Study of the Domestic Architecture of the Upland Area in its Social and Economic Context', PhD thesis, Oxford, 1976

Dodds, J.F., *Bastions & Belligerents*, Newcastle upon Tyne, Keepdale, 1996

Drummond Gould, H., *Brave Borderland*, Edinburgh, Thomas Nelson, 1936

Du Boullay, F.R.H. and C.M. Barron (eds), *The Reign of Richard II: Essays in Honour of May McKisack*, London, Athlone Press, 1971

Ducklin, K. and J. Waller, *Sword Fighting*, London, Robert Hale, 2001

Duncan, A.A.M., *Scotland, the Making of a Kingdom*, Edinburgh, Oliver & Boyd, 1975

Durham, K., *Strongholds of the Border Reivers*, London, Osprey 'Fortress' Series, 2008

——, *Border Reiver 1513–1603*, London, Osprey 'Warrior' Series, 2011

Eddington, A., *Castles & Historic Houses of the Border*, Edinburgh, Oliver & Boyd, 1926)

Eyeton, R.W., *Antiquities of Shropshire*, London, John Russell Smith, 1860

Eyre Todd, G., *Byways of the Old Scottish Border*, London, Macmillan, 1913

Fiorato, V., A. Boylston and C. Knusel (eds), *Blood and Roses: The Archaeology of a Mass Grave from the Battle of Towton AD 1461*, Oxford, Oxbow Books, 2007

Fisher, A., *William Wallace*, Edinburgh, Birlinn, 2007

Fletcher, C., *Richard II: Manhood, Youth and Politics 1377–1399*, Oxford, Oxford University Press, 2008

Getz, F., *Medicine in the English Middle Ages*, Princeton, Princeton University Press, 1998

Gillespie, J.L., 'Richard II's Cheshire Archers', https://www.hslc.org.uk/wp-content/uploads/2017/05/125-2-Gillespie.pdf

Given-Wilson, C., *Henry IV*, London, Yale University Press, 2016

Good, G.L. and C.J. Tabraham, 'Excavations at Threave Castle, Galloway, 1974–78', *Medieval' Archaeology* (1981); 25: 90–140

Goodman, A. and J. Gillespie, *Richard II: The Art of Kingship*, Oxford, Clarendon Press, 1999

Gravett, C., *Medieval Siege Warfare*, London, Osprey, 1990

Griffiths, R.A., 'Local Rivalries and National Politics: The Percies, the Nevilles and the Duke of Exeter 1452–1455', *Speculum*, Vol. XLIII (1968)

——, *Kings and Nobles in the Later Middle Ages*, Gloucester, Alan Sutton, 1986

Hales, J.W. and F.J. Furnival, *Percy Folio of Ballads and Romance*, 4 vols, London, De La Mare Press, 1905–10

Hall, Edward, *Chronicle containing the History of England during the reign of King Henry IV and succeeding monarchs to the end of the reign of King Henry VIII*, London, 1809

Hamer, E., 'Anglo–Scottish relations in the reigns of Robert II & Robert III', thesis, University of Glasgow, 1971, http://theses.gla.ac.uk/72755/1/10647029.pdf

Harrison, W.J., *The Geology of Northumberland* (proof notes), 1879

Hartshorne, C.H., *Memoirs Illustrative of the History and Antiquities of Northumberland*, 2 vols, London, Bell & Daldy, 1852, Vol. 2, *Feudal and Military Antiquities of Northumberland and the Scottish Borders*

Hepple, L.W., *A History of Northumberland and Newcastle upon Tyne*, Newcastle upon Tyne, Phillimore, 1976

Higham, N.J., *The Kingdom of Northumbria 350–1100*, Gloucester, Alan Sutton, 1993

Hingeston-Randolf, F.C., *Royal and Historical Letters of Henry IV King of England and France and Lord of Ireland: 1863–1864*, Cambridge, Cambridge University Press, 2013

Hislop, M.J.B., 'The date of the Warkworth Donjon', *Archaeologia Aeliana*, 5th Series, XX, 1991

Hodges, C.C. and J. Gibson, *Hexham & its Abbey*, Northumberland, Hexham Abbey, 1919

Hodgson, J., *A History of Northumberland*, 3 parts, Newcastle upon Tyne, Frank Graham, 1973, Part II, Vol. 1

Homer, *Iliad*, trans. W.H.D. Rouse, Edinburgh, Thomas Nelson & Sons, 1938

Hope Dodds, M. (ed.), *A History of Northumberland*, 15 vols, Newcastle upon Tyne, Northumberland County History Committee, 1893–1940, Vol. 15

Horrox, R., *Fifteenth Century Attitudes*, Cambridge, Cambridge University Press, 1994

—— with W.M. Ormrod (eds), *A Social History of England 1200–1500*, Cambridge, Cambridge University Press, 2006

Hugill, R., *Castles and Peles of the English Border*, Newcastle upon Tyne, Frank Graham, 1970

Hunter Blair, C.H., 'Harbottle Castle', *History of the Berwickshire Naturalists Club*, Edinburgh, Neil & Co., 1932–4, Vol. XXVIII

Jackson, D., *The Northumbrians*, London, Hurst, 2019

Kaeuper, R.W., *Holy Warriors: The Religious Ideal of Chivalry*, Philadelphia, University of Pennsylvania Press, 2009

Kapelle, W.E., *The Norman Conquest of the North*, North Carolina, Croom Helm, 1979

Keegan, Sir J., *The Face of Battle*, London, Penguin, 1976

Keen, M., *Chivalry*, Connecticut, Yale University Press, 1984

——, *English Society in the Later Middle Ages 1348–1500*, London, Penguin, 1990

——, *Nobles, knights and men at arms in the Middle Ages*, London, Hambledon Press 1996

—— (ed.), *Medieval Warfare – a History*, Oxford, Oxford University Press, 1999

Kinross, J., *Walking and Exploring the Battlefields of Britain*, London, David & Charles, 1988

Kis, D., *Encyclopaedia of the Dead*, Illinois, North-western University Press, 1998

Lander, J.R., *The Limitations of English Monarchy in the Later Middle Ages*, Toronto, University of Toronto Press, 1989

Lang, J., *Stories of the Border Marches*, New York, Dodge, 1916

Lloyd, J.E., *Owen Glendower*, Oxford, Clarendon Press, 1931

Loades, M., *Swords & Swordsmen*, Barnsley, Pen & Sword, 2017

Logan Mack, J., *The Border Line*, Edinburgh, Oliver & Boyd, 1924

Lomas, R., *North-East England in the Middle Ages*, Edinburgh, John Donald, 1992

——, *Northumberland – County of Conflict*, Edinburgh, Tuckwell Press, 1996

——, *A Power in the Land: The Percys*, East Linton, Tuckwell Press, 1999

Long, B., *The Castles of Northumberland*, Newcastle upon Tyne, Harold Hill, 1967

Lynch, M., *Scotland: A New History*, London, Pimlico, 1992

Macdonald, A.J., *Border Bloodshed*, Edinburgh, Tuckwell Press, 2000

Macdonald-Fraser, G., *The Steel Bonnets*, London, Barrie & Jenkins, 1971

McFarlane, K.B., *The Nobility of Late Medieval England*, Oxford, Oxford University Press, 1975

McFarlane, K.B., *England in the Fifteenth Century*, ed. G.L. Harris, London, Hambledon Press, 1981

McIvor, I., *A Fortified Frontier*, Stroud, Tempus, 2001

Mackenzie, E., *History of Northumberland* (Newcastle upon Tyne, Mackenzie & Dent, 1825

McNamee, C., *The Wars of the Bruces: Scotland, England and Ireland*, Edinburgh, Birlinn, 1997

McNiven, P., 'The Scottish Policy of the Percies and the Strategy of the Rebellion of 1403', https://www.escholar.manchester.ac.uk/api/datastream? publicationPid=uk-ac-man-scw:1m1843&datastreamId=POST-PEER-REVIEW-PUBLISHERS-DOCUMENT.PDF

Marsden, J., *The Illustrated Border Ballads*, London, Macmillan, 1990

Mathew, G., *The Court of Richard II*, London, John Murray, 1968

Meade, D.M., *The Medieval Church in England*, London, Churchman, 1988

Meikle, M., *A British Frontier*, Edinburgh, Tuckwell, 2004

Middlebrook, S., *Newcastle upon Tyne, its Growth and Achievement*, Newcastle upon Tyne, *Newcastle Chronicle & Journal*, 1950

Moat, D.D., *The North West Borderland*, Newcastle upon Tyne, Frank Graham, 1973

Morris, M., *Edward I – a Great and Terrible King*, London, Random House, 2008

——, *Castle; a History of the Buildings that Shaped Medieval Britain*, London, Random House, 2012

Neillands, R., *The Hundred Years War*, London, Routledge, 1990

Nicolas, Sir N. Harris, *The Controversy between Sir Richard Scrope and Sir Robert Grosvenor, in the Court of Chivalry*, 2 vols, London, 1832, Vol. II

Nicolle, D., *Medieval Warfare Source Book*, London, Brockhampton Press, 1999

Norman, A.V.B. and D. Pottinger, *English Weapons and Warfare 449–1660*, London, Arms & Armour Press, 1966

Oakeshott, R.E., *A Knight and his Castle*, London, Dufour Editions, 1996

——, *A Knight and his Weapons*, London, Dufour Editions, 1997

——, *A Knight and his Horse*, London, Dufour Editions, 1998

——, *A Knight and his Armour*, London, Dufour Editions, 1999

Oman, Sir Charles, *The Art of War in the Middle Ages*, 2 vols, London, Greenhill, 1924, Vol. 2

Paul, Sir J.B., *The Scots Peerage*, Edinburgh, 1905

Percy, Bishop Thomas, *Reliques of Ancient English Poetry*, ed. H.B. Wheatley, New York, Dover, 1906

Percy Hedley, W., *Northumberland Families*, 2 vols, Newcastle upon Tyne, Society of Antiquaries, 1968, Vol. 1

Pevsner, Sir N. and I. Richmond, *Northumberland*, 'The Buildings of England' Series, London, Penguin, 1992

Platt, W., *Stories of the Scottish Border*, London, Harrap, 1919

Pollard, A.J., 'Characteristics of the Fifteenth Century North', in *Government, Religion and Society in Northern England 1000–1700*, ed. C. Appleby and P. Dalton, Oxford, Oxford University Press, 1977

——, 'Percies, Nevilles and the Wars of the Roses', *History Today* (September 1992)

Prestwich, M., *Armies and Warfare in the Middle Ages*, Connecticut, Yale University Press, 1996

Ramsay, Sir J.H., *Lancaster and York*, 2 vols, Oxford, Clarendon Press, 1892

Ransome, C., 'The Battle of Towton', *English Historical Review*, Vol. 4 (1889)

Reid, N.H., 'Alexander III; the Historiography of a Myth', in *Scotland in the Reign of Alexander III 1249–1286*, ed. N.H. Reid, Edinburgh, John Donald, 1990

Ridpath, G., *The Border History of England and Scotland*, Edinburgh, Mercat Press, 1776

Robb, G., *The Debatable Land*, London, Picador, 2018

Robertson, Dr E.C., 'On the Skeletons exhumed at Elsdon and their probable connection with the Battle of Otterburn', *History of Berwickshire Naturalists' Club 1879–1881*, Berwick-upon-Tweed, Martin's Printing Works, 1882

Robson, R., *Rise and Fall of the English Highland Clans: Tudor Responses to a Medieval Problem*, Edinburgh, John Donald, 1989

Rollaston, D. and M. Prestwich (eds), *The Battle of Neville's Cross 1346*, Lincolnshire, Studies in North Eastern History, 1998

Rose, A., *Kings in the North*, London, Phoenix, 2002

Ross, C., *Edward IV*, London, Eyre Methuen, 1974

Sadler, D.J., *Battle for Northumbria*, Newcastle upon Tyne, Bridge Studios, 1988

——, *War in the North – The Wars of the Roses in the North East of England 1461–1464*, England, Partizan Press, 2000

——, *Border Fury – The Three Hundred Years War*, London, Longmans, 2004

Saul, N., *Richard II*, Connecticut, Yale University Press, 1997

Scofield, C.L., *The Life and Reign of Edward the Fourth*, 2 vols, London, Routledge, 1967

Scott, Sir Walter, *Border Antiquities*, 2 vols, London, Longmans, 1814

——, *Minstrelsy*, London, Ward Lock, 1892

Seymour, W., *Battles in Britain*, 2 vols, London, Sidgwick & Jackson, 1989, Vol. 1

Sitwell, W., *The Border*, Newcastle upon Tyne, Andrew Reid, 1927

Smith, T. (ed.), *The Itinerary of John Leland the Antiquarian*, Oxford, James Fletcher, 1768

Smout, T.C., *History of the Scottish People*, London, Fontana, 1969

Smurthwaite, D., *The Ordnance Survey Guide to the Battlefields of Britain*, London, Michael Joseph, 1984

Steel of Aikwood, *Against Goliath*, London, Pan Macmillan, 2008

Steel, A., *Richard II*, Cambridge, Cambridge University Press, 1941

Stewart, R., *The Marches*, London, Jonathan Cape, 2016

Storey, R.L., 'The Wardens of the Marches of England towards Scotland 1377–1489', *English Historical Review*, 72 (1957)

——, *End of the House of Lancaster*, Stroud, Sutton Publishing, 1999

Sumption, J., *The Hundred Years War*, London, Faber & Faber, 1990–2009

Tabraham, C.J., *Hermitage Castle*, Edinburgh, Historic Scotland, 1996

——, *Scotland's Castles*, rev. edn, London, Batsford, 2005

Taylor, C., *Chivalry and the ideals of Knighthood in France during the Hundred Years War*, Cambridge, Cambridge University Press, 2013

Thrupp, S.L., 'The problem of replacement Rates in Late Medieval English Population', *Economic History Review*, 2nd Series (1965–6)

Tomlinson, W. Weaver, *A Comprehensive Guide to Northumberland*, Newcastle upon Tyne, Robinson, 1863

Towson, K., 'Henry Percy, 1st Earl of Northumberland: Ambition, Conflict and Cooperation in Late Medieval England', PhD thesis, University of St Andrews, https://core.ac.uk/download/pdf/8763991.pdf

Tranter, N., *Fortalices & Early Mansions of Southern Scotland 1400–1650*, Edinburgh, Moray Press, 1935

Traquair, P., *Freedom's Sword: Scotland's Wars of Independence*, London, HarperCollins, 1998

Treece, H. and E. Oakeshott, *Fighting Men*, Leicester, Brockhampton Press, 1963

Trevelyan, G.M., *A History of England*, London, Penguin, 1975

Tuck, A., *Richard II and the English Nobility*, London, Edward Arnold, 1973

——, *Border Warfare*, London, HMSO, 1979

——, *Crown and Nobility, 1272–1462*, New York, Barnes & Noble, 1985

Veitch, J., *History and Poetry of the Scottish Border*, Edinburgh, William Blackwood & Sons, 1893

Wagner, P. and S. Hand, *Medieval Sword and Shield*, California, Chivalry Bookshelf, 2003

Warner, P., *Sieges of the Middle Ages*, Barnsley, Pen & Sword, 2005

Watson, G., *The Border Reivers*, Newcastle upon Tyne, Sandhill, 1974

Weiss, H., 'A Power in the North? The Percies in the Fifteenth Century', *The Historical Journal*, 19, 2 (1976)

Welford, R., *A History of Newcastle & Gateshead*, 3 vols, London, Walter Scott, 1884

Wesencraft, C., *The Battle of Otterburn*, Newcastle upon Tyne, privately printed, 1988

White, R., *History of the Battle of Otterburn 1388 fought in 1388 etc.*, Newcastle upon Tyne, Emerson Charnley, 1857

Wise, T., *The Wars of the Roses*, Oxford, Osprey, 1983

——, *Medieval Heraldry*, Oxford, Osprey, 2001

Woolgar, C.M., *The Great Household in Late Medieval England*, London, Yale University Press, 1999

Wylie, J.H., *History of England under Henry IV*, 4 vols, London, Longmans Green & Co., 1884–98

Index